Understanding Work-Based Learning

Understanding Work-Based Learning

Edited by
SIMON ROODHOUSE
and
JOHN MUMFORD

LONDON AND NEW YORK

First published in paperback 2024

First published 2010 by Gower Publishing

Published 2016 by Routledge
4 Park Square, Milton Park, Abingdon, Oxon OX14 4RN

and by Routledge
605 Third Avenue, New York, NY 10158

Routledge is an imprint of the Taylor & Francis Group, an informa business

Publisher's Note
The publisher has gone to great lengths to ensure the quality of this reprint but points out that some imperfections in the original copies may be apparent.

British Library Cataloguing in Publication Data
 Understanding work-based learning.
  1. Education, Cooperative. 2. Experiential learning.
  3. College students--Employment. 4. Education,
  Cooperative--Case studies. 5. Experiential learning--Case
  studies. 6. College students--Employment--Case studies.
  I. Mumford, John. II. Roodhouse, Simon.
  378.3'7-dc22

ISBN: 978-0-566-09197-1 (hbk)
ISBN: 978-1-03-283836-6 (pbk)
ISBN: 978-1-315-54906-4 (ebk)

DOI: 10.4324/9781315549064

Contents

List of Figures

List of Tables

Case Study Contributors

Jonathan Garnett, Director Institute for Work Based Learning, Middlesex University.

Lesley Harper, Director of Undergraduate Programmes, CETAD, Lancaster University.

Grant Harris, Sussex IT Manager (Operations), Sussex HIS (Sussex Health Informatics Services).

Helen Jones, McDonalds.

Cath Millington, Head of Service, Stockport Children and Young People's Disability Partnership.

Ann Minton, Work Force Development Fellow, School of Flexible and Partnership Learning University of Derby Corporate, University of Derby.

Penny McCracken, Higher Education Consultant.

Tony Wall, Head of Flexible Learning and Teacher Fellow, York St John University.

Janet Waugh, Playgroup Leader and student of Northumbria University.

Martin West, retired Police Superintendent, now working in the Publishing industry.

Glossary of Terms

Accreditation of Prior Experiential Learning (APEL)	This is the process by which an individual learner can obtain academic credits for learning developed from experiences at work or in professional practice. The university assesses the learning by comparing it with similar learning that might have taken place on campus.
Accreditation of Prior Learning (APL)	This is the process by which an individual learner can obtain academic credits for learning achieved on formal courses and training (for example, a HND counting towards a BA degree).
Admissions	The university department that takes enquiries from potential students, receives applications and processes these.
Blended Learning	A Mode of Study made popular by the Open University where learners mostly study at a distance, but with some campus sessions and some online learning. The balance between these can vary, and sometimes can be negotiated with your tutor.
Board of Studies	Official body in each university where teachers and learners discuss the concerns of learners and make a record of these for action to be taken. It is an important forum for the learner voice to be heard. All academics must demonstrate they listen to, and take action to address concerns raised at Board of Studies.
Credits and Credit Points	University qualifications are made up of specific amounts of credits. You need to complete the specified number of credits to achieve a particular qualification. So for example, to gain a Bachelor's degree with honours (BA Hons) you need to successfully complete 360 credits. Credits in higher education can be transferred between universities.
Distance Learning	A Mode of Study where you do not attend the university for 'lectures' but where the 'learning' and the 'teaching' are run in separate locations. Your tutor may be in her office at the university while you undertake your studies at home or in the workplace. Distance learners usually have learning materials specifically designed for this mode of study.
Enrolment	The process by which you agree to take the place on the programme and accept the responsibility to pay any fees.
Formative Assessment	This is where a tutor assesses a learner's performance or work to provide feedback on how improvements can be made. It is usually undertaken at points during the course of a module or unit.
Higher Education (HE)	This is the highest level of education available provided by special institutions that are either universities, university colleges or other specialist centres that deliver higher education. The term is interchangeable with 'university-level'.
Higher Education Institution (HEI)	A university, university college or other institution that has been granted the right to make UK Higher Education Awards by the Privy Council.

Induction	The process by which the university introduces you to its systems, regulations and support available to you as a learner. This is often campus based, but may be virtual or through documents sent to you by post.
Learning Materials	Handbooks and study materials given to you so you can follow a particular module or unit. This might include a Reader (see Reader) and a list of suggested reading.
Learning Resources	The term used to describe university services that support learning. These will include library services, email and access to the university network. Can also include placement services, careers advice and so on.
Mode of Study	Universities deliver their programmes in significantly different 'modes' which include 'Full Time'; 'Part Time'; 'On-Campus', "Flexible Learning'; 'Distance Learning'. This may have greater importance to the university and their funding arrangements than your experience as a learner. It may have fee and funding implications for you.
Modules or Units	The parts that make up a university qualification. They are usually followed in a specific sequence towards a specific qualification title. There may be 'core modules/units which you must successfully complete, and 'optional' modules/units which you can choose from as part of your programme.
National Qualifications Framework	The list of academic and vocational qualifications and an attempt to indicate the equivalence between vocational and academic qualifications (see the section on National Qualifications Framework).
NVQ	National Vocational Qualifications (NVQs) are work-related, competency-based qualifications. They do not reflect the higher-level learning skills of higher education, but place emphasis on specific skills and knowledge for particular jobs.
Negotiated Modules or Units	Modules or Units where the focus of the studies is negotiated between you, the university, and often your employer (if applicable).
Online Learning	A university programme run entirely using a web-based system.
Programme/ Programme of Study	The series of modules you undertake in order to reach your target qualification. The programme may include, or be made up entirely of negotiated modules/units.
Programme Leader	Member of academic staff with responsibility for leading the delivery of a whole work-based learning or traditional programme at undergraduate or postgraduate level.
Qualifications	These are 'certificated' awards made by universities, colleges and professional training organisations. University qualifications have a range of titles that are usually linked to the academic level (see National Qualifications Framework to compare vocational and academic qualifications).
Reader	A Handbook with extracts from books and other literature which you are expected to read and use as part of a module or unit.

Registration	The process by which you apply to become a learner at university. This means making an application for a programme of study, course or module. After sending in an Application Form, you are likely to be asked to sign a letter confirming you would like to accept the place on the programme.
Registry	The university department who holds the information on learners, the programmes they are following, their grades and their final award.
Semesters/Terms	Most universities organise teaching into two semesters or three terms. Each is followed by a period in which official assessment of learners' work is undertaken. Semesters run late September to end of December and late January to mid May. Terms normally run in the Autumn, Winter and Spring as in schools.
Summative Assessment	This is where a tutor (and sometimes the workplace manager?) assesses a learner's performance or work to grade it. It is usually undertaken at the end of a module or unit and 'sums up' achievement. You will normally receive feedback to help you understand how the grading has been made.
Tutor	The tutor is the academic who runs the modules you are taking as part of your course. They may also be known as: Programme Adviser, Academic Advisor, Academic Supervisor and so on.
Tutorial	One-to-one or small group meeting with a university tutor. It may be in person, by telephone, video-link or online.
University-level	A term that is usually applied to qualifications and learning. Qualifications are graduate level (that is, from Graduate certificate to Doctorate). When applied to learning, the term means learning of the highest level of complexity, breadth and detail.
VLE/Virtual Learning Environment	All universities have 'Virtual Learning Environments' which learners can access to support their studies. They will often have handbooks and other materials online. They can be accessed from any computer with web access. VLEs may also have specific tasks for you to undertake as part of your module or unit, and include Blogs or other methods of communication between learners. You normally need to be a registered and enrolled learner to access these services.
Worker Researcher/Insider Researcher	A very important concept in work-based learning which recognises the importance of the work-based learner as both a worker and researcher. Its main importance is in relation to ethical dilemmas that might arise, and the relevance of knowledge the learner may develop in the workplace or professional setting.

Acknowledgements

We would like to thank our colleagues in HE@Work, for their support in this project. The willingness of the universities actively engaged in work-based learning to provide advice on learners to approach is much appreciated.

In addition, this book would not be possible without the preparedness of the work-based learners who wrote the case studies in their own words so openly about their experiences. Thanks should also go to the Edge Foundation, who have supported HE@ Work, thus enabling us to draw experiences from working with large companies which has informed the book.

Finally, we would like to thank Alan Durrant, Garth Rhodes and David Young for giving permission to reproduce the glossary of terms from their book, *Getting Started with University Work Based Learning*.

Foreword

Everyone deserves the opportunity to realise their potential, further their careers and live a fulfilling and socially responsible life. Learning is critical in this, yet, all too often, learning is thought of as formal education, particularly in school, college or university, involving highly structured delivery and assessment mechanisms. We have an education system built upon examinations and qualifications: pass one level and move on to the next, pass that and move on up the ladder. The level at which you enter employment will likely as not be determined by the level of the final qualification.

Successive governments have invested heavily in such a formalised education system. The roots of this commitment can be traced back to the initiatives of far-sighted employers such as Titus Salt and Robert Owen and their view of the workplace in the nineteenth century. Robert Owen, the pioneering employer who established the model village at New Lanark for his workers, explained in his 'New View of Society' essays:

'Train any population rationally, and they will be rational. Furnish honest and useful employments to those so trained and such employments they will greatly prefer to dishonest or injurious occupations. It is beyond all calculation the interest of every government to provide that training and that employment; and to provide both is easily practicable.'

These sentiments stand up to scrutiny today, yet Owen puts his finger on the importance of non-formal learning derived from many experiences including the work. He is clear where this learning comes from, pointing out that it is not just traditional talk and chalk but, rather in today's terms, learning based upon experience:

'Where are these rational practices to be taught and acquired? Not within the four walls of a bare building, in which formality predominates ... But in the nursery, play-ground, fields, gardens, workshops, manufacture museums and class-rooms. ...The facts collected from all these sources will be concentrated, explained, discussed, made obvious to all, and shown in their direct application to practice in all the business of life.'

We have long been in danger of allowing these insights into the value of informal learning to be overshadowed. In the drive to maintain global competiveness and hence wealth creation, we place ever more stress on increasing the supply of graduates; meanwhile we risk neglecting those who do not thrive in an education system predicated on full-time courses, examinations and qualifications. Learning should not be simply a matter of cramming people. For some, learning starts when they leave full-time education and start work. It is as if the education system has written them off, not least because the university system is course-driven and biased in favour of the full-time student.

This book is for anyone who wants to make the most of work-based learning: employees, employers, educationalists, policy makers and researchers. It sheds light on ways of giving full-time employees the chance to take up learning opportunities which are of the same level and rigour as those on offer to the full-time student. It approaches the subject from the perspective of the learner, drawing on case studies. It suggests that universities already have in place much of the machinery needed to support learners who are in work: they just don't make enough use of it. Look closely and you will find a substantial legacy of this kind of activity by universities. This is a book about seizing opportunities.

Barry Sheerman, MP.

Introduction

The book focuses on the engagement of people in employment with university-accredited learning. It is about individual learning that occurs predominantly through work. References to organisational learning are included to provide a context for other forms of learning that occur in the workplace.

In the preparation of this the authors have consulted widely, run workshops and given presentations, consequently it is based on material evidence. The text thus provides an explanation of university work-based learning including definitional issues and theoretical perspectives. Validation, the process a university goes through to give credibility to its qualifications, is a fundamental function and deserves a distinct analysis in the context of work-based learning, and consequently there are two chapters; one providing an overview and the other explaining the mechanics of the business of validation and accreditation. Other key support mechanisms are investigated, including accreditation of prior learning and experience as well as university work-based mentoring. However, the centrality of the book concerns itself with the learner experience. We sought case studies from those who had used university-accredited learning in mid-career to provide a means of addressing a number of questions.

For example, when we consider the preparation of people to enter the world of work, university-accredited learning features as the gold standard. It is the most respected route into employment and is so highly prized that students with very low or no incomes put themselves into debt in order to achieve a university qualification. The Higher Education Funding Council for England (HEFCE) (2007) estimates that 42 per cent of 18–30 year olds in the UK currently participate in Higher Education (also known as HE) and the government target is to raise this to 50 per cent. Standard and Poor's (2008) estimated that 78 per cent of those with higher education were earning more than the median salary. However, upon entering the world of employment, the role of universities in meeting learning needs seems to change. Why should this be so? Why should institutions that are so valued by those preparing for employment feature so little with the needs of those in employment?

However, before considering the chapters and case studies, it is important to position the university contribution in the broader context of learning in the workplace and university engagement with business.

Learning in the Workplace

Learning in the workplace is focused on a job and the learning may be associated with training to gain the skills, experiential learning from doing a job, or reflection about the context of that job. Importantly, the work role automatically creates a social setting and competency framework. Performance assessment in the role is intuitively conducted by work peers and line managers, in a way that is both continuous and involuntary. In the world of employment there is an ongoing need to make a contribution in a work team that is valued by others and this need is central to the learning that takes place.

Structured support for learning in the workplace therefore focuses on interventions that allow the individual to see how what they are doing 'fits' with the activities of others; in other words, culture building. One typically sees:

- Employee orientation courses that teach the social norms of an organisation and explain the overall purpose of a company.
- Team-building events where employees learn to interact constructively in challenging settings.
- Feedback processes that expose the employee to the views of peers, bosses, subordinates, clients and so on.
- Away-days where employees can reflect either individually or collectively on the workplace context.
- Lessons-learned exercises at the end of projects or missions to disseminate experience in a way that is accessible to others.
- Training to ensure that the statutory obligations of the organisation are shared as obligations of the individuals.

These interventions are initiated and managed by employers as part of their human resource development process and respond to perceived business needs or gaps in organisational capability. The decision whether to initiate a specific programme is taken in the context of other business options and competing calls on the company's management resource. It's a business decision taken like any other business decision. The knowledge dealt with in the events listed in the bullet points above is very context specific and often only relevant to those participating in the event itself. They are usually regarded as quite private affairs.

This is a different approach to the one a higher educational institute might take when considering whether to run a course. Universities have a tendency to represent themselves as disseminators of knowledge to meet a societal need. By this they mean teaching codified generalisations of 'universal truths'. A higher education institute will make its business case for a course in terms of a perceived ongoing need to disseminate these truths in the student market. But the employer-structured support for learning in the workplace does not disseminate knowledge of that type. The learning experiences in the workplace occur naturally as part of an activity which has another specific purpose.

An organisation is a group composed of specialists working together on a common task, and its function is to make knowledge productive (Drucker, 1993). Knowledge always stays with the individual and a social process is needed between individuals so they cooperate in making their knowledge explicit (Nonaka and Takeuchi, 1995). Interventions that make a group of individuals work more effectively as a team are a crucial source of competitive advantage for the organisation.

University Engagement with Workplace Learning

Perhaps the biggest distinction between workplace training and a university education is that in workplace training less than 20 per cent of trainees are engaged on programmes leading to nationally recognised qualifications (King, 2007) and of these the vast majority will be working for QCF level 2 or 3 qualifications. By contrast, in a university or college 100 per cent of trainees are seeking recognised qualifications at higher level. It is therefore not surprising that universities barely feature in the workplace learning. As Connor and Hirsch (2008) observe, businesses spend at least £400m annually at universities on continuous professional development (CPD) and other short courses....it pales into insignificance with the £38bn businesses spend on training, £5.5bn of which is potentially accessible by higher education institutes (also known as HEIs). Also, it is the case that business spend with higher education institutes is heavily skewed to a few universities, 12 accounting for 50 per cent of the spend (King, 2007). Employers do tend to want to work with universities with a brand strength that can enhance their own.

So where are the examples of universities contributing to learning in the workplace? Much of the reason for higher education engagement in the workplace centres on increasing the student intake with new graduate entrants. Vocational training courses for new entrants and management skills training for those promoted to middle management feature strongly. As Connor and Hirsch confirm, investing in leadership and management continues to be seen as the priority in workforce development. Most businesses use internal resources for this but others turn to higher education institutes for specific management qualifications (especially Master of Business Administration (MBAs)) and short bespoke courses.

There are situations where individuals are making a career step for which the experiences in the current job cannot prepare them. Hence, there is a need to expose the individual to new knowledge to fast track their learning. This is a very different situation to that described in the first section of this chapter where the individual is essentially learning by exploring their own experiences. It is a form of learning which is easier to relate to a university course because it involves exposing the learner to knowledge and skills which are outside their current experience. However, even in this situation it is not evident that universities are the best provider. In many of the professions, courses provided by institutes have greater credibility in the workplace and, hence, appeal to learners. Universities often seek course endorsement by the same professional bodies to attest their relevance in the workplace. More recently, sector skills councils, bodies set up by government to represent industry skills needs, have also begun to play a role in this attestation process.

The spectrum of university engagement with job-specific learning can be summarised as follows.

CONVENTIONAL FULL-TIME COURSES

By definition, a full-time course is one where the agenda is controlled by the academic institution. It is a learning experience often described as academic, taking place within a set of closely managed framework of rules. By necessity, the time commitment for study is in direct conflict with the time commitment for full-time employment. However, in the past some employers sponsored staff to do full-time courses at universities as part of their career development. This is now a rarity and as the *Business Week* survey of part-time courses shows, the majority of provision is aimed at learners undertaking career breaks, not learners enhancing their current job roles. This need to leave employment in order to progress academically makes it an expensive investment in time and money and involves the risk of not finding suitable employment on return to the employment marketplace. For this to happen, there needs to be a strong expectation of a major career boost or lifestyle change. In addition, the employee goes to the university as a student with the benefit of their work experience. This prior workplace learning is rarely brought into the conventional full-time university programme in any meaningful way. The conventional full-time course is really a workplace-learning interruption rather than a workplace-learning progression, a timeout model.

CONVENTIONAL PART-TIME COURSES

The part-time course represents a step towards accommodating the needs of those in employment by at least recognising that the time commitment for study needs to fit more closely with employment and social commitments. It is probably the most common method that those in employment achieve academic qualifications. These courses range from day-release schemes to evening classes, and are often combined with distance, open and interactive learning. They often appeal to individuals who feel that their career prospects are limited by old out-of-date awards or the lack of academic qualifications, but cannot afford to disrupt their careers or lose earnings. MBAs are particularly popular in this respect, as are other postgraduate programmes. Individuals without degrees or even A levels can usually gain access to such postgraduate programmes based on a wealth of relevant work experience which can be articulated. It is an example of universities recognising non-academic experience as an entry qualification. It suggests there are processes and procedures which can support work-based learning. However the part-time course is still essentially an academic-learning experience staged in parallel with a workplace-learning experience. One of the criticisms seen in our case studies is that these courses do not take sufficient account of the student's workplace experience and the length of time is arbitrary (for example, a three-year full-time degree course taking six years part-time to complete).

DISTANCE LEARNING

Distance learning is a more flexible form of course for those who cannot attend regular campus-based lectures. Distance learning was pioneered by the Open University (OU), and remains the world's leading provider of this type of programme. Learning of this type is excellent for widening the participation of students from all walks of life in higher education. However, one suspects that a large number of people in full-time employment dabble in OU courses as a way of topping up their knowledge base, a more recreational activity. It must also be pointed out that distance learning, by itself, lacks the human interaction with peers which is such an essential part of a learning experience. Several of the case studies highlight the importance of getting away from the workplace to engage with other learners and experience an environment that places emphasis on collegiality, ideas, discussion and reflection. Distance learning features as an important element in many types of course but is combined with other forms often described as blended learning.

FOUNDATION DEGREES

Foundation degrees were set up as part of the UK Government White Paper 'The future of higher education' and their purpose is defined as follows in the HEFCE prospectus (2000):

> 'The foundation degree is intended to help education providers supply the labour market with the high-quality graduates needed to address the shortage of intermediate level skills, as well as making higher education (HE) more affordable, accessible and appealing to a wider range of students – thereby widening participation in HE and stimulating lifelong learning.'

These courses are thus fundamentally a preparation for entry to work, rather than learning through work, but nevertheless focus on the vocational skills associated with a job role. In these courses a period of work experience is essential so that the student can experience first hand what the job role entails. However, this type of learning is difficult to manage unless the student is already linked in some ongoing way to the employer. Many work placements are of doubtful value. It is notable that in many large companies (for example, BP) work placements for students are managed as a 'corporate social responsibility' exercise by the public relations department. Unsurprisingly, feedback from many students is that they don't feel they have been allowed to do anything substantive. Work experience comes from accountability for a job role, not the observation of the workplace. For this reason many of the early Foundation degree course fell well short of student expectations.

A recent development, where workplace training is recognised as part of the course, has opened up a route for people to take Foundation degrees while in full-time employment. For example the 'Tesco' Foundation degree and a similar programme by TUI (a large company in the holiday sector) both integrate company training programmes into Foundation degrees provided by partner universities. This model is ideal: companies recruit people who lack some of the theoretical knowledge or intellectual skills for the job role and want a university to help with training. These new developments are only now taking their first students but there are high hopes that this will be an effective learning model for those in employment. Nevertheless, they are still courses in the conventional sense of university provision bound by the same regulatory frameworks, assessment regimes, timetables and attendance constraints.

APEL AND SHELL COURSES

In France it is quite possible for someone in full-time employment to catalogue a portfolio of their workplace learning and have a university award a degree on the strength of this evidence (Garnett et al., 2004). However, in the UK this capturing of prior learning, accreditation of prior experience and learning (APEL) rarely, if ever, counts for more than a maximum of 60 per cent of an award. Also, it is perceived by students as overly time consuming (UVAC, 2005, p. 33) and thus defeats the purpose of exempting the student from coursework. Amongst the Russell Group, a self-selecting elite group of UK universities, there is strong resistance against recognising any learning that the university has not controlled. However, there are more progressive universities that see their role as supporting learning wherever it occurs and enabling students to build on their existing learning experiences. The model they use is the 'shell' course which is essentially a content-free programme. The university imports learning undertaken elsewhere into this framework. An example is the McDonalds degree course where the McDonalds' suit of management development programmes is treated as modules by the university. The university validates the courses and quality-assures student assessment but does not design the course or participate in provision. This is an extension of the model described in the 'Tesco' example above and relies heavily on the quality of human resource management provided by the employer. Nevertheless, it is a model which genuinely starts with a workplace development agenda and uses the workplace as the location of learning. It is the leading edge of accredited workplace learning.

Sabbaticals

Some companies, particularly large companies, re-energise their management cadre or upgrade a cadre of professional staff by exposing them to leading edge thinking in business. Short bespoke courses are often arranged at prestigious university business schools, but are rarely accredited. The prestige of the company and the university convey all the endorsement that is needed to make the course valued, and employers tend to think that formal accreditation might discourage staff participation. In essence this is the opposite end of the spectrum to the model in previous section. In the 'shell' system the workplace provides the learning experience and the university places it in an academic framework. In the sabbatical model the university provides an escape from the workplace and an experience that stretches the imagination of the employee, but there is no attempt to place it in an academic framework. It is interesting that Oxford and Cambridge universities report that 80 per cent of the course places sold to business are these non-accredited short sabbaticals.

Conclusion

It appears that there is a paradox. The formal educational system puts significant effort into generating learning experiences for students so that they are prepared for the labour market, yet once these students are in the workplace they lose track of their learning progression and the relevance of that provision becomes devalued. The learning process adopts a form which educationalists find difficult to relate to. It is as if they believe legitimate and verifiable learning can only take place within the confines of their campus. By the same token, those in full-time employment become accustomed to this different style of learning and often begin to see the academic alternative as out of touch, esoteric and lacking relevance. For them, the term 'academic' takes on a negative persona.

Yet this need not be the case. There is evidence taken from the annual HE@Work large company survey to confirm that those in full-time employment want to progress academically (Dunn et al., 2008). This survey also suggests that the alignment of workplace needs and academic provision is strongest in postgraduate areas. Postgraduate learning is where university research and business development interests often seek a similar type of knowledge. This may provide an insight into the academic nature of work-based learning and a rationale for learner progression. In the academic world, career progression entails becoming more focused in a specialist area of knowledge, thus becoming the expert. In the workplace, learning and progression is also very specific to a focused area of knowledge, but this knowledge is not necessarily recognised for its academic content. If this academic content remains unrecognised does it mean that content does not exist? No – it just means the academic content is not visible or has not been 'mined'. This suggests that the missing element may be a process for describing workplace learning in a way that demonstrates its academic worth. Understanding this process is the purpose of this book.

Making Sense of Work-Based Learning

1

The Genesis of University Work-Based Learning

SIMON ROODHOUSE

Following on from the introduction, this chapter introduces higher education work-based learning. The rationale for higher educational engagement is examined historically, from the perspective of the knowledge economy and the changing world of work. Many of the observations are taken from Employers, Skills and Higher Education, (Roodhouse and Swailes, 2007) and Getting Started with University Level Work based Learning (Durrant, Rhodes and Young, 2009).

A Brief Higher Education History

Waterhouse (2002) seeks to explain employer engagement by focusing our attention on technical education as the point of contact. He suggests that, 'A fundamental part of education, wherever it occurs, is technical. Technical education is not simply practical, it is about particular types of action to make and manipulate physical things. Technical learning begins at birth. Technical education as a specific social institution began when techniques had reached a certain level of complication and sophistication.' This gave birth in Europe to the apprenticeship system, with its overlay of secret knowledge and mystique. In spite of the printing press, the computer and communications technology, the restrictive practices of these medieval guilds are still with us – known today as professional bodies or associations such as the General Medical Council, the Law Society or the Institute of Civil Engineering. This concept of technical education as a social institution has often been distinguished from vocationalism; 'A vocation is a calling, and the highest vocation, certainly in Europe, is to the priesthood and the European universities were invented to deliver vocational education in the strictest of senses. They were set up by the Church to train clerks, i.e. clerics. Indeed, all the great civilizations of the old world had similar institutions with an identical purpose.' (Waterhouse, 2002) These origins are still evident today in the oldest universities. They were essentially the training colleges of their day.

The classic model of the late medieval university was the Sorbonne in Paris. Like other European universities the Sorbonne had four faculties. The lower faculty, the Faculty of Arts, generally trained young men in the skills of the clerk (church employee) and the three higher faculties were those of theology, medicine and law. The whole purpose was vocational, with the degree as a licence to practice and the doctorate as a licence to teach. However, much of this seems to have been forgotten. Medicine, law and theology as subjects worthy of study were the equivalent of the creative industries today.

As Waterhouse (2002) points out, 'Universities in the early modern period were in no sense technical. They were about language, social interaction, beliefs and ideologies.

They were not about making things or manipulating the physical world by action. (This even applied to faculties of medicine. If a surgeon was needed, people visited a barber not a doctor). By the 18th century the universities were largely moribund, their social function having become the perpetuation of the aristocratic elite.'

In 1792 the Legislative Assembly of the French Revolution abolished the Sorbonne and three years later the Hautes Ecoles were established. They were dedicated to practical and technical learning – astronomy, geometry, mechanics, applied arts, natural history, medicine, veterinary science and rural economy, the new industries of their day – comparable to media studies or business and management. These actions were indicative of an explosion in technical knowledge during the seventeenth and eighteenth centuries, which had occurred almost entirely outside the universities. Investigation, experimentation and learning had largely taken place without formal structures or teaching institutions; the Hautes Ecoles were designed to help put this technical knowledge into practice and fuel the Industrial Revolution.

However, the French model of the Hautes Ecoles did not sweep across Europe. With the notable exception of the University of Berlin, under Von Humboldt, existing universities were slow to change. Industrialists, Princes or enlightened regimes found it easier to establish new institutions of higher technical learning than to change the power structures of the universities. So, for example, England in the mid-nineteenth century saw the foundation of the University of London and the first of the civic universities, often driven (for reasons of public health) by the medical school. Elsewhere in Europe colleges of mines, engineering and commerce were being established. Later we had the development of technical schools and colleges; these were specialised professional schools for teachers, nurses, artists and designers, all of which eventually went to provide the heritage of the English polytechnic system.

None of these types of institution had degree-awarding powers, though various professional diplomas were created. Throughout the course of this development the word 'vocational', like the word 'professional', was used to give dignity and status to practical, socially useful, and in some cases technical, activities. The next stage of evolution, as suggested by Waterhouse (2002), requires universities to re-conceptualise themselves as a service industry, not a priesthood of occult technology, or a restrictive academic guild. In place of the student and teacher come the customer and facilitator of learning. Replacing the campus is the distributed system in which technology enables institutions to extend into the workplace. But, however, they have a long way to go, as Woolf suggests:

'There are two key characteristics of universities which undermine their ability to provide good education and training in some areas. First, they are self-contained and separate from the workplace. They cannot for either financial or practical reasons, possibly keep up with all the changes that take place in a fast-developing industry – the new machinery and techniques, new markets, the emerging competitiveness. And because they are separate their instruction takes place in environments which are not like the workplace. Universities use classrooms. They assess and mark people individually, which is the only fair thing to do – and what students, very reasonably, demand – since people then go out into the world as individuals, with their individual degree results. University rhetoric about developing teamwork is consequently not worth very much. When people in work are asked about the type of training they have found the most valuable, "on-the-job training", invariably comes out on top by a mile; and it is what universities cannot, by their nature, provide.

Secondly, university teachers, however vocational their speciality, are making their careers as academics, not as practitioners of the profession, trade or calling they teach. The tension, in university life, between teaching and research is a permanent one. Teaching is ultimately, what universities exist to do. But research is what academics like to do, and it is what helps to maintain the universities ability genuinely to promote understanding and, critically, it is something on which one can reach fairly objective judgements about people's quality and abilities. You cannot sit around a table looking at direct evidence of teaching skills in a way you can with research publications. So research publications inevitably get the most attention from the ambitious and able.' (Cited in De Burgh, Fazackerley and Black, 2007. pp. 278-9)

Consequently, the ultimate value proposition for universities, Waterhouse argues, 'is not that they can teach, nor even that they can sell research, but that they can assess: they accredit learning and are awarding bodies. It is this social certification of successful learning that individuals, employers and ultimately society pay for.' The next reinvention for the sector is contemporary vocationalisation and responsiveness to economic imperatives rather than learning. So what is being said here is that universities have engaged in a form of vocationalisation and that technical needs of business have generally been met outside the system, although the universities have engaged in the practice of the new industries.

The Reassertion of the Knowledge Economy

The arguments about university engagement in work-based learning are inevitably caught up with a wider debate about the purpose of these institutions and their role in economic development. Blunkett (2000), speaking on 'Modernising Higher Education' as Secretary of State for Education and Skills, argued that change was necessary: 'Higher education policymaking is now subject to new constraints caused by the rapidity of change, a situation unthinkable in the 1960s Robbins era. And this change is related to the fundamental socio-economic development of the last quarter of the 20th century: globalisation.' These views are echoed by the Institute of Directors:

'Education and skills are crucial ingredients for business success. Businesses need to have an educated and skilled workforce in order to enhance their productivity, quality of service and overall competitiveness. Business success is important because it can result in employment and wealth creation and so contribute towards financing the public services through taxation.' (Wilson, 2006)

In 2009, Mandelson, the Secretary of State for Business and Universities reaffirmed these themes:

'...the modern global economy puts a premium on specialization. It is an economy of supply chains and niches. The sectors in which British firms have potential comparative advantage in the next decade – low carbon, digital communications, life science, the creative industries: these are all absolutely reliant on high levels of knowledge, of skill and innovation. They will also draw heavily on our capacity for research and our ability to commercialise it. So our universities

are inescapably central to our economic future.' (Mandelson, 2009, speech at Birkbeck College, University of London)

The interest in globalisation has created the environment for the knowledge economy. For the purposes of clarity, in this case, globalisation is understood to mean, 'The growing interdependence of countries world-wide through the increasing volume and variety of cross-border transactions in goods and services, and also through the more rapid and widespread diffusion of technology. Not just an economic phenomenon, but frequently described as such.' (New Zealand Ministry of Foreign Affairs and Trade, 2006). In higher education policy terms it has been interpreted as a need for virtual universities, international alliances, expansion with diversity and excellence, wider participation and expanded student numbers, and a role in securing economic competitiveness and social cohesion. Vocational relevance to improve competitiveness and social inclusion, and generate wealth may then be summarised as the New Labour higher education strategy.

As Brennan (2005) suggests, in this setting, learning is seen as an integral and ongoing feature of working. This is reflected in the DfEE Green Paper (1998) which highlights the rise of the knowledge economy, or the learning society. Brennan argues, in this version of human capital theory, that intellectual capital has become critical to economic success. This approach focuses on the importance of knowledge creation, and the application and manipulation of 'new' knowledge in the workplace. Garnett describes it as:

> *'It is intellectual capital that is the true measure of the wealth of an organisation. The importance attached to the concept of intellectual capital is indicative of a revolutionary shift from the company as a place of production to being a 'place of thinking'. At one level this could be thinking to improve what is it being done or at a deeper level a fundamental change in what is being done.' (Garnett, Costley and Workman, 2009, p. 226)*

He develops this theme by suggesting that knowledge can only have a value to the organisation if it contributes to the aims of the organisation. This he says 'places an emphasis for the organisation on identifying, utilising and measuring the performance of the value of knowledge' (Garnett, Costley and Workman, 2009, p. 228).

The authors of a High Level *Review of Training Packages in Australia (Australian National Training Authority, 2003)* suggest that this new knowledge is different such that:

- The production of new knowledge within organisations and enterprises is different from the knowledge outlined in traditional subjects or disciplines, and common in educational and training programmes.
- New knowledge is high in use-value for the enterprise or organisation. Its deployment has immediate value but, as it is context specific, its value within the enterprise or organisation may be short-lived.
- New knowledge is not foundational and cannot be codified into written texts such as competency standard descriptions, procedural manuals or textbooks; rather it is constructed within the context and environment of the immediate workplace.
- New knowledge is therefore rarely the product of individuals but is constructed through collaborations and networks that exist within specific sites and particular contexts.

Brennan (2005) reasons that this new knowledge is conceptualised as practical, interdisciplinary, informal, applied and contextual rather than theoretical, disciplinary, formal, foundational and generalisable. She posits that relevance no longer equates with the 'application' of knowledge to the workplace, but instead, the workplace itself is seen as a site of learning, knowledge and knowledge production. When this view of the nature of knowledge in the workplace is linked with an analysis of the skill requirements generated by changes to the way work is organised, it would appear that a higher proportion of workers are now expected to use their technical and generic knowledge and skills to contribute to the production of new knowledge within the workplace. The application of skills previously learned outside the work context may no longer be sufficient.

A view proffered by Brennan is that current demands for work-based learning differ from those involved in formal university award courses in that they:

- do not rely on the intervention of institutionally-based teachers or organizationally-based workplace trainers;
- are not structured around predetermined vocational outcomes;
- are not determined by qualification frameworks and endorsed training packages;
- are not guided by specific content;
- are not organised around the 'enabling' disciplines.

Instead, the main characteristics of work-based learning, as identified by Brennan (2005), are that it:

- is context bound, driven by specific and immediate work requirements;
- emphasises learning over teaching or training as a defining characteristic;
- depends on the responsibility for learning being spread between a number of people within the workplace;
- is consistent with new learning concepts such as learning networks, learning organisation and communities of practice.

The changing nature of work is relevant to the integration of work-based learning into higher education in that it points to significant changes in the 'content' or curriculum of higher education programmes, as well as where and how it should be delivered or achieved. It also suggests that the historic dominance of universities in knowledge production is being eroded, and that knowledge production increasingly becomes a collaborative activity based in and around the workplace. As the University Vocational Awards Council (UVAC) indicates, if higher education is to continue to make a contribution to the knowledge economy, it becomes necessary for higher education to expand work-based learning and recognise the workplace as a legitimate site of knowledge production and commercialisation. In order to realise this universities need to build formal and informal relationships with the creative industries, employers, operatives, students and their own staff.

In this context partnership and collaboration between employers, employers' organisations, workers, further and higher education providers assumes a particular significance. The concepts of lifelong learning and learning for work, at and through work, also highlight the importance of continued training, individual personal and professional development and workforce development. In turn, the notion of continuous learning and its recognition emphasise the need for vocational progression routes in and through higher education. These elements have become cornerstones of recent policy affecting higher and further education (Brennan, 2005) along with the need to commercialise university activity.

However, it should be noted that there is scepticism about the extent and nature of changes in the work context and its implications for the development of knowledge and skill, regarding them as primarily aspirational, rather than descriptive of the current contexts of work. Nevertheless, as so many elements of these analyses have become incorporated into the policy agenda for education and training in the UK, they effectively become a reality for both learners and providers. The HEFCE inevitably reflects this:

> '*A key role for universities … is … activity to meet the needs of business and the community, contributing to economic and social development both regionally and nationally. We are committed to encouraging and rewarding partnerships between HEIs and business, the transfer of knowledge and expertise, and the development of employment skills.' (HEFCE, 2004)*

So, what does this mean for the university as a corporation? As Mould, Roodhouse and Vorley (2006) state, the role of the university has changed in the last 25 years with the (re)emergence of a 'third mission' (teaching and research being the first two) which is concerned with the commercialisation and transfer of academic activities to the economy, a process known as knowledge transfer. Charles (2003) describes how the former blue-sky priorities of ivory tower institutions are increasingly challenged by demands for vocational training and employable skills, which is arguably unsurprising in light of the transition from elitist to mass higher education. Further to this, Claes (2002) notes that while the core function of the contemporary university is currently blue-sky research-based teaching, this is subject to increasing negotiation. Gray (2001) aptly identifies this amidst the transition from tradition to science as the source of intellectual authority. Indeed, Kerr (1963) observes the 'multiversity' to be a more appropriate interpretation of the contemporary university on account of their increasingly diverse remit and function. The shift from a historical and societal institution to an innovation-led and commercially orientated institution can be seen as a result of the third mission outlined by the 1993 Government White Paper 'Realising our Potential' (Cabinet Office, 1993).

Mould, Roodhouse and Vorley also point out as a result of this transition, Gumport (2000) finds the universities attempting to (re)legitimise their role as a societal institution, and shed the perception of higher education as an industry. As societal institutions, universities assume a broad range of social functions which Gumport finds to include 'cultivation of citizenship, the preservation of cultural heritage(s), and the formation of individual character and habits of mind'. In contrast, Gumport also identifies the corporate model of the university as to 'produce and sell services, train some of the workforce, advance economic development and perform research'. Kerr (1987) describes this tension between higher education as a societal institution and higher education as an industry, as the 'accumulated heritage versus modern imperatives'. He continues to note these conflicting ideologies as critical to the future form of the university and to higher education in industrialised nations. Undoubtedly this ongoing transformation of higher education in the UK has become dominated by the dawn of third-stream activities as universities endeavour to resolve, reassert and (re)legitimate themselves as quasi-public institutions. Indeed, Godin and Gingras (2000) observe universities to be highly significant to the knowledge-based economy, finding them to be at the 'heart of [knowledge production] systems and that all other actors rely heavily on their expertise'.

However, while the ideology of the entrepreneurial university is largely accepted, it is important to note the more moderate interpretations of 'academic capitalism' (Slaughter and Leslie, 1997) and the 'enterprise university' (Marginson and Considine, 2000), which contest the extent of the entrepreneurial university's role and capabilities, and how organisational contradictions are resolved. Further to this, employer engagement and commercialism, in the context of an entrepreneurial university, was reinforced through alternative sources of public finance including the University Challenge Fund and the Strategic Development Fund, to realise their value to the knowledge-based economy. These alternative sources of 'third-stream' funding do not, and are not intended to, replace diminishing teaching and research income, but create the opportunity for greater future financial autonomy through generating alternative income. Geuna and Nesta (2003) identify the paradigm shift associated with the rise of the entrepreneurial university as having resulted in the dominant norm becoming the management of industrial research agreements, assessment and protection of intellectual property, and the commercial translation of science rather than blue-sky research.

It is these imperatives which are driving public education and training policy, particularly employer engagement and workforce development, thus work-based learning.

The Influence of Changing Employment Patterns and Work Organisation

A better understanding of the economic and policy drivers referred to earlier can be achieved by briefly examining their impact on organisations and the people working for them. The most significant of these structural changes can be summarised as:

- Increased use of collaboration such as outsourcing to manage non-core functions, whereby a number of individual firms collaborate with each other to manage production of an end product or service.
- Flattening of traditional bureaucratic hierarchies, creating fewer layers of management, with the consequence that, in many occupations, workers are required to take on broader responsibilities. In addition to technical tasks, workers then develop a wider range of skills in order to enable them to contribute to the strategic performance of the organisation by engaging in quality management, teamwork, and interpersonal and inter-organisational collaboration.
- Restructuring and downsizing as a strategy for maintaining flexibility in order to respond quickly to changing market requirements.
- A rise in non-standard work as a consequence of restructuring and downsizing as organisations seek to adjust the size and composition of their workforce in response to market requirements.
- Breakdown of traditional occupational demarcations leading to multi-skilling across all major occupations.

In summary, as reported by the Organisation for Economic Co-operation and Development (OECD), a survey of the relevance of education to work indicates that these contemporary organisational workplaces are now characterised by: further increases in job complexity; multi-tasking and multi-skilling; increased requirements for qualifications as evidence of skills; ongoing use of enterprise training for skill formation; further reduction in organisational hierarchy; increased distribution of responsibility to individuals and teams; and increased use of performance-based pay (OECD as cited by CMEC, 1998).

It is also worth noting that restructuring, downsizing and outsourcing have resulted in a decline in the number of large companies and organisations, and a growth in small to medium-sized enterprise (SME) employment, often providing a specialised product or service. This had led to an increasing demand from SME employers for workers with higher-level skills and support to help them train and develop their staff. Since SMEs have limited numbers of staff (10 to 250 employees) it is difficult for employers to 'release' them for education and training away from the workplace. For these enterprises, work-based learning may be the only way forward.

In this context, higher education has always been associated with preparation for work or a vocation, particularly in relation to entry to professions as explained by Waterhouse (2002). Once entry was achieved, being a member of a British profession was regarded as a 'job for life' and in consequence, preparation for work prior to entry into employment, usually followed by some kind of probationary period in employment, appeared to be an appropriate model. In addition, until recently, only a relatively small proportion of the population needed to have a university education to prepare them for work. However, employment patterns, and the ways in which work is organised, have changed considerably over the last 30 years. Far more areas of employment are now considered to be areas of graduate employment such as nursing and require a degree or equivalent for entry into employment or to be achieved during employment. Higher education needs to respond to the growth in the scale of graduate employment, and in the range of work sectors to which the description applies.

On the other hand, analysis of the structure of the labour market over the last 15 to 20 years suggests that employment patterns in most industrial societies have undergone considerable upheaval (De Grip, Loo and Sanders, 1999); traditional career patterns are breaking down and full-time permanent employment is no longer the predominant pattern. For example, there are 3.7 million self-employed individuals who account for 2.6 million jobs in the UK economy, out of a total of 26.2 million (Cowling, 2003). Although this may not be true of all work sectors, this analysis has been widely adopted with the result that recent government policies, such as the commitment to creating patterns of lifelong learning, are based on such premises.

In a number of enterprises, full-time employment has been replaced by 'non-standard' work, particularly part-time, casual and contract work. Of particular relevance to the present context is the rise in 'portfolio' or 'free-agent' contract workers who must take on the responsibility for managing their own careers and skills development in order to become, or remain, employable. Up-skilling and lifelong learning become the new buzz words associated with the move away from the 'job for life' and the need for individuals to develop new skills and to update existing skills throughout their working lives as the job market dictates.

For individuals who are self-employed or managing their own businesses, lifelong learning becomes essential if they are to be successful; at the same time they face pressures to limit the amount of time spent away from work. For this reason, strategies to engage in programmes tailored to their specific needs and based within work become crucial. The facility for higher education to provide work-based programmes for the purpose of personal development, either leading to a qualification or to meet specific skills needs, offers a mechanism for addressing the needs of the portfolio worker, whether that person is self-employed or working within an organisation.

The changing shape of the labour market is considered to be a direct consequence of changes to the ways that work is organised, shifting from bureaucratic patterns to more flexible modes of organising work through collaboration. Organisations are now required 'to be more agile, to be able to respond quickly to changing market conditions and to develop new collaborative capabilities both within and between organisations' (Australian National Training Authority, 2003).

2 Defining and Theorizing University Work-Based Learning

SIMON ROODHOUSE

This chapter sets out to provide an explanation of the boundaries of work-based learning for the purposes of this book and the dominant theories underpinning the concept. These observations are then placed in the context of the institution, employer and individual as the key actors in the work-based learning story.

Definitions

Turning to 'work-based learning', as explained by Costley (2001), the term is part of a cluster of concepts, including 'lifelong learning', 'employability' and 'flexibility'. Unwin and Fuller (2003), elaborate these distinctions by concentrating on workplace as opposed to work-based learning:

> 'The term "workplace learning" is used to embrace all types of learning which are generated or stimulated by the needs of the workplace including formal on-the-job training, informal learning and work-related off-the-job education and training.' (Unwin and Fuller, 2003, p. 7 cited in Evans and Kersh, 2006, p. 4)

Boud and Symes (2000, p. 14, cited in Evans and Kersh, 2006, p. 4) take this further by making a distinction between these two terms:

> 'Work-based learning needs to be distinguished from work place learning, that form of learning that occurs on a day-to-day basis at work as employees acquire new skills to develop new approaches to solving problems. No formal education recognition normally accrues to such learning, whether or not it is organised systematically.'

One of the challenges which results from this is to attempt to introduce some clarity about what work-based learning at this level involves and the contexts in which it occurs:

> 'It is evident there can be no single or simple definition of what work based learning entails beyond the notion that it is about learning (not teaching) and occurs in the workplace (rather than on campus). As such, work based learning can, and should be, distinguished from the notion of work related learning; the latter, in the form of vocational programmes designed to prepare people for employment which often includes employer-determined competencies e.g. national

occupational standards, and does not necessarily require significant areas of the curriculum to be completed in the work place itself. Neither should it be assumed that work based learning in the higher education context is specifically about training; work based learning may take many forms and be undertaken for a number of different purposes; it is not restricted to performance-related learning in a narrow sense. Instead, the emphasis is on identifying and demonstrating learning that has occurred through work based activity, wherever and however this may have been achieved.' (UVAC, 2005)

This position is underlined by the Higher Education Academy's guide to learning and employability:

'It is not necessarily the experience of work itself that is paramount – rather it is the learning that an individual derives from that experience of work and from reflecting upon it. A government-sponsored review recognised that work based learning could take many forms including a full-time undergraduate undertaking a work placement planned as part of the curriculum; a full-time undergraduate doing a part-time job; a full-time employee seeking to explore work focused and work-related issues in the context of the knowledge, skills and values of a higher education institution. The common factor linking these forms was that the individual would be doing a job of work, or would be undertaking a work role.' (Little and ESECT, 2004)

However, confusion remains over work-based learning terminology for employers and higher education, and as a result it is recognised as essential that a common language is established:

'… it is critically important to establish a shared understanding of the particular area of focus from both an academic and employer perspective, irrespective of the terms used.' (Nixon et al., 2006)

It is also clear that the work-based learning landscape has become more densely populated in recent years, with diverse partners, players and cultures now located on its territories. However, one concept that is frequently used in discussions of work-based learning is 'flexibility'; all organisations, including higher education, are expected to respond flexibly and rapidly to labour market changes. Flexibility may require working in partnership or collaboratively with other organisations in order to achieve desired goals most effectively. With this drive to create flexible organisations has come a corresponding emphasis on flexible learning, within and across organisations, which includes different learning levels, contexts, and modes of delivery and assessment methodologies.

As Garrick and Usher (2000) state:

'Organizations are expected to respond flexibly and rapidly to market changes and a premium is now placed on the need for flexibility not only within workplaces but also between them. Within this context are located interlinking discourses of flexible organizations, flexible workers and a consequent perceived need amongst managers (at a range of levels) for flexible structures, modes and contents of learning to service these organisations and workers.'

Flexible learning and work-based learning are used almost interchangeably by government agencies; for example, in a DfES White Paper (DfES, 2005) there is reference to progression taking place through 'flexible, i.e. work-based learning routes'. Along with online and distance learning delivery mechanisms, work-based learning routes have come to be regarded as an important part of flexible learning processes.

Work-based learning is an emerging discrete university subject which is taught, studied and researched, 'a field of study', (Gibbs and Garnett, 2007, cited in Garnett, Costley and Workman, 2009, p. 3) in its own right. It is not a traditional part-time course undertaken whilst at work but rather:

> *'The demonstration of your ability to reflect upon your skills, knowledge and approach to your work, often called your 'professional practice'. In some situations, learners will develop occupational competence alongside the WBL programme and this is usually assessed separately by the employer,' (Durrant, Rhodes and Young, 2009, p. 2)*

The emphasis in this model is on what has and can be learnt at work by carrying out the job, interacting with colleagues and identifying and reflecting on processes and procedures, the corporate memory relies on being employed. In this respect, employment is defined as:

- 'paid work;
- underpaid work, which could include voluntary work or working within a family business them receiving remuneration;
- full-time or part-time employment;
- self-employed workers and business owners – from actors, artists and builders to farmers, gardeners and restaurateurs.

In short, work-based learning is for anyone who is regularly engaged in work (or undertakes periods of contractual work sufficiently long enough to complete a programme of study), whatever the nature of that work.' (Durrant, Rhodes and Young, 2009, p. 19)

Some Theoretical Perspectives

This focus on the work-based or workplace learning has not unexpectedly been theorized. Much of the literature is derived from studies into different forms of learning which have been of interest to university Schools of Education, Adult and Continuing Education, Business, Management Studies and, more recently, newer higher education subjects such as nursing and allied health. The increasing interest in professional practice has also stimulated study and writing particularly about contextual knowledge and transfer (Evans, Guile and Harris, 2009). In addition, social scientists such as Bourdieu have been interested in the workplace practice culture and its relationship to theory.

Kolb, Schon, Boud and Eraut perhaps can be recognised as key thinkers and influencers in this field. Kolb developed the Experiential Learning Model composed of four elements:

- Concrete experience.
- Observation of and reflection on that experience.
- Formation of abstract concepts based upon the reflection.
- Testing the new concepts.

These four elements are the essence of a spiral of learning that can begin with any one of the four elements, but typically begins with a concrete experience. His model was developed predominantly for use with adult education, but has found widespread pedagogical implications in higher education.

Schon was largely responsible for introducing reflective practice which is a continuous process and involves the learner considering critical incidents in his or her life experiences. As defined by Schon, reflective practice involves thoughtfully considering one's own experiences in applying knowledge to practice while being coached by professionals in the discipline. In education, it refers to the process of the educator studying his or her own teaching methods and determining what works best for the students. He additionally argued that organisations and individuals should be flexible and incorporate lessons learned throughout their lifespans, into what is now a well-established discipline in management and business studies: organisational learning.

Boud is interested in how people learn and the fostering of that learning through mechanisms such as problem-based and negotiated learning incorporating reflection and reciprocal peer learning. He has developed models for learning from experience and the role of those who intervene in learning whether or not they are identified as teachers. Problem-based learning (PBL) is a student-centred instructional strategy in which students collaboratively solve problems and reflect on their experiences. The characteristics of PBL are:

• Learning is driven by challenging, open-ended problems.
• Students work in small collaborative groups.
• Teachers take on the role as 'facilitators' of learning.

Students are encouraged to take responsibility for their group and organise and direct the learning process with support from a tutor or instructor.

How professionals learn in workplace settings has been Eraut's focus. He found that most learning occurs informally during normal working processes and that there is considerable scope for recognising and enhancing such learning. As mentioned earlier, the current focus is on developing an 'epistemology of practice where knowledge is created and used rather than codified' (Costley and Gibbs, p. 221, cited in Garnett, Costley and Workman, 2009).

Institutional Work-Based Learning

In higher education, workforce development is often referred to as work-based learning and is increasingly recognised as a field of study. Defining workforce development as work-based learning, Costley (2001) argues that it enables higher education to incorporate, in particular, the learning people do, for, in and through work into the learning provided. She also draws our attention to the longevity of engagement in work-based learning in the sector:

'Some universities have been involved in work based learning for a long time, for example, through placements and sandwich courses. Some universities have structured courses where continuing professional development with the knowledge gained through experience is accepted

implicitly. Others use the processes of accrediting prior and experiential learning (APEL) to formally recognise such knowledge….Learning contracts are becoming familiar instruments. These activities are variously described as work based, work related, placement activities, elective modules, independent study, APEL, reach out, CPD, work based learning among others. It is worth noting that work based learning in higher education is nearly always part of an existing university programme with its own disciplinary frameworks and approaches to higher education. Learning outcomes and criteria for assessment are therefore within the subject knowledge born of research and scholarly activities that already are embedded in the universities.' (Costley, 2001)

What is difficult to conceptualise is the lack of sustained engagement by higher education in workforce development, when there have been long vocational learning traditions in theology, law, construction and medicine. This may be to do with a traditional university interest in entry-level education for the professions, 'liberal' adult education or social function. However, from a contemporary business employer perspective, the Institute of Directors concluded:

'The quality of the UK's education system and the skill deficiencies in our workforce remain disappointing elements on the country's scorecard. Until this sorry state of affairs is tackled, too many individuals will fail to develop their potential, too many businesses will suffer from skill shortages and skill gaps and too many organisations will fail to improve productivity, thereby impeding the country's economic performance.' (Wilson, 2006)

A description of well-meaning misunderstandings and cultural distinctions perhaps pinpoints the underlying causes for a slow and partial response to work-based learning:

'We somehow seem to be incapable of learning from experience. Succeeding generations of employers are still marooned in tedious development project steering committees whose proceedings take place in academic jargon. Frustrated academics are still struggling to secure placements and projects with the very companies who are lambasting the quality of their graduates' work readiness.' (UVAC, 2002)

It could also be concerned with intellectual scepticism amongst the academic community, that employability which is associated with work-based learning is nothing more than a continuous conflict between individuals, market demands and fluctuations: 'Employability not only depends on fulfilling the requirements of a specific job, but also on how one stands relative to others within a hierarchy of job seekers.' (Brown, Hesketh and Williams, 2003) In other words it has little relevance to the understanding of the subject or discipline, a primary function of learning in universities.

There is no doubt that higher education has been highly successful in developing and delivering entry to work programmes for many years; that is, qualifying people for work at higher levels. The sector continues to engage in giving graduates 'the relative chances of acquiring and maintaining different kinds of employment' (Brown, Hesketh and Williams, 2003) which 'involves both the capacity and the willingness to be and to remain attractive for the labour market, by anticipating changes in tasks and work environment and reacting on them'(De Grip, Loo and Sanders, 1999).

However, continuous professional development, retraining, part-time provision, learning diagnostics, assessment and certification, all work based, remain marginal. Why is this the case, when the national economic and social demands are as strident as ever? Part of the story is a general lack, at a local university level, of an overall institutional work-based learning strategy and lack of relative importance attached to this type of activity, including making links with business compared with developing academic research and international standing (Connor, 2005). This could be attributed to public sector funding priorities which, until recently, have not encouraged higher education engagement in workforce development.

In this respect, it is noticeable that national work-based learning government initiatives, such as modern and graduate apprenticeships, have failed to become integral components of further and higher education progression routes (UVAC, 2003a). A lack of employer awareness of higher eduation, and the perception that higher education is out of touch, impractical, and unresponsive to employer needs, continues to act as a barrier to higher education engagement with employers (Faithorn, 2005).

However considerable effort has been made to develop work-based learning, particularly by institutions such as Middlesex, Anglia Ruskin, Portsmouth, Derby, Glamorgan and Northumbria universities. It has been achieved through the individual and organisational desire to respond to local and regional needs. This is despite the paucity of coincident policy directives from agencies with responsibility for business, skills, education and learning. Whatever the national policy drive, mechanisms to connect business needs with higher education provision are generally disorganised and confusing.

What Does this Mean for the Individual, Employer and University?

There is increasing interest by employees, employers and universities in workplace learning. Those in work are increasingly undertaking work-based learning qualifications because they:

- 'Are able to see direct relevance between studying for a qualification to work-based learning and their role in the workplace.
- Can obtain support from their employers.
- Are able to develop the programme around their own professional development needs and individual interests.
- Are able to negotiate the focus, context, timescale and assessment of their work.
- Can fit this flexible form of study into their working and personal lives.
- View studying for an accredited qualification as evidence of commitment to their professional role.
- Seek career progression and the potential for increased earnings.' (Durrant, Rhodes and Young, 2009, p. 10)

Durrant, Rhodes and Young (2009, p. 11) explain the value of work-based learning and accreditation to the employer as:

- Staff undertake real work projects which offer direct benefit to their organisation.

- The workforce becomes motivated and focused on organisational challenges.
- Staff on the work-based learning programmes become more closely engaged in organisational processes.
- Increased loyalty results from the visible and tangible investment in the development of the workforce.
- Staff retention rates are improved and enhanced capabilities of existing workforce can help with recruitment – both as a means of attracting new employees, but also as a means of promoting from within the organisation.
- Studying on a work-based learning programme to help employees to achieve their full potential.
- They can work with the university to develop a programme which not only supports the professional development of their staff which also focuses on organisational improvement.
- Organisational and cultural change can be effected through small-scale developments via work-based learning projects.
- Work-based learning can be a means of addressing and meeting an organisation's business plans.

It is equally important in this tripartite arrangement to recognise that: universities have a stake in workforce development; the labour market and employer demand hence work-based learning. However, there is no common language between universities and employers; and there are national structural faults in the system. Consequently it is no surprise that work-based learning as 'the new kid on the curriculum and qualification block' in higher education is less well developed than perhaps it should be.

3 Legitimising Work-Based Learning Programmes of Study

PENNY MCCRACKEN

This chapter discusses the complex business of legitimising work-based learning in universities. It is the 'hard wiring' required to assure the quality and standards of university degrees in the interests of the public. In particular, the chapter focuses on the recent developments of the Quality Assurance Agency for Higher Education (QAA), national skills policy initiatives and public funding challenges regarding work-based learning being delivered in the UK. It is important to have some understanding of this because the QAA effectively determines the climate for the universities to operate their qualifications which in turn impacts on the forms of delivery, curriculum and relationships of those awards.

Introduction

In the UK all degree programmes, whether Foundation, Bachelors or Masters and Doctorates, can only be awarded by higher education institutions (also known as HEI) granted the appropriate degree awarding powers by the Privy Council. All such awards have to be formally approved by the university or higher education institution before students can be enrolled. In this chapter, this process is referred to as validation, although the universities themselves may use other terms. Since 2000, validation has been guided by the QAA Academic Infrastructure (AI) and, in particular section 7 of the *Code of Practice for the Assurance of Academic Quality and Standards (the Code)* which covers programme design, approval, monitoring and review (QAA, 2006). The AI is a set of nationally agreed external reference points in use throughout higher education. Universities use various parts of this at relevant points in their monitoring and approval processes to assure themselves of the academic standards and quality of learning opportunities of their awards.

The AI does not require compliance but provides a set of precepts which represent good practice. Within the UK, where higher education institutions are autonomous, each institution providing higher education programmes decides how the precepts most effectively apply in its context. As a result, although all higher education institutions carry out processes of approval, it takes different forms in each. Nevertheless there are several broadly similar stages: initial approval in the light of market research to proceed with the development; an initial internal scrutiny of the developed programme; and a final approval process. This last stage is often, but not always, an event when a panel of internal staff from outside the subject area, together with an external expert, often a subject expert from another university, read the paperwork and have a discussion with the programme team and relevant senior staff. Even when there is not an event, external peer input is an essential part of the process.

A Context

During the early development of the AI, work-based learning (also known as WBL) was a minor feature of the sector. So for example, sandwich years in industry and a year abroad for language students were always a discrete element, rarely assessed, and validation panels were familiar with these traditional elements of programmes. It was not until 2001–02 with the introduction of the Foundation degree with its strong vocational orientation, that universities were required to address the work-based learning agenda at validation in any significant way. It is, as a result, important in the context of university work-based learning to consider this new qualification. It should be noted that work-based learning is not exclusive to Foundation degrees but is significantly different from the traditional placement schemes and sandwich courses. Work-based learning for part-time students in employment was unusual, especially at undergraduate level.

In 2000, the Government initiated the development of a completely new higher education award in England, the Foundation degree. The HEFCE invited higher education institutions to bid for funding to develop and run this new award (HEFCE 2000/27). The Foundation degree consists of 240 credits at higher education levels 4 and 5 and it is an intermediate-level award on the Framework for Higher Education Qualifications (FHEQ) (QAA, 2008). In addition it has a number of defining characteristics, all of which previously existed separately but not together in one award. These included: employer involvement in the design and review of the programme; the opportunity for learners to study in the workplace; integration of work-based learning and academic study; guaranteed progression to an Honours degree with a maximum period of additional study of 1.3 years full time (pro-rata by part-time study); and flexibility. In addition, the intention was to encourage partnership arrangements across higher education providers, employers, employer organisations such as Sector Skills Councils (SSCs) and professional bodies (QAA, 2002 and 2004) to meet the UK intermediate labour market skill shortfalls (QAA, 2002).

In the first year of operation, 4,320 students enrolled on Foundation degrees of whom 2,530 were full time (HEFCE and QAA, 2007). This was no surprise since the developments were essentially supply-led with funding from the HEFCE. The development time for the first tranche of awards was short and, as such, unhelpful to institutions as it left little opportunity to consider the full implications and potential variations for the new award before enrolling the first students. Universities employed their normal validation processes for the new awards. However, the main operating difficulties for some of these qualifications lay in the choice of panel members engaged to validate them. Universities generally used internal and external panel members who were predominantly subject-based and did not necessarily have sufficient work-based learning experience. The number of university staff in the sector with work-based learning experience was itself limited.

In 2001, universities and their partner colleges still tended to think predominantly in terms of full-time students and programmes rather than facilitating learning and criterion-referenced assessment using competence frameworks. The introduction of nursing degrees also brought the combination of competence frameworks and academic learning outcomes together at undergraduate level but these programmes tended to remain within the relevant faculties and the experience was rarely shared across the institution. There had also been a trend in the post 1992 universities, formerly polytechnics, some with a strong vocational and technical orientation, to convert their Higher National Diplomas (HNDs) into degrees. However, further education colleges with an interest in higher education also had experience of HNDs, which often had placements, and Higher National Certificates (HNCs), which were normally studied by students in employment on a day-release basis. Because of the availability of additional student numbers (ASNs) from HEFCE and the associated funding to support the introduction of Foundation degrees, a number of institutions converted HNDs to the new qualification. This was particularly the case in areas such as art and design and sports studies, whereas programmes in sectors where the HND was widely accepted by employers, such as engineering, saw relatively few conversions. As noted in the QAA survey of 2005, the majority of institutions who took this route did not consider the different distinctions between placements in the HND and the integrated work-based learning and academic study needed in Foundation degrees (QAA, 2005a).

The short development period for the early Foundation degrees meant that institutions had little time to engage in detailed discussions with employers, particularly with new employer partnerships or new employment sectors. They were, as a result, validating programmes in the late summer or even early autumn at the same time as marketing the programme and recruiting students. Some were initially approved for perhaps two or three years, giving the university the chance to review the programme in the light of the early implementation experiences. The QAA survey of 2005 found that five of the 34 programmes reviewed in 2002–03 were revalidated by their higher education institutions after two years (QAA, 2005b). Other programmes were originally validated for the normal five or six year period although again the QAA survey noted that by 2004-05 most of the original programmes had undergone significant changes as institutions learnt from the course operation and changing external circumstances.

HEFCE commissioned two special reviews of Foundation degrees in 2002 and 2004. In addition, in the same year, it commissioned two surveys, one considering HNDs converted to Foundation degrees and the other following up the programmes reviewed in the first special review of 2003–03 (QAA, 2005a and b). These reports provide details of the range of issues providers experienced in launching the first professionally focused higher education intermediate award integrating work-based learning and academic study. A number of these observations concerned validation.

The earliest Foundation degree overview report (QAA, 2003) covered a sample of 33 programmes, accounting for about a third of the total number of Foundation degrees which had enrolled students in 2001. These were selected to cover a range of subjects, modes of attendance, size of consortia and geographical distribution. Because the award was new, the reviews were undertaken in order to identify whether the qualification was working as intended, or would do so when fully operational. The individual reports were not published but remained confidential to HEFCE, QAA and the individual providers. However, an overview report was published in order to share with other providers the learning experiences of the early Foundation degrees. This identified a number of problems concerned with implementing the programmes which could have been resolved earlier or even prevented if recognised at the university validation stage. The survey following up these programmes two years later identified that these had not entirely been resolved. The areas identified for further development included:

- finding strategies for responding appropriately to industry needs for short-term programmes and rapid changes in the sector
- ensuring that the distinctive nature of the Foundation degree is achieved and monitored
- ensuring there are intended learning outcomes (ILOs) for work-based learning and that students can demonstrate achievement of the ILOs by appropriate assessment of modules and work-based learning
- ensuring that the integration of work-based learning and academic study is carefully planned into the curricula of all programmes.

The emphasis on such areas reveals that some higher education institutions had still not fully grasped the characteristics and potential of work-based learning programmes and were treating them as traditional courses with conventional full-time student cohorts. Similarly the 2005 overview report of a different and larger sample of Foundation degree programmes identified that 'in a few audit reports..., auditors have identified weak procedures in the validation of Fds and raised concerns about the effectiveness of higher education institutions' oversight of the awards' (QAA, 2005b). Analysis of the reports indicates that the areas identified by QAA for development included processes such as institutional validation processes rather than matters concerning the operation of the Foundation degree.

What is it about this qualification which caused the well-practiced and familiar institutional validation processes to work less effectively? The early stages of implementation exposed a combination of issues:

- characteristics of Foundation degrees not being fully included by the programme team
- the validation panel not identifying the missing characteristics
- inexperience with work-based learning on the part of some programme teams and the central unit dealing with validation
- the choice of external and internal panel members
- underestimation of the challenges of working with employers
- an incomplete understanding on the part of employers as to their role (QAA, 2003).

The second review of Foundation degrees found that, generally, higher education institutions learnt quickly and adjusted the programmes and procedures in the light of experience. More institutions were developing Foundation degrees and had to start from scratch since in the early years there was no central forum to facilitate the sharing of experience. Indeed this was one of the purposes of the first QAA overview report in 2003. *fdf* (Foundation Degree Forward) was not established until 2004 when it took on aspects of this role. So the second overview report of 2005 also found that validation was an area for further development. Other factors occurring around the same time period helped to promote a more widely shared understanding of work-based learning in university qualifications.

Higher-level Skills and the Leitch Report

The Leitch report was commissioned by the Government in 2004 and published in December 2006 (Leitch, 2006), focusing on the need to develop skills in the workforce for the UK to keep pace with its economic competitors. Leitch suggested that by 2020, over 40 per cent of adults should be qualified to level 4 and above, from 29 per cent in 2005. He also suggested that the balance of skills below this should move from level 2 to level 3, requiring over 1.3 million extra level 3 achievements over the period and increasing the number of apprenticeships to 500,000. However 70 per cent of the 2020 workforce is already in the workplace so it was clear that these goals were never going to be achieved simply by the progression of students through the traditional formal education system.

These figures in the Leitch Report and their implications were reinforced in the Higher Education Consultation Paper published in 2008 by the Department of Innovation, Universities and Skills (DIUS, 2008): 'Around three-quarters of the 2020 workforce have already left compulsory education. So we need more people currently in the workforce to acquire high level skills.'

This, however, is a complex and poorly understood component of Government policy, and does not lend itself to generalisation. Part of that complexity is the individual nature of businesses with their distinctive cultures. This is also mirrored in the university sector with high levels of individuality reflected in the respective missions. Meeting national or regional economic needs might only be one component of corporate university activity and of limited interest to academic departments.

Following this the Government requested HEFCE, in its annual grant letter to higher education institutions, to encourage ways of upskilling the workforce; Foundation degrees were one obvious avenue for this. However, employers, from a university perspective, were slow to engage, not clear about what they wanted and unused to working together. Not surprisingly the public sector Foundation degrees, made up almost entirely of teaching assistants and early years Foundation degrees, had the largest number of programmes and enrolments, at least until 2005 (HEFCE and QAA, 2007). In addition, employer organisations were not always geared up to being a representative voice for their sector in discussions with the higher education providers. Not all SSCs could persuade their employers or seriously engage with universities, some preferring to focus on the further education sector which was seen as being more employer-friendly and responsive. At the local level, some of the British Chambers of Commerce were prepared to work with providers to help SMEs, always the most challenging part of the workforce, to access training and development. However, much of the training provided was short course, unaccredited and delivered by private sector training companies. Universities were not seen by employers as a natural source of training expertise but rather as providers of new work entrants, a place for company high fliers to enhance their careers and network with peers, and a source of subject and technical expertise.

HEFCE Employer Engagement Strategy

In response to the 2007–08 grant letter and the Leitch report, as well as other national skills policy developments, HEFCE established an employer engagement strategy, setting out how it intended to work with higher education to deliver employer engagement.

Although there is a long and varied history of working with employers, often at the postgraduate and research level, the new emphasis here results from an attempt to increase the global competitiveness of the UK (see Chapter 1). The intention of this strategy was to support individual higher education providers to engage more effectively with employers. What form engagement took was left to each higher education institution as long as it was compatible with the institutional mission. The aims of the policy were to develop the capacity of universities in working with diverse employers; provide learning programmes for employees, many of whom will not have previously experienced higher education; and increase the resources for higher education through cash and in-kind contributions from employers. This individualistic approach was seen as the most effective method of meeting employer need while recognising the cultural dynamics of the sector. In effect it was a policy to allow innovation, recognising that some would succeed better than others.

Consequently, the strategy included an employer engagement fund of up to £148 million. Higher education institutions were encouraged to bid for this funding by providing HEFCE with project proposals that would enable them to transform their capacity to respond to employers' higher-level skills needs and to grow learning provision co-funded by employers. In all, the money was allocated to 45 projects, involving well over a third of all institutions in the higher education sector.

In addition higher education providers were engaged in employer responsive provision through other HEFCE funded initiatives such as Lifelong Learning Networks and Higher Level Skills pathfinders. To increase the employer 'in-kind' contributions, a number of universities signed up to deliver over 10,000 new employer co-funded places for the 2008–09 academic year, so increasing the input made by employers through cash and in-kind contributions.

As a result of this significant impetus to engagement with employers in a wide variety of initiatives, those universities involved faced different demands on their corporate systems and procedures. Significant among these were timescales for the approval of programmes, quality assurance and costs. When universities and colleges began active dialogues with employers there were two important messages. More employers were interested in short blocks of learning rather than a degree, at least initially; and they wanted the learning and development now. The idea of waiting a year for the programme to be developed and approved was out of the question.

A number of institutions and organisations began shifting their approaches and systems for working with employers along these lines. Amongst the first to undertake pioneering work were Middlesex, Chester, Anglia Ruskin (then Anglia Polytechnic University), Derby and Portsmouth with Learn Direct and with encouragement from the Employer-based Training Accreditation (EBTA) project initiated by *fdf*. The higher education institutions involved had to reconsider rapidly their award approval processes and ways of offering university accreditation to higher education-level company-delivered training, which employers provided for their employees and for which the latter receive no recognition. Traditionally there was very little verification of how much of this training was applied and used in the workplace and this provided the area which could be assessed at higher education levels. It also helped employers to identify whether the training had been appropriate and effective. Key issues for the higher education institutions were not only the timescales for approving programmes but also devising procedures for doing so since this was a new area of activity. Universities all had procedures for the accreditation of prior learning, both certificated and experiential, in existence, but as the reviews of Foundation degrees found, they were not often used or even promoted (this system is discussed in detail in Chapter 6).

There was a need to develop processes and frameworks for learners in the workplace to accumulate credits towards an award. Initially, much of the employer training, and other continuing professional development programmes, which employers wanted from providers were less than existing awards the universities offered; 240 credits for a Foundation degree or Diploma of Higher Education and 360 credits for an Honours degree. The 120 credit Certificate of Education at level 4 was still an exception and used largely as an interim exit award. Some institutions offered programmes such as continuing professional development courses, which were not awards in higher education institution terms and so remained 'in limbo' outside programmes included in QAA institutional audit. Some responded positively by introducing new awards which could be given for smaller amounts of credit, 60 credits, for example, at various levels, including Master's level. So various smaller components, normally of 10–20 credits could be accumulated into a nationally recognised higher education award from a university.

A group of north-west higher education institutions, working together with EBTA, realised that accrediting a 20 credit module did not carry the same risk to the university as a whole degree. As a result they created a ladder of employer engagement which separated out the various categories of products which might come forward for accreditation and assessed the relevant institutional risks for each. These included:

- validation of bespoke courses
- credit recognition (specific credits)
- credit recognition (general credits)
- learning through work/CPD awards
- articulation agreements
- shell modules
- accreditation of prior experience and learning
- kite-marking or endorsement.

Although this is not the only ladder which might be created, its production helped higher education institutions to realise that they did not need to carry out the same procedures for each product because of the differing levels of risk. Nevertheless, it could take time for the university senior management team to be convinced that this was worth doing, sometimes up to a year. University senior managers and central quality units are understandably inherently cautious about risks to the institution's brand and reputation. One risk they wish to avoid is public criticism in a QAA audit report on the QAA website. This may generate adverse publicity and be detrimental to the institution. So there is a tendency to be cautious, and delay innovation. As the HEFCE/QAA task group found in 2008, financial risks were also an important consideration (see below).

Many employees undertaking training and the assessment of the learning they had gained in the workplace had rarely, if ever, considered higher education or thought they were competent enough to cope with it. The initial short awards provide a crucial route to rewarding achievement and increasing confidence of the employees. Some employers then continued working with their university partner to create larger dedicated awards which learners may continue with, often work-based degrees, diplomas or certificates.

Through these mechanisms learners who were work based were encouraged into university and received national higher education awards for their achievements. As a result new progression routes into and through higher education are being opened up and the workforce increasingly upskilled to higher levels in response to the Leitch report recommendations.

The university validation process requires the scrutiny panel to consider the alignment of the programme/modules with the relevant parts of the QAA AI as well as any other relevant external reference points. In the context of work-based learning, National Occupational Standards (NOS) are clearly relevant. These have been produced by the SSCs and describe the knowledge, competences and personal attributes which someone needs in order to be good or competent in their particular sector (Roodhouse and Swailes, 2007, p. 93). These are most familiar to university faculties in subjects such as social work, in its broad sense, and health-related disciplines. However, they are often less well known, or actually unknown, to those in central university functions, and they rarely feature as a prompt to validation panels as an area to look at. The **fdf** endorsement scheme pilot in 2007–08 specifically asked endorsers to look at the use made by the provider of any relevant NOS, and it emerged that this had not been explicitly covered at the validation in all cases. Opportunities to ensure alignment of the programme with the sector requirements and enhance the employability of students are therefore being missed.

A further dimension to this is accrediting learning which occurs almost entirely through the workplace. Here the content of the programme is work itself. It can be made up of training, projects carried out as part of the normal role at work and other work-based activities. Reflective practice is often used to help learners stand back and consider what they have learnt through carrying out certain activities. They evaluate what they learnt and what they did in order to make the process more effective on another occasion. University staff sometimes find this content disturbing because it does not resemble a traditional curriculum but an increasing number of universities have gained experience with this type of learning. It is an effective way for employers to be able to offer a recognised award to employees who in turn feel supported and encouraged by the employer. They are therefore motivated to work harder, more effectively and tend to stay with the employer longer.

Some institutions made a strategic decision to become more employer responsive/ business-facing institutions and were challenging the degree to which the current quality assurance framework supports or inhibits their ability to be more responsive. QAA undertook work which responded to these concerns, including increased level of activity under HEFCE's employer engagement agenda and issues raised by some institutions about constraints on them by the AI. In 2007, the QAA revised section 9 of the *Code of Practice* to reflect the expanding environment of work-based learning and employer engagement. Work-based and placement learning have become increasingly important elements of many higher education institutions' activities. They involve particular forms of collaboration and can involve a variety of arrangements, for example, between a higher education institution and one or more other bodies, or between a student and a work-based or placement provider. Section 9 of the *Code* is intended to provide guidance on these specific aspects of a higher education award and to support such arrangements where they are a predetermined and integral part of the award, and where their learning outcomes clearly contribute to its overall aims. The section of the *Code* was renamed

Work-Based and Placement Learning, to recognise these developments. The introduction to Section 9 stated that this section of the *Code* was concerned only with arrangements made for identified and agreed learning that typically takes place outside a higher education institution in either a work-based or placement situation.

It became clear too that some institutions had deliberately separated their short-course provision for employers, where it already existed, from their HEFCE-funded courses for students in order not to have to cope with the complexity, as they saw it, of the quality assurance process for this kind of provision.

A Response: The HEFCE/QAA Task Group

Nevertheless, institutions committed to working systematically with employers debated the degree to which the current quality assurance framework might inhibit their ability to be more responsive to employer need. As a result, in autumn 2007, HEFCE and QAA set up a task group to investigate these concerns and HEFCE published the findings in August 2008 (HEFCE and QAA, 2008). The headline findings relating to validation include:

- the current quality assurance framework is regarded by institutions as still fit for purpose in this environment but should be kept under review
- the AI and in particular the *Code* were seen as supportive to institutions in developing their quality assurance procedures but felt by some that too many processes are predicated on the traditional full–time three-year undergraduate
- some institutions commented that [their own] overly prescriptive procedures may make it difficult to design bespoke experiences. They felt that there needs to be greater internal flexibility to enable a more rapid response to developing and quality assuring new provision that satisfies the employer's needs. The findings here reiterate that employers do not understand why approval of even short courses should take as long as it does
- the academic year is not conducive to developing new and innovative partnerships which may require a 52-week calendar and 24-hour timetable
- institutions recognised that robust quality assurance procedures are necessary to protect standards of the credit/awards given and that these should be scrutinised. However, internal procedures were often seen as a barrier to responsiveness and innovation in design and delivery. Respondents expressed the need to develop clear and responsive approval processes within a validated framework.

The report also presented some strategies that have been subsequently adopted by institutions to help them overcome the difficulties of quality assuring employer responsive provision. These include:

- ensuring early involvement of Academic Registry staff who have responsibility for quality assurance
- developing clear frameworks for accrediting provision
- having a dedicated central team; ensuring that high-level staff have responsibility for quality assurance and employer engagement

- ensuring ongoing negotiation and maintaining dialogue with employers and other partners
- involving employers in course development and delivery
- ensuring good cross-institutional linkages between staff responsible at operational level for quality assurance and employer engagement.

The report highlighted the variety of approaches that institutions are taking in terms of where employer engagement/responsiveness relates to the strategy of the institution. The importance of taking a strategic approach, of being prepared to be flexible and working in a genuinely collaborative way was identified by some higher education institutions.

The findings of the task group echo in many ways the report of James Kewin, Director of Skills and Innovation at CFE, 'Known Unknowns: the demand for higher level skills from businesses':

> 'There is now an expectation that training can be tailored to the needs of an individual business and delivered at a time and place that is convenient to the employer. The challenge for universities is to develop a more flexible approach to delivery without compromising the quality of course content.'

This argument for change is not for every university; nonetheless those with an interest face barriers according to Connor and Hirsch (2008):

'We know from a number of studies that there are difficulties faced by higher education, employers and employees in expanding engagement, especially for workforce development. These include:

- high risks involved for universities entering new markets (development costs, lack of experience outside of student market, short-termism of some employer demand, uncertainty on continuity)
- language and culture barriers for employers and HEIs to overcome
- motivating employees to see value in engaging in higher learning with a university or college
- relevance of provision for meeting employer demand
- accepting the different domains of learning (academic, workplace), and integrating academic and work based learning better
- customer service
- flexibility in processes and products (need to offer customisation, scheduling, smaller units but retain high quality'.

It is also helpful to remind ourselves that employers do not need to know the detail of quality assurance processes such as validation. They are happy to know that there are such processes, and be prepared to take part at the relevant points. The detailed wiring of the processes can remain hidden.

There are a growing number of universities, committed to working with employers and employees, who have changed their offer and procedures. A number are able to validate a programme within six weeks from the initial approach and achieve this in different ways as set out by Tony Wall (see Chapter 5). However, there is still some way to go in terms of raising the awareness of employers as to what universities can offer them in comparison to the private providers of training and professional bodies. Higher education institutions are rarely represented at key events for HR Directors and Directors of Learning and Development. This message is reinforced in the CBI, Universities UK and HEFCE joint report on the contribution that higher education can make to workforce development: 'Workforce development programmes will not be a priority for all universities. But those that do see it as a key activity should regularly tell employers what they can offer and who to contact. As one course provider put it, "The key is visibility".'

Each university will decide whether this is a route it wishes to take. Once the decision is made in favour of work-based learning, the institution benefits from strategic direction from the top to ensure that all departments, not just those who deal directly with the employers, are able to provide appropriate processes. Validation is a key process which assures and secures the academic standard and quality of the university offer. However it should be fit for purpose, and can be and is being adapted to ensure that the interests of both institution and employer are served in the interests of developing the UK workforce.

4 University Models of Work-Based Validation

TONY WALL

Building on the previous chapter, consideration is now given to the practicalities of delivering work-based learning in a university setting to conform to the QAA guidelines, and respond to policy initiatives. This explanation of the different forms of delivery provides a complex picture of the requirements placed on university staff engaged in delivering work-based learning awards. It is this complexity, often described as bureaucracy, that leaves employers and employees bewildered when exposed for the first time to a university work-based qualification. However, it illustrates the torturous processes and procedures university staff have to go through to deliver these awards and in part explains why universities have the models they do. It is also apparent that flexibility and responsiveness, although getting better, remain tricky to deliver. Finally, it provides a useful context for the case studies.

Introduction to Validation

Universities are empowered by the Privy Council as autonomous institutions to design and deliver awards, in line with the QAA AI, which, as mentioned in the previous chapter, includes a Code of Practice for Quality and Standards, the FHEQ, Subject Benchmark Statements and Programme Specification. In this context, validation is the process of securing quality and meeting standards for new provision, such as a module or a full award. In practice, the term validation is being used interchangeably with the term 'accreditation'. Accreditation has typically been used in two contexts: a university accrediting a college, whereby the university is agreeing that the partner can and is securing quality and standards; and accreditation of prior learning, whereby the university is agreeing that the learning is of an appropriate quality and standard to be awarded credit towards gaining an award. Validation and accreditation are both forms of approval, or agreement, that quality and standards will be, or are, being secured. More precisely here, though, accreditation is a specific form of validation when the learning is not predominately facilitated by a university, hence relevant to work-based learning.

Universities have developed work-based learning validation models since the 1980s with Middlesex University pioneering work, and more recently in response to the government-employer engagement policy. This chapter highlights the principal validation practices and the key work-based approaches which structure the offer to learners. It is this process that sets the parameters for universities, or in other words, what they can and cannot do. These are:

- mainstream provision;

- creating bespoke provision;
- 'shell' award provision;
- cooperative relationships and collaborative provision.

It should be noted that one practice cuts across these approaches; short awards. University Certificates or Professional Certificates, which typically consist of 60 credits at various levels, engage employers and learners more readily than larger provision such as Foundation degrees which are 240 credits. This is partly because of the pressure on the learner (time constraints, holding a job down, having a family life) or pressures of the business which means time away from work is costly and inefficient. These shorter awards successfully operate within a variety of validation environments outlined below.

MAINSTREAM PROVISION

Many universities now offer work-based learning modules validated as part of their core, undergraduate provision, for example, in the middle of a full-time degree (second/third years) often to provide access to employability skills. These are distinct from sandwich years, mentioned earlier. The validation of the module occurs as part of the wider validation of the award, which replicates the higher education institution's existing processes and frameworks for all its awards, and can take up to 18 months to complete. In this way, the module is treated as a standard module within an award. This type of module can operate distinctively as:

- A negotiated learning module, with 'open' content (for example, developing a learning contract with learning determined by the individual learner).
- A negotiated learning module, with specific careers, work-related skills content (for example, developing communication skills and career path).
- A content-driven module (for example, psychology).

There is a common theme around negotiation and a number of the case studies highlight the benefits of this (see the Local Authority Manager and Learning Architect in particular). Within this context, the role of a facilitating tutor is crucial. They guide the learner into areas of investigation and generation of evidence to meet the learning outcomes of the module, but also to do this at the right level on the FHEQ, part of the AI. Although this approach enables employees to engage with university learning it is usually found to be insufficiently flexible. The QAA *Code of Practice, section 9, Work-based and Placement Learning* provides detailed information on how to design and implement this type of provision (QAA, 2007).

BESPOKE PROVISION

When employers require specific provision to meet an articulated business need, there are generally three ways in which universities can respond to this:

- slightly customise existing mainstream provision;
- hold specific, separate validation processes and events;
- create specific routes through existing shell frameworks.

In the first of these, 'minor modification' processes are utilised through the appropriate academic faculty or institutional quality service structures. This can be a relatively simple way to meet needs within standard institutional validation and quality approaches and processes. However, it may be as constrained as the mainstream provision alternative. It can be a slow process if the university only operates an annual system of validation geared to the academic calendar and traditional provision.

The second approach is to design a bespoke award for specific employers which rely on 'guaranteed' minimum numbers of learners. The Care Commission for the Regulation of Care Award case study is an example of this. Higher education institutes can establish additional validation events, specifically for client programmes, utilising existing validation approaches and processes. This is an expensive approach, hence the need for student cohorts, partly due to the developmental processes and the time it can take to get full agreement from all stakeholders and the client. It not always particularly successful either – employers want more than quality provision – they *also* want speed *and* affordability, especially given the volatile trading environment their businesses operate in.

A variation on this which has proved more successful is the production of a programme for the employer, approved and operated across several institutions. This is useful where there is a large pool of demand. In this case, each higher education institution carries out an approval process and has a proportion of the students registered on its system. So each student gains the award of the university where she or he is registered. An example of this approach is the Foundation degree for the Royal Air Force (RAF), approved and run by four higher education institutions. The programme includes some leadership, management and other modules which were already available. The second example was validated in 2008 for the travel industry by six institutions. *Fdf* organised a joint validation event where each higher education institution was represented, together with a panel consisting entirely of members external to the six institutions. In some cases higher education institutions carried out a supplementary internal process and used the report of the validation event which shortened the process. For others, the process carried out jointly was sufficient. The development of this award identified the areas where some institutions had to change their assessment regulations for this programme in order that systems were consistent for students, whichever institution they registered with.

However, this is difficult to operate for smaller pockets of demand and small organisations, or when *actual demand* is lower than expected. Higher education institutions must ensure that there are appropriately flexible systems in place to safeguard against financial or other risks which might compromise academic standards or the quality of learning opportunities, but this should not discourage innovation.

The third approach, using shell frameworks, has been particularly successful in being responsive to the needs of employers and employees across all sizes of organisation.

'SHELL' FRAMEWORKS

The shell framework is a long-established concept. Some have been operating for over a decade and variants have been running successfully in range of higher education institutions, including at the Universities of Chester and Derby, Middlesex and York St John Universities. This number is increasing with the expanding interest in employer engagement. Shell frameworks allow the agile negotiation of awards, content, modules and award titles. They extend the idea of the negotiated learning module, as described earlier, to the full programme. Shell frameworks are therefore demand-led, aimed at delivering the personal and professional needs and aspirations of individuals and groups in the workplace. The benefits of shell frameworks to employers and universities are recognised as:

- an agile response to employers for bespoke and/or workplace provision;
- an agile response to organisations wanting [higher education institution] recognition or accreditation;
- a managed, structured approach to cross-faculty, multidisciplinary flexible learning;
- credit accumulation;
- inclusive access;
- a professional development framework for internal staff;
- a shared understanding across higher education institution departments, such as marketing and registry, about commitments to employer engagement and work-based learning as a legitimate mode of learning.

In this model, the framework, its operation and associated processes are formally validated once and then reviewed periodically. When required, the specific content or the structure of a learning pathway is agreed or approved on-demand. Frameworks generally include the following:

- generic award aims and outcomes, clearly stating the particular focus of the framework;
- generic level aims and outcomes, and are clearly based on the FHEQ;
- access to most, if not all, awards available within a higher education institution;
- associated generic shell modules at various credit values and levels.

A key feature of shell frameworks are the generic aims and outcomes. They are instrumental in establishing the flexibility to construct routes negotiated with employers or employer groups (for cohorts), and even routes negotiated with individual learners (with or without employer input). Importantly, it also means that validation can occur within six weeks, rather than 18 months. However, this flexibility increases complexity and potential risks to quality which need to be overseen and managed. The models to achieve this can be a centralised approach (for example, Chester, Derby Universities), decentralised approach (for example, Middlesex University) or a mixed approach (for example, York St John University). Whichever model is chosen, shell frameworks need to have:

- clear reference to FHEQ levels;
- clear written processes of operation (they can become complex);
- clarity over how the above is maintained through negotiation processes (for example, through learning contracts, approval panels, and so on);
- clear process and justification for external examining arrangements;
- clear communication flows between approving mechanisms to ensure an up-to-date record of provision;

- clarity and shared understanding of who is responsible under different modes of operation and, where relevant at different stages of the process.

Employer negotiated routes

This approach is characteristic of the University of Chester model, which operates the Work based & Integrative Studies (WBIS) framework at undergraduate and postgraduate levels. In this model, the responsible organisational unit, which may be a subject or a multidisciplinary team, approaches the corporate Approval Panel to carry out approval of the specified provision. This could be for the approval of a Foundation degree for a specific client or a client group (for example, to market to a group of retailers with a known need). After scrutiny by the Approval Panel, successful approval and any requested amendments have been made, the provision can be delivered. This is represented in Figure 1.

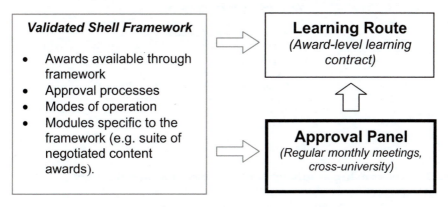

Figure 1   Approving employer routes through a centralised model
Source: Wall, 2009

One of the challenges of this approach is that the Approval Panel may not have the authority to approve new resources or capacity to deliver, as the management structures are located elsewhere, such as faculties. Another approach is to have a mixed model which can link directly into these wider structures.

The mixed model approach for validating employer provision, see Figure 2, is characteristic of the York St John University model, which operates the Independent & Professional Studies (IPS) suite of awards. Within this model, the central Approval Panel has a different role. Here, it is focused on:

- overseeing the IPS student experience;
- overseeing the quality assurance, enhancement and risk management arrangements of IPS; and more specifically
- approving cross-faculty provision (including employer and flexible provision).

When work-based learning delivery is required in one faculty (an employer may have approached a specific subject area such as community health or business), the IPS can be adopted by programme or subjects teams as required. IPS then feeds directly into faculty-based scrutiny and approval processes which typically take place every 3–4 weeks.

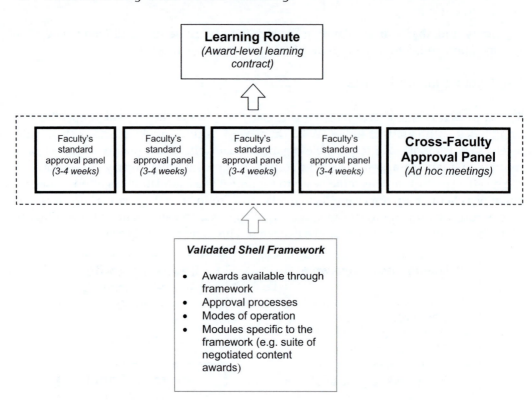

Figure 2   Approving employer routes through a mixed model

Source: Wall, 2009

Employers work with the teams to develop specific provision, and may feed in to the approval process (Figure 2). This not only exposes these approaches and methodologies across the institution, but also facilitates a direct link to senior management teams in faculties when additional resources are required. When the requirement is cross-faculty, the corporate Approval Panel is focused on cross-faculty approval, based on the recommendations from the faculty-based approval processes referred to earlier. An employer, again, feeds into the design of the programme, and may be involved in the approval processes. An IPS Pathway Leader (client route) is identified for every pathway to maintain the relationship, ensuring that the employer is involved as appropriate, and makes arrangements for monitoring and evaluation.

Routes negotiated with individual learners

The previous models focus on employer and higher education institution negotiated awards for cohorts. It is also possible for individuals to negotiate their own award, based on identified personal and professional needs, interests and aspirations. From an adult learning perspective, it can be argued that such an approach encourages greater motivation and hence deeper approaches to learning. The Open University has pioneered this approach. However, LearnDirect's *Learning Through Work* initiative promotes this approach, with a particular focus on work-based learning. An extract from the *Learning*

Through Work website states: 'Learning through Work can help you to devise a tailored and flexible learning plan by:

- Assessing your current work practices and relevant industry experience.
- Evaluating your personal, professional and career objectives.
- Considering your personal and lifestyle commitments.
- Identifying the strategic directions and priorities of your employer.
- Negotiating your own learning plan with support from a tutor.
- Organising work based projects.
- Recording your progress and achievements.' (Learning Through Work, 2009).

Although this is a common approach across the higher education institution partners, there are variations. The University of Chester and York St John University approaches are outlined in Figures 3 and 4.

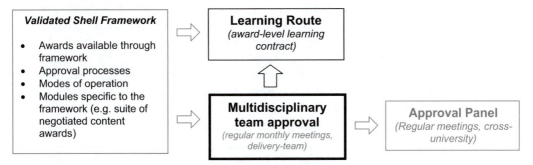

Figure 3   Approving individual routes through a centralised model
Source: Wall, 2009

The University of Chester model allows individual students to negotiate their learning route or contract in their first module, called Self Review & Negotiation of Learning, with a tutor (see Figure 3). The tutor is important in guiding this experience, as it can include a complex mixture of:

- taught, work-related modules in the faculty;
- work-based projects;
- accreditation of prior learning.

The selection of these components needs to take into account the level of the award the learner is studying at (based on the FHEQ). For example, a BA (Hons) degree usually requires 120 credits at higher education levels 1, 2 and 3 and a Master's degree is normally 180 credits at Master's Level. The selection of subject content for the award (as taught modules, work-based projects or prior learning) will determine the title of the award. For example, a learner may decide to accredit 15-years worth of developmental projects in a business and take some related modules in management studies. The learner might negotiate with the team that an MA in Organisational Development (WBIS) would be a useful award and award title. The multidisciplinary team involved in the delivery/teaching of the Framework then review this proposal, along with all of the other proposals, on a regular, normally monthly, basis. The role of this team is to ensure consistency of the award titles, and reference to subject benchmark statements as relevant. This is a crucial process in safeguarding the reputation of specific named awards, the institution, and higher education more broadly. Upon approval, the list of pathways is then reported to the formal Approval Panel, mentioned earlier.

It is essential to recognise the importance of the multidisciplinary team involved in teaching delivery. This team, although having different specialist backgrounds and academic expertise, includes expertise in work-based learning and experiential learning concepts, theories and practices. This is a crucial feature of the process as they are better able to make judgments appropriate to the particular ethos and processes of work-based learning and negotiated learning.

Similarly, in York St John University's IPS suite of awards, individual students negotiate their learning route/contract in the first module, Learning, Recognition and Negotiation, with a tutor (see Figure 4). IPS learners, too, can negotiate a mix of work-based projects, accreditation of prior learning and taught work-related modules, but they may also select specialist modules and other content-based modules across participating faculties. These modules may or may not operate in a work-based learning mode. The IPS Pathway Leader for individual learners ('individual routes') then arranges scrutiny and approval of the route/contract from the relevant faculties that deliver the modules. The IPS Pathway Leader (individual routes) oversees all of the learners studying across two or more faculties (if the learner is clearly located within one faculty for their entire pathway, an appropriately qualified IPS Pathway Leader can be identified at the faculty level).

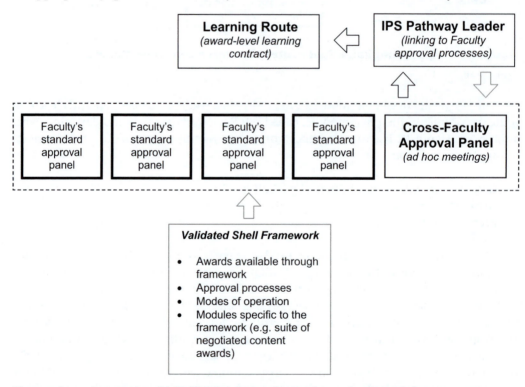

Figure 4   Approving individual routes through a mixed model

Source: Wall, 2009

For example, if a learner decides to accredit five years of professional learning in educational project management, with some formal learning in management (in the Business School) and learning (in the Faculty of Education & Theology), a BA (Hons) in Leadership & Project Management in Education might be proposed. The IPS Pathway Leader (individual routes) then seeks scrutiny, feedback and approval from the associated faculties. The expertise in the faculties ensures consistency with their other awards and reference to benchmark statements.

COOPERATIVE RELATIONSHIPS AND COLLABORATIVE PROVISION

The examples so far have focused on delivery by the awarding institution. In practice, however, there is increasing interest in working more collaboratively to engage organisations and their employees in higher-level learning. Part of the growth has been pioneered by the work of HE@Work and *fdf*'s EBTA. These recognise and promote the concept that higher-level learning can and does happen outside the classroom, in organisations who deliver their own training, through private training organisations, and in the learning that happens in the workplace outside training and development events.

The validation arrangements in these circumstances draw on the models above, but again, there is diversity in practice and variation of the types of relationship adopted to validate these activities. A major factor in this process is who delivers and assesses. A range of these arrangements are outlined below.

Full accreditation agreements

This is familiar ground for many universities who formally accredit further education college higher-level learning programmes. However, there is also a move towards accreditation of external organisations outside the higher and further education sectors, such as businesses and training providers. They have to meet explicit criteria including:

- The general suitability and financial stability of the partnering organisation.
- The specific suitability of the partnering organisation, its staff and other resources in delivering the particular provision proposed.
- The readiness of the partnering organisation to engage with the appropriate higher education processes to secure standards and quality.

This usually involves a detailed partnership analysis, visit and the specification of a contract. This is typically a detailed document setting the full terms, conditions and parameters of the relationship. Again, there are different approaches but rapid response models can successfully respond to cooperative working. In both the Chester and York St John University models, the collaborative partnership's staff are a separate team with specialist policy and procedure knowledge, but can draw upon external committees as required.

Rapid approval of partners can be facilitated through various practices. These include:

- Creating a team from central services to evaluate the partner (such as registry, academic quality, partnerships). It is important that these individuals are familiar with working with external organisations, as this can compromise the relationship that has been developed through other contacts.
- Creating a team, constituting a person/people familiar with the provision and at least one other who has not been involved with the relationship, but who is familiar with collaborative provision. The impartiality is extremely important, to ensure the external partner is sufficiently familiar with higher education expectations.

The key issues identified when implementing collaborative arrangements are:

- Ensure the educational compatibility of partners, and take due diligence in ensuring they are in good standing.
- Ensure each partner is clear about their roles and responsibilities (when working with non-higher education organisations it is important to ensure they understand the particular language and processes of higher education).
- Develop and agree processes to ensure staff in partnering organisations are suitably qualified for their role.
- Monitor external communications of partners regularly, as these may change more quickly than in higher education institutions.
- Franchising arrangements can become complex and serial franchising has to be avoided as it can compromise the higher education institution's control over academic standards. The higher education institution is ultimately responsible for its awards, so needs to ensure very clear processes to retain control in academic quality processes.
- The higher education institution is ultimately responsible for ensuring that the learning opportunities offered are adequate to enable a student to achieve the academic standard required for its award.
- Award specifications should be readily available and comprehensible to stakeholders (including award, level and reference to relevant subject benchmark statements).

Further details can be found in the *Code of Practice, section 2: Collaborative provision and flexible and distributed learning (including e-learning)* (QAA, 2004).

Credit recognition

While full accreditation agreements usually validate work-based learning in terms of complete awards, credit recognition can be more flexible for the needs of employers and employees. This is where learning and development activity in an organisation or a private training company is allocated a credit value and level. Credits can be distinguished as:

- Specific credits – learning that fulfils specific content-focused learning outcomes (perhaps of an existing module).

- Generic credits – learning that can be designated against a level, not necessarily specific content-focused learning outcomes.

Validating work-based learning through generic credits enables the higher education institution to allow the potential partner to retain their current practices, and places greater demands for flexibility on the assessors and those involved in quality assurance. This form of negotiated learning is possible, but it is important to recognise the importance of the expertise of the team involved in the delivery, and that there are processes in place to monitor the experience.

The process for validating this type of work-based learning includes:

- identification of core content, learning strategies and existing evidencing strategies;
- allocation of a *potential* credit level and value;
- discussion around level and value – including additional requirements to secure the level and value within the higher education institution's regulations (for example, assessment policies);
- determination of credit type – generic or specific;
- development of module specification in line with the higher education insitution's standard procedures.

The discussion component is particularly important to ensure consistency of the level and credit values within and across the higher education institution, and because there are no hard and fast rules for making these judgements. There will then be important discussions about the delivery of the credits, including:

- Who will be delivering the learning activity?
- Who will be assessing it?
- Who will be quality assuring it (for example, second-marking, moderating)?
- What are the progression routes from the credits accumulated (the shell frameworks are particularly useful in this context, as progression routes at the higher education institution can be provided by default)?

Depending on the answers to these questions, there are various relationships that can be employed to ensure the university confidence in the learners attaining the credit and level required. For example:

- Associate Tutors (at the partner organisation) deliver – higher education institution staff assess.
- Associate Tutors deliver and assess – higher education institution staff assess.
- Associate Tutors deliver, assess, and assure – higher education institution staff moderate.

Indeed, there can be a mix of these over time, as confidence in the partner grows. Whichever the model, it is imperative that all parties are clear about the roles within the collaboration agreement.

Two other forms of validating work-based learning are relatively undemanding in terms of development work and formal validation activity. Consequently they may be better described as a 'cooperative relationships' rather than 'collaborative provision'.

Accreditation of Prior Experiential Learning (APEL)

APEL validates work-based learning that was developed elsewhere, in the past, as part of an award (see Garnett, Portwood and Costley, 2004). The cases in this book give examples (see the Local Authority Manager and Learning Architect in particular). These concepts are explored in greater detail elsewhere in the book, however, it is useful to consider the difference between specific and generic credit here:

- Specific credits – prior learning that can easily be mapped against a specific (existing) module's learning outcomes.
- Generic credits – prior learning that can be designated a level, not the specific learning outcomes of an existing module (this enables the focus to be on the work-based project or learning activity, and the associated experiential learning, rather than specified outcomes).

As mentioned earlier, the generic credit approach provides greater flexibility, but has implications for the staff involved in facilitating the claim. Generic credits used within shell frameworks provide a high level of flexibility, but can be challenging in ensuring consistency of assessment practice. Clear guidance must be available within a higher education institution in this case. All higher education institutions have APEL policies but evidence suggests that they are less often used than they might be (QAA, 2004). The processes can be complex, require evidence, and the higher education institution receives no funding for carrying out this work, and students are discouraged from applying even when it can shorten the length of their award.

Access and articulation agreements

This form of cooperative relationship may not usually validate work-based learning in a technical sense (although it may do at a pre-higher education level), but allows access to a higher education institution's provision. In this way, therefore, it is recognising that the learning that has occurred with an external provider (in-house training in an organisation or a private training organisation) is a suitable preparation for continued higher education learning. Within this relationship, it must be absolutely clear what the relationship is entitling learners to, for both the learners and the parties involved in the relationship.

External Memberships in Validation

In all of these models, there are decisions about when to include external membership to approval events. There are at least three distinct roles:

- External assessors – making judgments about the quality and academic standards of a proposed provision.
- External panel member – as above, but not necessarily making academic judgments.
- External examiners – assessing and moderating a higher education institution's academic judgments of assessed pieces of work, aiming towards consistency across higher education institutions.

It can be challenging to find appropriate people to satisfy these roles. Crucially, those involved need to have a clear understanding of the work-based learning ethos and values to make meaningful comments. For example, 'traditional' notions of coherence (that is, based around content, not experiential/need) may limit any negotiated provision from developing further. In terms of academic members satisfying these roles, in addition to 'buying' in to the ethos, they must also have expertise in both subject knowledge and work-based learning knowledge. This is an ongoing area of enquiry by the QAA (see QAA, 2009).

Conclusions: Achievements and Challenges

There can be no doubt that higher education institutions are beginning to change their corporate systems and procedures. For some, it is no longer a fringe activity but much more integral to the mission and focus of the institution. This is not surprising given the current policy climate. What is surprising is why it did not happen earlier, faster and across more institutions given the increasing cries from employers for graduates who were ready for the workplace, and from government about the economic imperatives of a more highly skilled workforce.

The picture is typically diverse when it comes to the higher education sector. This is inevitable given the independence of institutions, something our EU compatriots find hard to understand. However, this diversity ironically makes it more difficult for the sector to engage with employers because the terminology and processes are different. Those in the sector are able to see the commonality but for 'outsiders' like employers it is much more difficult. Nevertheless, it is possible, and in some cases highly beneficial, for clusters of higher education institutions to work together to meet a defined strategic business need. The examples of the RAF programme developed with four higher education institutions and the common Travel Management programme validated by six universities prove the point. There are usually four pinch points where the detail matters and these will mainly be in assessment.

Finally, QAA intend to publish their position on work-based learning in order to promote further the emphasis on the flexibility of the AI, particularly to central quality assurance units. Their initial statement published in the summer of 2008 emphasises the flexibility of the AI to encompass a wide variety of practices. The key learning points from these experiences are:

- Better sharing of practices across the sector accelerates the development of more responsive but robust procedures.
- Developments in processes and frameworks should be clearly situated within the strategic positioning of the higher education institution; different higher education

institution histories, structures, aspirations and strategic ambitions will partly determine what is appropriate.

- Developing more inclusive conceptions of 'coherence' based on experiential learning, need or interest, can create opportunities for innovative practice and learning.
- More experience of work-based learning in the sector increases the pool of informed validation panel members in institutions.
- Readiness to use additional external assessors/panel members from the employment sector, often in addition to an academic.
- Changes in the funding regime assist the development of bite-sized chunks of learning.
- Involvement of central services with the development of work-based learning programmes and systems enhance the business offer of a higher education institution.
- Business-focused units can work with all parties to assess the appropriate processes.

But perhaps above all else, a joined-up approach within a higher education institution can help develop a full, coherent range of offerings working with employers, thus benefitting employees, and these activities can build trust and develop opportunities for future cooperation and collaboration.

5 Recognising, Assessing and Rewarding Work Experience

JONATHAN GARNETT

A fundamental component of work-based learning for the individual is experiential learning, as explained in Chapter 2. It is recognition of the workplace as the generator of learning. This chapter explains the background to a mechanism designed to capture prior experience and convert it into a language the university can understand and assess. It is placed in a context of assessment generally with a helpful explanation of the French Government system, not least because assessment is at the heart of university education and as highlighted in the case studies important to learners. The practical delivery of this procedure is then discussed using Middlesex University as the example.

The assessment of work-based learning is a central issue for all higher education institutions trying to engage in work-based learning. Chapter 4 explains the quality structures within which UK higher education operates and the responsibilities institutions have for maintaining the academic standards of higher education qualifications. Work-based learning brings new challenges as it attempts to meet the performance imperatives of work and the time-bound needs of employer stakeholders. In addition, Chapter 3 outlines that learning which is work based can be seen as different in nature from subject-based knowledge. The challenge is to find assessment tools and procedures which not only assure the higher education institution that appropriate academic standards are being met but also that the assessment adds value to the work-based task, and thus enhances and reinforces the relevance of the learning not just for the individual work-based learner, but also ideally for the benefit of the employer organisation. A number of higher education institutions have approached this problem by recognising that work-based learning is not likely to fit neatly into subject disciplinary divisions and that the nature of learning generated by work is often transdisciplinary (Boud and Solomon, 2001) in nature. This leads to the validation of learning outcomes which are generic in nature (for example, effective communication, planning and use of resources, demonstration of analysis and synthesis) which can be validated at the level of the higher education programme and applied to shell modules (see Chapter 4).

Three-way learning agreements between the individual work-based learner, the employer and the higher education institution are often key to the customisation of shell modules and generic outcomes to specific work contexts. The learning agreements themselves would often be assessed and could identify appropriate forms of assessment for customised shell modules (for example, a work-based project negotiated in a shell module might be assessed on the basis of a handbook produced for use within the workplace and a critical commentary on the need for the handbook and the research and development work which underpinned the development of it). There is an increasing emphasis in higher education generally to see assessment as not just a means to measure attainment for the purposes of awarding a qualification, but also as an integral component of the teaching and learning process (for example, Bryan and Clegg, 2006). This is particularly true of work-based learning and it is particularly important to ensure than there is a good alignment between the assessment task and assessment criteria and the learning needs and development of the work-based learner and their organisation. This involves developing the work-based learner as an active participant in their learning through developing their understanding of academic as well as work-based performance standards (Workman, 2009). When the learning being considered took place before the individual engaged with the higher education institution it is described as APEL.

APEL stands for the Accreditation of Prior Experiential Learning and is a process by which learning from experience is identified, evaluated and, if appropriate, given formal recognition. Experiential learning includes knowledge and skills acquired in an unplanned way through life and often as a result of the learning demands of work (both paid and unpaid). The description of such learning as 'prior' means that it has happened in the past and in the UK context is often taken to mean prior to entry to a course or commencing a vocational qualification. The individual case studies in this book illustrate the richness of work as a source of learning but only case study 7 the 'Learning Architect' makes explicit the role of recognition of learning from work as a core part of the programme. This dichotomy of opportunity but limited application, also highlighted in Chapter 4, is a central theme in rewarding experience through APEL.

The development of APEL in the UK was stimulated by the pioneering work of the Learning from Experience Trust in the early 1980s. Many of the early developers of APEL at higher education level benefitted from participation in Learning from Experience Trust study tours of the USA. A major milestone in the acceptance of APEL was achieved in 1986 when the Council for National Academic Awards (CNAA), the body which validated degree qualifications in the polytechnic sector, published regulations for APEL for use in relation to its awards. The 1990s saw a favourable policy context for APEL as there was a focus on increasing participation in higher education and widening access. APEL was seen as a valuable tool to widen access by recognising the achievements of mature students and providing an alternative basis for entry to higher education. In 1996, the South East England Consortia (SEEC) of higher education institutions produced a code of practice for APEL which was endorsed by 37 member institutions. In 2005 the QAA, which oversees standards in higher education, produced, drawing upon existing good practice, APEL guidelines for higher education institutions.

APEL is often championed as an important way of recognising lifelong learning and enhancing social inclusion by providing access to academic and vocational qualifications for those who might otherwise be excluded by lack of formal qualifications or the demands of work. The importance of recognising the workplace as a site for learning has grown in significance during the 1990s and continues today as the Government places a premium on the economic imperative to up-skill the UK workforce. In the context of current debates about the role of higher education, it is equally important that valuing the learning from experience of the individual learner is a sound starting point from an educational point of view (see Osborne, Davies and Garnett, 1998) and fits well with aspirations of learner autonomy and the high-level cognitive skills of analysis, synthesis and evaluation which are typically associated with high-level learning. The recognition of learning, wherever it has occurred provided it can be demonstrated, fits well with the academic awarding function and expertise of higher education. Increasingly, what makes universities unique is not teaching or research but their function of formally recognising learning achievement.

The 2004 UVAC report on APEL (Garnett, Portwood and Costley, 2004) highlighted that while APEL in the UK has at least a 20-year history and is espoused by over 90 higher education institutions, the number of students taking APEL nationally averaged at only 100 for each education institution. Similarly, while APEL was embedded within the system of National Vocational Qualifications (NVQ), which allowed for full awards to be made on the basis of APEL, the take-up rate was modest. The report highlighted a number of limitations to the take up of APEL. Even institutions which reported that they offered APEL acknowledged that the opportunity to do so was not always highlighted. There was also concern that experience, expertise, advising on and assessing APEL claims was often concentrated in a few members of staff. Some institutions were concerned that APEL was very labour intensive, both to support and assess, and was thus not cost effective for the institution. Despite the longstanding nature of APEL practice some institutions also reported lingering doubts about the reliability and validity of APEL assessment and concern about the quality of the learning assessed.

Nevertheless, Wailey (2002, p. 35) helpfully identifies widely accepted assessment criteria as:

- Validity – relating to the match between the evidence presented and the learning outcomes claimed.
- Sufficiency – relating to sufficient breadth of evidence, including reflection, to demonstrate the achievement of all the outcomes claimed.
- Currency – demonstrating that what is being assessed is current learning.
- Quality – relating to the evidence demonstrating the required level of learning achievement.

Assessment often involves making a judgement as to how far the claimant has been able to match and evidence the learning outcomes of specific modules. However, this matching approach does not necessarily do justice to the full range of experiential learning of the individual claimant.

The UVAC report (Garnett, Portwood & Costley, 2004) drew attention to the development of uses of APEL in Canada and France which suggested that APEL processes had the potential to be used more creatively as the basis for qualifications of vocational relevance. France has, arguably, the most advanced system for identifying, assessing and recognising skills that is focused on the labour market and the enterprise, an outcome of national legislation, methods of financing lifelong learning and private sector initiatives.

In January 2002 France passed a law of social modernisation (no. 2002-73), Validation des Aquis de l'Experience (VAE), which set up a new APEL system. This followed a series of Ministry initiatives and laws since the 1960s in relation to APEL. The VAE system allows those with a minimum of three years employment history (paid, unpaid or voluntary) to make an application for exemptions towards, or for a complete award of, diplomas or professional titles awarded by the State. The award by the State is the *bilan de competence* which is awarded by an accreditation panel following an interview. To prepare their application and development of a portfolio, and to meet the panel, candidates can benefit from a new official 24-hours accreditation leave from their work (Collot, Pagnani and Guteskunst, 2003).

In contrast to the position in France, the UK position for learners can range from hostility to recognition of learning from the workplace (see Case Study 1), lack of information about the opportunity or a sense picked up from higher education staff that it would be easier just to do the whole course! However, there are now a growing number of higher education institutions committed to developing courses through engagement with employers and employees. APEL is growing as an important way in which course content and provision can be customised to be more cost and time efficient and to align individual learning with organisational objectives (see Garnett, 2007 for a detailed case study).

Middlesex University, one of the longstanding institutions engaged in work-based learning has a policy to actively promote the accreditation of learning wherever and however it has been achieved provided it can be identified and assessed as being at higher education-level. This led the university to develop and approve regulations for the accreditation of experiential learning in 1991 and to establish quality assurance principles and procedures to enable this work to be conducted within the mainstream quality assurance framework of the university. The procedures put in place cover supporting the development of an accreditation claim, assessing the claim and awarding and recording the academic credit which might result from that claim. These procedures are important as the Middlesex accreditation quality assurance principles start from the premise that the university is responsible for all academic credit awarded in its name and thus all learning for which credit is awarded must be assessed with equal rigour. In the case of APEL, this means that that credit is only awarded on the basis of demonstrable learning achievement and not on the assumption of learning due to undertaking a particular job for a particular period of time. Comparability of rigour of assessment also means that the same process of internal moderation and external examiner scrutiny which applies to the assessment of university-taught courses must also be applied to the assessment of APEL claims. The university importantly provides staff development for both APEL adviser and assessor roles.

The main use of APEL at Middlesex University is as part of a negotiated programme of work-based learning. Work-based learning is learning which is through, at and for work which is explained in Chapter 2.

The Middlesex approach to work-based learning (irrespective of the level of programme) focuses on four key stages. The common starting point for most work-based learning programmes is a forward-focused review to establish what relevant knowledge/skills the individual brings to the programme (this can lead to formal accreditation via APEL). The Middlesex focus on the facilitation of a learning review leading to general credit has freed the traditional APEL process from the tyranny of only recognising learning which closely matches existing validated programmes (Garnett, 1998). This is highly significant as it provides for fuller recognition of the learning achievement of learning (from experience or taught) which is external to the university and hence leads to enhanced customisation. Once the individualised starting point has been established this leads into a programme planning stage which takes fully into account stakeholder interests and requirements as well as resources (for example, of time, information, materials) (Garnett, 2000) to produce a customised programme demonstrating coherence and progression from learning identified and certified via APEL to a work based programme designed not only to meet the academic requirements of the university but also to be of value to the employer or client. A key input from the university into such a work-based programme is to equip the work-based learner/researcher with appropriate techniques to undertake real-life projects that are focused on knowledge creation and use. The work-based projects are often the focal point of the work-based programme and have the potential to impact upon the workplace (Garnett, 2005).

The case of the 'Supermarket Dotcom Training Manager' (Case Study 3 tells the story of a Middlesex work-based Learning Studies graduate who has progressed to a higher degree. The training manager is a specialist in driver education who was able to gain significant advanced standing at Honours degree-level from recognition of learning from experience and a range of professional development courses. The challenge for the Middlesex APEL process was to identify and assess a diverse range of achievement extending from significant taught professional courses and a diverse range of learning from experience. The training manager worked with a university adviser to put together an APEL portfolio following a standard Middlesex University format. The APEL portfolio includes a curriculum vitae (resume) extended to focus upon key learning episodes (for example, establishing a small business) and a current job description expanded to focus upon the knowledge and skill requirements to perform the job. These documents serve as the basis for advising on the development of the claim, help to focus the claimant on differentiating between recounting the experience and identifying the learning from experience, and serve to put the accreditation claim in context for the assessor. The heart of the portfolio is a number of claimant defined 'Areas of Learning'. For each area the claimant will identify a title and explain how they acquired knowledge and skills in the area (often this will be a combination of short training courses and learning through carrying out a work role). The claimant is required to clearly identify what it is that they know and are able to do (that is, their claim for knowledge and skills) and crucially to provide evidence for this claim of learning achievement. The Middlesex programme framework allowed the training manager to build upon the learning from APEL and negotiate a personalised route to an Honours degree. Without the combination of APEL and negotiated work-based learning, Middlesex University would not have been able to contribute to the training manager's continuing professional development. The university has extended this approach to qualifications at undergraduate, postgraduate and doctoral level. The case of the 'Learning Architect' in Case Study 7 tells the story of a graduate of the Middlesex Doctorate in Professional studies who benefitted from a work-based learning approach and the opportunity to gain APEL at doctoral level.

The UVAC report (Garnett, Portwood & Costley, 2004) suggests that APEL be reconstructed as a tool not for admission to a course but for Learning Recognition and Development (LRD) to enhance the productive capability of individuals and the organisations in which they work. The argument is that while in the age of the 'knowledge economy' the belief is widely expressed that organisations are only as good as their people, much of what an individual knows and is able to do has been learnt from experience and is often held as tacit knowledge by the individual rather than explicit knowledge that can be shared for the benefit of the organisation (Stewart, 1997). The value of reflective practice has recently been highlighted by an international team of writers considering 'Productive Reflection at Work' (Boud, Cressy and Docherty, 2006). Reflection is held to be 'a key human mechanism in understanding our experience and deriving lessons from it'. Central to reflection is the notion of standing back from experience to derive meaning with a view to informing future action. Two vital parts of self-reflection are the ability to critique your own thought processes and to take into account your feelings, for example, role of inference, distortions of reality. Coghlan and Brannick (2001, p. 31) describe reflection as 'The process of stepping back from experience to process what experience means, with a view to planning further action ....it is the key to learning as it enables you to develop an ability to uncover and make explicit to yourself what you have planned, discovered and achieved in practice.'

Higher education institutions have considerable expertise in developing the reflective practice of students as part of higher education courses, especially those requiring periods of professional practice (for example, education, health) and programmes specifically designed for adults in work (for example, work-based learning programmes). Reflection is central to APEL as it is specifically focused upon structured reflection on experience to identify, describe and evidence learning achievement relevant to a particular course. This form of reflective practice has been developed over a 20-year period but its application has been largely limited to determining admission with advanced standing to prescribed university courses. An increased focus upon work-based learning to enhance productivity would enable APEL to be freed from the shackles of looking at experiential learning to meet the needs of higher education course entry to consider it as a tool to assess an employee's experiential learning (for example, identifying and prioritising learning opportunities and sources; honing the employee's reflective and evaluative skills) and thus to relate individual knowledge to an organisation's appraisal/performance management system. In this way, rewarding learning from experience could truly be transformed!

6 *Supporting Learners Through Mentoring in the Workplace*

ANN MINTON

As many of the case studies cite, learning support is critical to sustaining the study and succeeding. This can come in many forms such as friends, family, networks or university academic tutor. This chapter focuses on one mechanism which has proved to be a success in university work-based qualifications, mentoring. It explains what mentoring in the workplace can be, what needs to done to put a scheme in place, and how to operate it, with a useful insight into what problems to avoid.

What is Workplace Mentoring?

The workplace provides a rich learning environment, whether it is new staff induction to the workplace or the acquisition of new knowledge and skills by existing employees for career promotion purposes or in response to organisational change. As explained in Chapter 1, the modern workplace is also changing and evolving – and so those in work are all constantly learning mostly implicitly, by applying newly acquired information to develop the knowledge and skills necessary to fulfil the work role. Developing a community of learning within an organisation, or between an organisation and education provider, maximises the opportunities and potential for learning and provides a variety of support mechanisms to promote work-based learning. 'Learning communities give students the chance to deepen and diversify their education, connect with others who share their interests, and actively participate in the educational process.' (Shapiro and Levine, 1999)

In this context, university work-based learning programmes enable learners to utilise their working environment to inform the curriculum within a defined programme of study. Sometimes the learners engaged on a work-based learning programme of study find there is a gap between the university and workplace, where neither organisation fully understands the needs of the learner. Mentoring can bridge this gap, as it is about helping a person (learner) to achieve, by providing support and encouragement and a 'safe space' to try out ideas to discuss alternatives and solve problems. It also helps to develop a community of learning, as it widens the interface between the organisation and the university beyond tutor and learner. Mentoring can also develop a community of learning within the organisation, as mentors can then come together to identify potential for supporting learners within the organisation as well as enhancing and developing the role of mentor themselves. The SME owner, for example, in Case Study 1 recognised the need for someone to fill the gap, as she had no experience of higher education, and felt that her lecturers had little appreciation of the context in which she worked, to be able to provide the kind of support needed. A useful mnemonic for what mentors do is provided by Ross (2007):

Manage the relationship
Encourage the learner
Nurture
Teach
Offer
Respond to learner's needs

However, mentoring is not a new concept – Greek mythology tells us that Odysseus, during his years of travelling and adventure, appointed a nobleman, Mentor, to act as guide and friend to his son Telemachus. Odysseus was keen that Telemachus should have a trusted friend to support him through his learning transition into manhood. Although modern mentoring in the workplace focuses on the development of knowledge and skills related to the work environment, it has a common foundation with Telemachus and Mentor in that a relationship, based on trust and support, exists between two people.

Gibb (1999) comments that employers support mentoring for the following reasons:

- 'Better induction and socialization (for example, new graduate trainees).
- Complement formal learning processes (for example, professional development).
- To improve performance (for example, grooming for promotion).
- To realize potential (for example, equal opportunities).'

All of these factors also impact on recruitment and retention, because someone takes an interest in the individual, by listening to their points of view, helping them to see the wider picture to enable them to make informed choices about their future. This is often achieved by providing encouragement and sharing enthusiasm for the job without the tension of maintaining discipline and measuring performance associated with a line management function. This mentoring approach, when a learner is involved in a programme of study, can be used to translate the requirements of their programme into the workplace and to apply the learning that they have undertaken in the workplace to meet university requirements. In this respect the mentor can act as a source of help by understanding the requirements of the programme and articulating learning through their own life and work experience. Learners find that having a role model and a link into the organisational network and wider community, the mentor, in the workplace is invaluable in helping to settle into an organisation.

Parsloe (1999, p. 8) provides a useful definition of mentoring:

'To help and support people to manage their own learning in order to maximise their potential, develop their skills, improve their performance and become the person they want to be.'

As employers and universities increasingly recognise the learning opportunities generated by the workplace, this chapter seeks to provide an overview of the use of mentoring to support successful employee development (both for mentors and learners), by suggesting practical ways in which mentoring can be applied and developed.

How is Mentoring Used?

The growth of mentoring has in part been a response to the changing role of training and development within organisations and an increased responsibility for the human development function by line managers (Megginson et al., 2005). It is, for example, used extensively within the health professions to support and develop trainee practitioners, and there is a significant body of academic literature to support this (Ramani, Gruppen and Kachur, 2006; Bligh, 1999). Coaching and mentoring are frequently used within business as a career development tool (Friday and Friday, 2002) often in association with company appraisal systems. The growth in popularity of work-based learning courses at university has also led to an increase in the role of mentoring in the workplace, recognising that higher-level knowledge and skills can be developed and enhanced whilst at work, building on the traditions in health education and business coaching previously mentioned. It can then be argued that any programme utilising work-based learning as a teaching and learning strategy, requires by default, a mentoring scheme, to ensure learners are maximising the opportunities available to them and are supported in their learning at work. It would seem that the programme illustrated in the police officer Case Study 2 would have benefited from a mentoring scheme run in association with the programme. This would have helped to clarify the purpose and outcomes of the pre-MBA course as well as helping him in the application of theory to practice. Mentors could also have supported the learners with their 'insurrection' with less stressful results for all concerned.

Organisations use mentoring schemes in different ways, to reflect their own culture. For example, in some organisations mentoring is seen as an intrinsic activity within the line management structure, whereas for others it is an anathema to the openness of the employer/employee relationship and mentors are recruited expressly outside the line management system. Experience suggests that having a mentor, who is not a line manager, offers different opportunities; a regular dialogue with the line manager, supportive of the learner's studies, as well as having an independent person to share concerns with. In Case Study 8, the IT operations manager notes that having the boss for a mentor provided much needed practical help, such as study leave, and moral support, but there was limited mentoring of the subject matter and assessment regime.

Hansford, Ehrich and Tennant, in their 2003 evaluation of mentoring impact, note that 13.9 per cent of companies claim increases in productivity and efficiency and 4 per cent improving workplace communication and relations satisfaction. The University of Derby experience of supporting programme learners by workplace mentors reflects similar outcomes; enhanced performance, improved morale in their studies and at work, with greater job satisfaction. Employer partners also report increased morale, productivity, efficiency and career progression with their mentors.

For mentoring to be successful it should have a clear purpose, roles and objectives for the mentor and learner (Gibb, 1999; Ramani, Gruppen and Kachur, 2006). In the civil servant Case Study 5, the mentoring system was informal and down to individual mentors to 'go out of their way' to assist the student, with no training, guidance or evaluation system. The civil servant suggests that this opportunity to support learners could be developed, by simply having formal guidance and structure for the relationship. If neither learner nor mentor is sure what they are aiming for and the relationship has no direction, then the meetings between the actors lack focus, energy and purpose, becoming of secondary importance and thus easy to rearrange or cancel in a busy diary. Where the mentoring scheme has clarity of purpose, this provides an overarching structure and framework for the relationship to develop. The company appraisal system can easily be used as the framework in this case. If the scheme is linked to a formal programme of study, the mentor must understand the requirements of the programme and any associated assessment regime. Often where organisations and universities have jointly developed a programme, specific training courses for mentors are delivered by the university. It may also be provided on a more individual basis depending on the nature of the programme. The key to successful workplace mentoring is that there is training and support available for both mentors and learners to clarify expectations and boundaries and to ensure that they get the most out of the relationship with support available if difficulties arise.

Billett (2000) notes that 'participation in everyday working activities makes the most significant contribution to the mentees learning', thus where mentoring is linked to appraisal systems, having a mentor to guide and focus mentees through their identified objectives can be of great value, highlighting access to key resources and networks.

How Can an Organisation Support Mentoring?

When the company and university wish to set up a mentoring scheme to support their learners, there are three key elements to the mentoring scheme; the scheme and its place in the organisation, the mentors and the learners. Senior line managers need to provide demonstrable support for mentoring as a central pillar of the staff development strategy, linking it to the appraisal system, as well as being an intrinsic part of the university education programme for the learners, by promoting the benefits through the company communication channels. It is useful to have an overall champion for the scheme at board level, but also an operational coordinator, who oversees the running of the scheme, organises training, and matches mentors and learners, working with the university where appropriate.

For mentoring to be successful, a structured programme provides an effective vehicle for mutual negotiation and agreement of the purpose, ground rules, duration and resources (Clutterbuck, 2004, p. 28) which assists in the facilitation and enhancement of the learning experience. It also adds value if the mentoring scheme fits into the wider organisational staff development programme as well as university course.

All parties need to recognise the time commitment, with managers ensuring that both the mentors and learners are allocated time for the mentoring to take place, and that this is a scheduled part of their workload, rather than relying on good will, implying additional unpaid activity. Thus it is argued that mentoring activity should be valued by managers, recognising that it provides a contribution to the efficiency and effectiveness of the organisation (Hansford, Ehrich and Tennant, 2003) and therefore given equal importance to other aspects of their role.

Whilst it is recognised that an effective mentor-learner relationship has intrinsic rewards for the mentor, it can also be the cause of additional work and pressure. To have the mentoring role recognised by senior managers and celebrated overtly, within and outside the organisation, helps to reward the mentors by knowing that their work is acknowledged and valued. Some managers can further support this by protecting the time allocated for this activity, or encouraging the mentors to protect the time that they set aside for learner support, without putting pressure on them to squeeze this in around other aspects of their work. Finally, consideration can be given to financial rewards such as attendance at conferences or events. Ramani, Gruppen & Kachur (2006) summarise the three aspects of mentor development in Table 1.

Table 1   Developing, Rewarding and Supporting Mentors (Ramani, Gruppen & Kachur, 2006)

Developing mentors	Rewarding mentors	Supporting mentors
Mentor staff development	Academic recognition	A peer-support group
Heighten awareness of gender and culture issues	Protected time	Mentors for mentors
Education on professional boundaries	Financial and non-financial rewards	Referral panel: study skills counsellors, psychologists etc.

Preparation of mentors begins with the selection of the 'right' people. Not everyone in a position of seniority has the necessary skills to be a mentor. Clutterbuck (2004, p. 57), in Figure 5, provides a useful checklist of the ideal characteristics in a mentor.

Look for someone who:
- Already has a good record for developing other people
- Has a genuine interest in seeing younger people advance and can relate to their problems
- Has a wide range of current skills to pass on
- Has a good understanding of the organisation, how it works and where it is going
- Combines patience with good interpersonal skills and an ability to work in an unstructured programme
- Has sufficient time to devote to the relationship
- Can command a learner's respect
- Has his or her own network of contacts and influence
- Is still keen to learn.

(Clutterbuck, 2004)

Figure 5   A checklist, ideal characteristics to seek in a mentor

Once identified, mentors need to be prepared for the role, ensuring that they understand the purpose and organisation of the scheme, the expectations placed upon them and their learners, the 'ground rules' for the relationship, the importance of keeping to agreed meetings and undertaking agreed actions and, of crucial importance, where to go for help. (Gay, 1994)

Whilst initial training is important, ongoing development is vital, to ensure the development of best practice by discussing and accessing the key skills associated with mentoring. Mentors should be aware of the pitfalls such as gender and cultural issues, including understanding body language.

Mentors also need to be aware of the professional boundaries within which the relationship exists (Kay and Hinds, 2007, p. 74). The learner may raise personal issues which are outside the scope of the relationship; knowing and understanding where to seek further additional help, will assist the mentor in reinforcing the limitations of the relationship. The organisation should not expect the mentor to be a facilitator not an expert. A referral system or similar mechanism to deal with some of the key issues, such as acquisition of study skills or personal counselling, should be in place to assist the mentor in utilising and accessing specialist help.

The organisation can also support mentors further by developing a support programme or network, where areas of concern or specific issues can be discussed in a 'safe' and confidential environment and advice offered. As each interpersonal relationship is different, skills and approaches previously used may not be effective, however, learning from other mentors may lead to alternative solutions.

If the scheme is related to a university course, and the university and organisation do not share clear expectations for the scheme and it is not proactively supported by senior managers, allowing time and space for learners and mentors to work together, then difficulties quickly emerge to challenge even the most successful of relationships. Also, as discussed earlier, the importance of recruiting and preparing the *right people* to be mentors will also affect the success of the scheme, choosing mentors on seniority and business success, rather than looking for those who have an interest and talent in developing others as described in Figure 5, will inevitably lead to difficulties. However, many of these issues can be addressed through regular monitoring and evaluation of the scheme by the scheme organiser and senior managers, to identify issues and take the appropriate remedial action.

Learners also need to be prepared for the scheme, to ensure they make the most of the opportunities available to them and understand the purpose and scope of the scheme. Ideally this should form a part of the course induction. They too must have clear expectations of their role and that of their mentor and the relationship boundaries, particularly being sensitive to the difference in the relationship between the mentor, tutor and line manager.

In this respect they are the 'driver' in the relationships with their tutor and mentor, taking responsibility for meeting arrangements and setting the agenda, ensuring that they are prepared for the meetings with key questions and issues to be discussed. However, it is important that they do not see the mentoring session as 'teaching' or being told what to do – they must expect to be questioned and challenged, and that their response to such questions and challenges should be framed with respect and openness. Billett (2003) notes that the most effective relationships are those with proactive mentees and relatively reactive mentors.

Matching Learners and Mentors

For a mentoring relationship to be successful there should be some compatibility between mentor and learner, and the scheme coordinator (where this exists) should ensure that there is a strategy in place for the matching process, together with a mechanism for gathering information from interested parties. The university and organisation should do this in partnership, where the scheme is jointly organised, but where mentors are provided on an individual basis by an organisation, clear criteria for choosing a mentor should be available. This can include information about the styles and personalities of both parties to ensure compatibility, although Alleman et al. (1984) demonstrated that it's not essential for the mentor and learner to have similar personalities and backgrounds. Kay and Hinds (2007, p. 32) make practical suggestions about matching the parties:

- Access – it should be relatively easy for the learner to contact the mentor directly, by an agreed method. If the parties work on different sites, or have no direct means of contact, this can be a barrier to the relationship.
- Finance – the mentor should be able to makes independent and objective recommendations about development requirements, which would not be possible if they are responsible for the budget from which it is financed.
- Line management – as previously noted, the mentoring function can be compromised if the mentor is also the line manager.

Clutterbuck (2004, p. 63) also comments that a large hierarchy or experience gap between the parties should be avoided. If the gap is too great, the mentor's experience may seem irrelevant to the learner and the learner will not feel that the mentor understands the challenges that they face as they are too far removed from the situation to be able to help them to apply their work to the university programme.

What Makes an Effective Mentor?

An effective mentor always emphasises empowerment and personal accountability and provides space for reflection. By introducing the mentor to reflective questioning techniques, they can challenge the learner to ask more rigorous and objective questions, often from a wider perspective, to produce a more efficient and effective analysis of the situation.

Mentors should be selected with the objectives of the programme in mind so the mentor should understand the key concepts of learning in the workplace, whereas if the mentoring is related to induction, the mentor needs to understand the key processes policies and procedures of the organisation. However, irrespective of the focus of the scheme, ensuring that the mentor can empathise with the situation of the learner as well as, to some extent, act as a role model for the purposes and behaviours expected of the learner is the key to success. The qualities, then, for a mentor are: relevant experience, enthusiasm, commitment, approachability and ability to open doors, noting that the ability to maintain confidentiality is essential. Kay and Hinds (2007) quotes Gerald O'Callaghan from BP:

'Most mentors are experienced, well-rounded professionals and managers who are interested in developing young people and broadening their own contribution to the company.'

Fundamental to the mentoring relationship are communication skills; without good communication the mentoring relationship will founder, due to lack of understanding and trust between the parties. Of all the aspects of communication Parsloe (1999, p. 58) suggests that listening, questioning and feedback are the most important communication skills for the mentor.

LISTENING AND OBSERVING

Active listening is important in the mentoring relationship, as it demonstrates to the learner that the mentor is concentrating on what is being said and giving it thought. Body language is important in this respect as well as cultural norms, particularly with respect to eye contact (Parsloe, 1999, p. 63).

Listening to the tone of voice of the learner can convey as much about the mentor's needs as the content of their conversation – if the learner sounds tentative or confident this can relay how they are feeling about their role or studies.

Mentors have to strike a fine balance when the learner is speaking, probing specific areas for discussion and clarification; this can sometimes be interpreted as interruption, which is dispiriting for the learner. Remaining objective throughout the discussion, without arguing or taking the views of the learner personally, can challenge the mentor, but focusing on the needs of the learner and giving them space to express controversial views, in a safe environment, is one of the strengths of the mentoring system. Making notes also demonstrates active listening and will help in the recall and summarisation of the key points prior to identifying the agenda for follow up questions and discussions.

QUESTIONING SKILLS

At the outset of the relationship the mentor should clarify with the learner that they will be asking a series of questions to help the learner clarify their thinking and ultimately make decisions and solve problems. Explaining that these questions will often be used to help the learner see issues from a different perspective. Mentors must not only support their learners, but should challenge them too (Clutterbuck, 2004, p. 16).

It is suggested that questions should be asked in a friendly and supportive manner, acknowledging answers positively otherwise it might feel like an interrogation. Open questions (for example, what, why, where, how) should be used, gently probing for clarification. Such questioning could have been useful to the IT operations manager Case Study 8, to aid in the translation of theories into real life experience. The learner could have explained the theory to the mentor during a session and the mentor, using a series of questions and probes, would help the learner to identify how this was applied in practice.

FEEDBACK

Feedback can motivate a learner to continue to learn from experience, acquire new skills and knowledge by developing themselves. However, it also has the potential to undermine confidence and demotivate, and this is largely to do with appropriate delivery in terms of time and place. Discussion should, wherever possible, be constructive, focusing on how to improve but also indicating where the learner is succeeding.

The mentor should encourage the learner to take responsibility for analysing the feedback, and identify ways in which it can be used to enhance future performance. In the BP Case Study 4, the learner recognised the value of encouragement from a tutor/ mentor, even when the work was not yet ready (he later realised it was 'rubbish') but it enabled a trusting relationship to develop, where the learner could analyse the iterative feedback received to enhance his writing.

Where the learner is undertaking a formal programme of study, it is important that the mentor understands the roles and responsibilities of the course team. For example, it may be that there is a 'mentor coordinator' to whom he should relate comments about the operation of the scheme and a personal tutor for discussion about the learner, sharing concerns about progress, or particularly highlighting areas of excellence in practice.

The Mentoring Process

Irrespective of who 'owns' the mentoring scheme, the process is focused on the development and enhancement of the skills of the learner, by a process of support meetings, targeted on the personal development needs of the learner. It is helpful to schedule meetings regularly, and ground rules set about how the meetings will be organised as well as the contact methods agreed (Kay and Hinds, 2007, p. 51). Whilst the mentor generally manages the meeting to ensure that progress is made and identified issues discussed, the content and themes for the meeting are organised by the learner, normally based on the information provided by the university about the course requirements. It is advisable to give consideration, where involved in a formal course, to assignment hand in dates to ensure that support is provided at the critical times in the assessment cycle, allowing time for reflection, drafting and redrafting of work as this is often where crises occur. Whilst the onus should be on the learner to provide this information, a good working relationship with the course team will facilitate the sharing of information. Where mentoring is associated with in-company appraisal systems, then timing of meetings should be linked to milestone events with the system, giving time for reflection on feedback prior to formal review meetings with the manager.

At each stage there should be an evaluation of where the learner is in relation to the goals to be achieved, for each module within the course, within the appraisal cycle, and what actions have been taken. Consideration should be given to what learning techniques have been successful, and those that have worked less well. Parsloe (1999, p. 38) defines the mentoring process as the following:

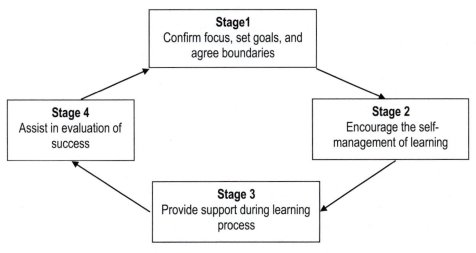

Figure 6   The mentoring process

It is accepted as good practice that the mentor prepares for the initial meeting by reviewing the overall programme objectives, analysing them, to identify and, as Parsloe (1999, p. 38) comments, to 'anticipate the likely needs of the learner'. Where a learner is involved on a formal course, the university is expected to provide relevant information to the mentor such as the learner handbook. If the mentor is not clear about the requirements of the course, then they should contact the course tutor to clarify any areas to avoid misunderstanding and confusion for the learner. Where courses are designed with a company, with mentor support as an intrinsic component of the teaching and learning strategy, then it is useful to develop a mentor handbook alongside the learner handbook, which provides additional information about the support available for mentors and key aspects of mentoring process, together with some guidance on useful techniques for mentoring. It is the University of Derby's practice to invite mentors to the induction session for the learners, so that they too are aware of the university facilities and to get to know the staff involved. In addition, the university offers a separate mentor session during the day, to talk through the support available for mentors and to answer any outstanding questions that the mentors may have. This also enables the course team to verify that the mentors are able to fulfil their role.

Where the relationship is related to the company appraisal system, it is important that the mentors are clear about the procedures and processes of the appraisal scheme as well as clarification on how their role fits within this.

At the beginning of the mentoring process the focus and objectives for developing a mutually supportive relationship are outlined and clarified. One of the important elements is a brief insight into both the mentor and learner background (Kay and Hinds, 2007, p. 39). This can also include interests outside work to develop mutual respect, understanding and how this experience can help to influence the relationship. It is the responsibility of the mentor to put the learner at ease and encourage an open dialogue.

If the relationship arises from a formal university-approved work-based learning programme of study, the mentor does not set the objectives, or determine the focus, but helps the learner to confirm and clarify the requirements, by asking open questions and providing the feedback mentioned earlier, so that the learner is clear in their own mind about the purpose and direction of the learning plan. When the relationship arises from the appraisal scheme, then the mentor may be able to help the learner in the preliminaries of objective setting, ensuring that they are 'SMART' (Specific, Measurable, Achievable, Relevant and Time constrained) and suitably challenging. The mentor provides a supporting framework of contact opportunities to enable the learner to structure the learning experience. Experience suggests that a form of SWOT (Strengths, Weaknesses, Opportunities and Threats) analysis can be introduced here to enable the learner to identify priorities and opportunities for learning.

At the first meeting the ground rules of the relationship will be set and agreed typically this will include:

- Mentors role to respond to developmental needs rather than impose own agenda.
- Confidentiality as appropriate to the context.
- Both parties to be open and truthful about the relationship.
- Mentors being aware of their limits of competence.
- Mentors undertaking CPD activity related to mentoring.
- Learner manages the relationship and the mentor empowers this, promoting the learners autonomy.

- Awareness of data protection act. (From Clutterbuck, 2004, p. 111).

At the beginning of the relationship it is also important to identify a timeframe and the circumstances under which the relationship will end, this may relate to a particular module or the duration of the whole course. As Kay and Hinds (2007, p. 82) note:

'A properly thought-out exit strategy will reduce many of the difficulties that can arise out of the ending of a relationship.'

In the second stage, the mentor facilitates the learning planning process, explained in greater detail by asking questions, making suggestions for contacts and helping the learner to identify learning opportunities within the workplace and suitable resources to support the learning process, during a regular series of meetings. A review of a SWOT analysis enables the mentor to help the learner establish their development priorities and begin to develop support networks which are crucial to success as evidenced in the case studies, by identifying aspects of the business that are important to further support the development process. By breaking down the overall aims into a series of manageable tasks, the learner can begin to self-manage the process. Once again the mentor acts as a sounding board for the learner to make suggestions and formulate plans and receive feedback on their ideas. In Case Study 8, the IT operations manager notes that it was difficult in some modules to reflect on real-life experience to translate this into assignments. The availability of a mentor here could have been useful to identify opportunities that did exist, to provide access to a network that could offer an insight into the relevant areas or to share their own experience for the student to reflect upon.

In the third stage, during the module/course when the learning plan or objectives related to appraisal is implemented, the mentor provides support by utilising the previously agreed framework of meetings and impromptu contacts to support the development. The timing and pace of these meetings, offering advice and guidance when requested, should be matched to the learner's need, rather than the needs of the mentor. When mistakes or setbacks occur the mentor has an important role in turning this into an opportunity for learning in a non-judgemental environment.

At these regular meetings it is important that the mentor begins the process by re-establishing the rapport. Each issue is then explored from the learner perspective with the mentor:

- clarifying key points;
- challenging any assumptions;
- facilitating learner analysis;
- drawing from their own experience.

This will enable the learner to formulate a plan by which to address the issue. At the end of the meeting the mentor will:

- highlight learning points and progress to build confidence and motivation;
- encourage the learner to identify actions for both parties, with milestones;
- ensure that the learner has identified a date for the next meeting.

If our Tesco dotcom training manager, Case Study 3, had had a mentor then the frustration of 'relatively long periods of inactivity from the university' would not have been an issue and project completion deadlines been an intrinsic part of the discussion. It would also have helped with some of the questions on 'how the university works' in the initial stages.

In the final stage, when the programme or module is nearing an end, or the appraisal review date approaches, the mentor encourages the learner to undertake formal evaluations, and helps them to prepare by asking reflective questions to identify any barriers to learning as well as the progress made and the benefits the organisation has noticed during the process. Arrangements for bringing the relationship to an end should also be finalised during this stage.

Much of the good work done during the mentoring phase can be quickly be undone if the learner feels that they are 'cast adrift'. They can become more demoralised and demotivated if, after a successful period of mentoring, suddenly there is no one to turn to for support and advice. It is important, therefore, to give the learner the confidence to work independently and a gradual withdrawal from the mentoring relationship can signify the organisations' confidence in the capabilities and competence of the learner.

Expectation about the informal phase of the relationship can be clarified – the mentor can offer reassurance of willingness to give any help and advice, as any colleague would, but that the mentoring relationship is no longer in place. At this final meeting it is useful to briefly review the tools and techniques that have helped the learner to learn successfully, noting the importance of reflection on learning and critical questioning, recognising the successful aspects of the relationship to enable both parties to move on with confidence.

Problems in the Mentoring Relationship

Problems associated with the relationship can be more difficult to identify and address, as the main participants are almost 'too close' to the problem to be able to evaluate it objectively. Thus it is important to have if possible a mentor coordinator who can monitor the individual mentoring relationships to identify potential problems early in the cycle. For example, the senior police officer in the Case Study 2 had said from the outset, 'I don't really have time to get involved... tell me what I need to do and if something needs writing write it for me.' Had there been a mentor coordinator then these sentiments could have been quickly identified and addressed. The situation simply ended up with the learner being under more pressure. The business school insisted upon a mentoring relationship, but did nothing to ensure that the relationship worked, so the learner had to complete not only his own work, but also that of his mentor or 'sleeping partner' as he so aptly described him. In this situation having no mentor is almost preferable, as the university would then have to take steps to support the learner in identifying an appropriate individual.

Potentially the most obvious problem is the failure to establish a rapport between the parties. Clutterbuck (2004, p. 124) suggests that if the parties have not 'clicked within the first two meetings' then the relationship is unlikely to be successful; at this point it may be useful to hold a review meeting with the scheme organiser to check that each are clear about their roles and to help the parties to develop trust and confidence in one another.

Alternatively, it may be necessary to put the learner together with a different mentor, if it is felt that the relationship will not work. Timing the intervention is difficult but crucial, too early and a potentially successful but slow-burning relationship will not have had time to develop, too late and the mentor and learner will both be demoralised and demotivated.

All the literature agrees, and personal experience confirms, that one of the most significant problems the mentoring relationship faces is lack of time (Billett, 2003). Typically those who are ideally placed to be mentors are busy and ambitious people, following the old adage – if you want a job done ask a busy person! Fixing a series of meetings ahead and regularly reviewing the dates can help to prevent 'diary drift', as will prioritising the mentor meetings. This latter strategy will only work if the meetings are carefully scheduled from the outset. The police officer Case Study 2 example cites the lack of availability of his mentor, who was also his line manager, a barrier to learning. Not only did his 'coach' not have time to coach him, he did not have time to familiarise himself with the requirements of the course to pass on to his learner. He was invited to a briefing session at the business school. During this session the course team should have included time within the programme to enable identification of any potential mismatches in expectations and address the issue.

Dependency can also pose a problem, where the learner or mentor is reluctant to allow the relationship to end, or in the case of the learner comes to rely too heavily on the mentor for advice and support during the relationship. This problem can be prevented by agreeing an end date for the relationship from the outset and then keeping to it.

Summary

Effective mentors balance support with challenge by providing opportunities and setting positive expectations. A formal scheme provides an infrastructure that should support this ethos, by offering the mentors the tools, techniques and opportunities to undertake mentoring activity in a supportive and challenging manner. Learners should have the space in which to grow and develop their potential by utilising their mentor effectively. Furthermore, a scheme should enable the individual mentoring relationships to be evaluated for their effectiveness, ensuring that they meet the needs of the learner and provide sufficient support for the mentor.

Many of our learners within the case studies comment upon the need for someone like a personal tutor who is allocated to them throughout the programme, who understands how the university works generally and can offer initial help with academic writing, but also understands the context in which they work, so that they can help them with the translation of theory into practice, as well as identifying opportunities to evidence their learning and opportunities to develop work-based projects. A good mentor, aligned to a mentoring programme, would provide just such support.

Whilst the mentoring relationship and the roles of mentors can appear complex, it is important to remember that no one expects the mentor or learner to be perfect and that the key to successful mentoring is in keeping the relationship simple. Parsloe (1999, p. 71) cites six Rules of Simplicity:

- Meetings – successful mentoring requires that the learner has time and space to share ideas, thoughts and concerns, and that the mentor has time to listen and ask reflective questions to enable the learner to choose the best course of action. Planning ahead is important – cancelling is easier than squeezing time into a non-existent space in a diary.

- Keep it brief – short, focused meetings are of more use to the learner, but they should be given time to talk, without pressure. If meetings are regular then the length can be varied according to need.
- Stick to the process – the learner chooses the issues to talk about and the mentor listens and asks questions. The mentor should take responsibility for structuring and the time management of the meeting once the learner has identified the key areas for discussion, either by way of a prepared agenda or an agreed list at the beginning of the meeting.
- Mentors should ask – not tell! – Parsloe suggests that it's 80 per cent asking questions and 20 per cent answering them. For mentors who are managers this can be a difficult hurdle to overcome.
- Remember it's about learning – and learning can happen outside a classroom. Finding opportunities and resources to support this will enrich the learner experience.

Mentors can gain from the process themselves – by learning new techniques to work with others and the benefits of feedback from colleagues. There are some useful websites concerned with mentoring as follows:

- Coaching and Mentoring Network: http://www.coachingnetwork.org.uk and http://www.coachingnetwork.org.uk/ResourceCentre/WhatAreCoachingAndMentoring.htm (accessed 26/08/09).
- European Mentoring Council: http://www.emccouncil.org (accessed 26/8/09). Gives access and an overview of the *International Journal of Mentoring and Coaching*.
- Mentors Forum: http://www.mentorsforum.co.uk (accessed 26/8/09).
- Mentoring and Befriending Foundation: http://mandbf.org.uk (accessed 26/8/09). Offers access to *Rapport,* the organisation's magazine, featuring in-depth reports, case studies of good practice, news and views on mentoring and befriending, information on government policy and the latest research studies and book reviews.

The Learner's Experience

7 *Introduction to Case Studies*

The preceding chapters have discussed work-based learning from the perspective of the university experience of managing work-based learning. However, relatively little attention is given to the work-based learning learner experience. It is useful to frame the following case studies by reflecting on the preceding chapters.

The book commences with an understanding that universities originated as places of training and reflection in a vocation, the Church, however, over the centuries have become more concerned with the generation of subject or discipline knowledge and expertise at the expense of vocational and technical learning. They have evolved into institutions that find it increasingly hard to relate to the workplace experience and the forms of learning found there. The task of preparing people for entry to work has taken precedence over meeting the educational needs of those in work. As a consequence, the first question to ask the individual in the case studies is, 'What role did the learners' workplace experience play in the engagement with the university?' Did the university have the capacity to recognise non-traditional forms of learning such as reflective learning or was it simply ignored and conventional forms of learning employed?

The premise that the knowledge economy has changed the nature of employment is also explored, not least because it is a major plank of government policy. Workplace learning used to be all about acquiring competence to perform prescribed tasks, in other words technical education, but the knowledge economy requires people to understand these tasks and seek ways to improve their effectiveness. This is important because it suggests that work-based learning is not simply a lower-order learning activity, such as an apprenticeship, but provides opportunities for higher-level progression regardless of point of entry to work or the level of qualification. The question to ask is, 'Do we see our learners returning to university engagement with a much higher-level capability than their formal qualification suggest?'

Companies used to manage employees as if they were cadres on prescribed career paths. There were clear parallels between the way the education establishment managed learners and the way employers managed these cadres. So employers were the natural partners for universities wishing to engage with learners in full-time employment, and vice versa. Nowadays, even in the biggest companies most employees are expected to take charge of their own career management and, in any event, most actually work for small organisations that have no capacity to manage careers. So do the case study learners fit this model of self-directed progression or are they part of an employer-managed programme?

The actual learning process also raises exploratory questions. Much has been made in the preceding chapters about recognition of prior learning and mentoring as a support mechanism. Did the learners want these mechanisms? Were they provided by the university, and if they were, did they work well? Were there other support mechanisms that would have added value?

Finally, we have the most important question of all; why did they do it? Those in full-time employment know their careers depend first and foremost on job performance, so why put that at risk by devoting energy to engaging with a demanding cultural-differentiated university-oriented learning world? Clearly the case study learners thought that the university experience would more than compensate this risk by providing something they needed. What was it? Was it extra knowledge? Was it intellectual development? Was it the formal qualification?

The case studies were gathered together by approaching universities noted for work-based learning and asking them to volunteer students who had completed accredited programmes while working full time. Not surprisingly the cases clustered around conventional part-time courses, with a combination of classroom and distance learning. These are the longer-established forms of work-based learning. Also, although the learners represented very diverse backgrounds, they all came with significant workplace experience and there were no learners who were new in the world of work. Again this is not surprising. University admission procedures tolerate those without entry qualifications who have deep workplace experience, but are stricter with those who are new to work (an issue for those who are trying to progress through apprenticeships). The cases are characterised as follows:

Table 2   Case characteristics

Case	Type of Workplace	Workplace role	Course
1	Small business	Managing Director	MBA
2	Police Force	Operations Manager	MBA
3	Supermarket Chain	Dotcom Training Manager	M Phil
4	Major Oil Company	Country Vice president	PhD
5	Civil Service	Internal Audit Manager	Degree
6	Regulatory Authority	Care Commission Officer	Degree
7	Training Company	Director of Learning	PhD
8	National Health Service	IT Operations Manager	FD
9	Local Authority	Children's Services Manager	MA
10	Children's Playgroup	Leader	BA Hons
11	University	Lecturer and trainer	MA
12	Restaurant chain	Store Manager	FD

In compiling the cases, the learners were given free rein to say what they felt and, as the case studies demonstrate, to focus on the issues they felt were important. The cases are narratives by learners expressing what it feels like to be working full time and doing a university degree. However, the volunteers were given some headings to guide them:

- What was the learner situation?
- Why did I decide to do something like this?

- What were the barriers to learning?
- What sort of workplace environment was I coming from?
- What supplements and tools did I use?
- Did capturing workplace experience work?
- Did the assessment method work?
- What was the outcome and what were the benefits?
- How much did it cost and who paid?
- What are the lessons learned?

The case studies are presented as the volunteers wrote them and treated as direct evidence. Chapter 20 draws on these case studies and presents a number of themes that emerge. The reader may wish to go to Chapter 21 first and then refer back to the case studies. In addition the case studies have provided examples for other chapters.

8 Case Study 1: An SME Owner and an MBA

© Istockphoto / Chris Hellyar

My Learner Situation

I left school with a Diploma in Business and joined the army at 18 years old. Having spent 8 years in the army and a further 5 years within a specialist department of the UK Government, I decide to embark on my lifelong ambition of setting up my own business. The business which provides counter-espionage services is now well established and in its eleventh year of business. I have grown my business organically, initially I was working alone on a consultancy basis, now we have a team of people including some graduates and a solid infrastructure from which we can continue to grow. My business is in a niche but yet growing sector of industry and keeps me very busy. In addition to this I am a Director of a number of trade association boards within my business sector.

I am an SME owner and my own boss and in order to progress, I intend to grow my business. To enable me to do this, I felt that whilst I could buy business expertise in most areas, it would be beneficial both to the business and to myself if I broadened my own abilities. I was keen to expand my knowledge base and consolidate my skills to support the development of my business ambitions and broaden my career. I submitted a personal profile and business case to Surrey School of Management and in September 2007 I started an MBA. I have just completed that programme.

Why Did I Decide to Do Something Like This?

During the early years of starting my business, I attended a number of short courses by the DTI, Business Link and other government schemes to improve my business knowledge. These had given me everything I needed to perform the basics of running a company, but as my career and business developed I had taken on other director roles in addition to running my business, for which I had legal responsibilities and wanted to expand my knowledge base further.

Not being a graduate has not concerned me and has not knowingly affected my career adversely, but I was keen to underpin the knowledge and practical experience I had gained over the years by obtaining formal qualifications which would also assist in my personal development.

I had considered an MBA about five years prior to starting the course, but at that time I was so busy developing my business I did not have either the physical or thinking time required for intensive periods of study. I had done short courses that gave me all the vocational/practical skills I needed. I knew everything I needed to know about my business and had strong general knowledge of the business world, but felt I wanted to extend my knowledge base further and use the terminology used by senior industry professionals.

I selected the Surrey MBA because it was focused on business and claimed that it would provide learning in a way that I could integrate into my business. I knew MBAs were well-respected academic qualifications but it was only after I was on the started the course that someone said, 'Oh, you're not just doing a Masters then.'

What Were the Barriers to Learning?

Fortunately, I was able to fund the course myself and was also awarded a scholarship. My main barrier was time. My business had to take first priority on my time and I was working around 70 hours per week. I am also married and we were rebuilding a house which was also taking up significant time, so I delayed starting the course till I felt I could manage the commitment to do further study. Anyway, the time availability was the main barrier to being able to do a course like the MBA. Paradoxically, time management is one of the skills that has most advanced while I have been on the programme. I used to think I was very good at time management, but I have progressed several levels further.

Once I was on the course I encountered another obstacle, which was the lack of practical business experience shown by some of the lecturers. Some had never worked outside academia and although most were great whilst imparting academic knowledge, some seemed unable to relate academic information to a business environment in a practical context. There was a wealth of practical experience amongst the other MBA students in my cohort, some of which had very senior roles within global organisations, and sharing practical knowledge was an important part of our learning process, however, a very small number of lecturers treated the group as though we were young recent graduates. This led to a great deal of frustration. We were all used to dealing with heavy schedules, but the administrative support was badly coordinated and a small number of the lecturers were unhelpful by not providing electronic copies of their lessons.

This was a disappointment. The ability to link my learning into the workplace was a big driver for choosing the course. I personally felt that there was little consideration given to part-time students. Most of us were working full time in addition to our studies and therefore the need to manage time effectively was critical. Unfortunately, the university administration was such that semester timetables were being issued and changed at the last minute, affecting business schedules of those students like myself who needed to travel for business. Over time, we managed the university's processes to make it workable for ourselves.

What Sort of Workplace Environment Was I Coming From?

In one sense I have a lot of job freedom. I am the boss and I own the company. But in another sense I am very limited in time I can spend. I typically work 60–70 hours per week and I am very clear that my job has to come first. Any learning that I do has to fit round these and other commitments. The course typically required me to spend ten hours per week in private study. Fortunately I am an early bird so I used to get up at 5am and do a couple of hours study before going to work.

Another feature of my workplace environment is that, although I have some staff, I am really working on my own. One of the things I really gained from the programme was having a group of peers that I could discuss business issues with. I learnt a great deal by discussing things with fellow course members and this was a real benefit of attending the MBA. I did a couple of evenings per week at the university and these interactions were important. I needed the regular physical contact with the class and hence geography was quite important. Surrey was a convenient location to come for meetings.

Finally as an SME, I had none of the support that people coming from global organisations might have, for example, HR support and advice. This sense of having to do everything yourself is an important consideration for anyone in my position who is thinking of doing a course like this. You must be 100 per cent committed to the course from the outset. It is very hard work and it will test your motivation to the limit.

What Supplements and Tools Did I Use?

Probably the most important supplement was finding a support system. Because I didn't have work colleagues who could support me, I needed to build a network of friends and other work contacts who could act as advisers and mentors. I found people who had done programmes like this before and enlisted their help. Another aspect that worried me greatly was that I had no experience of higher education and didn't have any idea how to do research or academic study. I had to learn this at the start of the course. I contacted one of the professors at the start of the course because I knew about his mentoring network and he helped enormously.

It would have been very good to have had a university tutor to act as a mentor throughout the course; however this was not available. There was a course lecturer for each module and some of these directors were very helpful. The ability to take a practical problem to the course director and chat it through was extremely valuable. However, I didn't feel that there was anyone who knew both my work side and my academic side and could act as a bridge. I really needed to relate what I was learning to utility in the workplace and a university mentor would have been helpful and improved my learning experience.

Did Capturing Workplace Experience Work?

The main mechanism for capturing workplace experience was the ability to bring work issues and case studies into the classroom as practical examples to work on. It was good to bring work problems into the classroom and socialise them with other course members. I found it very helpful to compare experiences with others who had different jobs. It really broadened my business understanding. I also applied what I was learning in my job. I found myself thinking about the theories I had learned and seeing where I could use them. The course involved a lot of project work, both individual and shared. There were assignments such as doing business plans, and these were very helpful.

However, there was no formal capture of my prior experience other than through the admissions process. They accepted me on the course because of my workplace experience. I wasn't a graduate, and it was my work experience that substituted for these qualifications. Unfortunately, I felt there was little recognition on the course that people had come through this route. The lecturers seem to presume experience in academic study, which implied they knew little about the student attending their lectures!

The stated aim of the course was to be able to communicate at a business level, but many aspects of the way the courses were run did not function at that level of professionalism. Some tutors may have been academically qualified but they lacked practical experience to help students relate their learning back into the workplace. In a lecture we might ask how we could relate a particular a particular academic study or model and in some cases the lecturer was unable to answer this. Some lecturers were very vocal and functioned in one direction only. We gradually changed that and got more of a focus on the things we needed.

When you have already spent 12 hours that day working as a managing director you don't want to sit in a room being lectured by someone who doesn't know how the business world functions. It is not what you have paid for in an MBA course.

Did the Assessment Method Work?

The main form of assessment was through project assignments. These were assessed as written reports and there were also assessed presentations. I felt these gave a good assessment of knowledge as they allowed you time to develop what you knew. Some of the projects were done in groups and this proved a good way of assessing how you worked in a team. These could be quite challenging as you had to go along with the consensus in the way the project was tackled. Often we worked by audio conference and, whereas I am an early bird, others are late birds. Often I found myself on an audio till well after midnight and was then getting up at 5am to do my own work. But this is what happens in the real world so being assessed under these conditions was realistic.

We also had exams; two exams of three hours each covering three subjects. These were fine as a test of how you coped with pressure. In the real world you don't often find yourself having to solve complex business problems in extremely short timescales and without references. You have time to think and explore and consult others. This is how knowledge is applied in the workplace. Once in a while you are faced with a stressful situation where you have to react quickly on your own and this seemed to be what the exam environment was testing.

What Was the Outcome and What Were the Benefits?

The experience has certainly boosted my business skills. I would not say I was one who lacks confidence but this has boosted my ability to handle senior-level interactions. I have also applied a lot of what I have learned directly to business situations. The experience has certainly broadened my knowledge base and developed me as a person. I now feel confident that I can build my business career in the way I want. The experience has broadened my horizons.

In particular, I have used the strategic models quite widely in my business. These have underpinned my business experience. The knowledge is packaged in a way that I can use it and I can understand where it works and where it doesn't work. This ability to put theory into practice is the main benefit for me. You can learn by rote but that doesn't give you ability to apply and understand. For me the ability to adapt what I learnt in the classroom so that it works in a particular business situation is the most important thing I gained.

I came from an environment where any meeting I was in I was generally chairing. On the course you are not always in the leader position and you learn to accommodate other people's working styles. You find out how people perceive situations differently from you and understand there are other aspects to a situation. It highlights the way you conduct yourself in different situations. I find I am now consciously bringing my staff forward to take more of a lead. Others have commented on how my communication skills have benefited. I can see things in wider context and that means I can position how I communicate.

I think the company has benefited hugely. It has given me a lot of food for thought and I have been consciously looking at how to apply things to the business. I am applying what I learnt – no question. From my experience it was an excellent thing to do. It was a huge learning curve. I developed skill level and I developed my time management hugely.

How Much Did it Cost and Who Paid?

The course cost £15,000 for the two years. I did get a £3,000 scholarship and my company paid the remainder.

What are the Lessons Learned?

The key question people ask me is, does a programme like this help SMEs? My answer is unequivocal – it is well worth doing and it can boost your business as much as you want. People said, 'Why would anyone from an SME want to do an MBA – they are designed for large corporations?' True, the materials are geared to major corporations but actually all the things you need to take into consideration as a big corporation you need to think about as an SME. It maybe not on the same scale but you do need to know the same information.

Then there is the whole question of time management which is so crucial to anyone in an SME. I selected Surrey partly on academic record but more on geography. I wanted quality but I had to have accessibility. I also wanted to be able to structure my time carefully so that I could balance all my commitments.

If someone in an SME is going to do something like this, I would say to them, 'Is there any doubt in your mind that you can commit the time?' If the answer is yes then I would say it is probably not the time to be doing this. The important thing to remember is that people have different learning styles and time could be much greater than that is stated on the programme. Certainly the time commitment was much greater than I expected. At the end of the day I could not afford my business to suffer and I had to do the course which meant compromises on my family and social life.

The thing that I valued most from the learning experience was the opportunity to work in groups with peers and share business experiences, which is something you lack when running a small business. As an SME, the main lesson is to pick a programme which gives you high-quality interaction time with like-minded peers. For me, a simple e-learning programme would not have provided me with the same value.

My final comment is that the university should understand that it is dealing with experienced business people, who want to be able to share work experiences in the classroom and see which academic theories add value. In this context, having lecturers who understand how the academic ideas apply to business in a practical context is critical. Workplace utility is the key deliverable.

CHAPTER **9**

Case Study 2: A Police Officer Undertakes an External MBA

Starting Point

© Istockphoto / Andy Medina

I became a Police Officer at the age of 19. I had not been to university despite having had a grammar school education and achieving good GCE A level grades. On leaving school I thought I had convinced myself that the right thing to do was to get out into the 'real' world at that point, but with hindsight I think I was more heavily influenced by my parents believing that than I realised at the time.

By 1995, at the age of 42, I had 23 years police service that had embraced a variety of roles and specialisms and I was the Chief Inspector on a rural division in one of the Home Counties. I was married, with a wife with a full-time job in the Probation Service, two children aged 12 and 9, and the usual range of domestic and householder responsibilities.

Motivation

When I joined the police, graduates were a rarity and they were generally fast tracked to the higher ranks by way of a 'graduate entry' scheme, some would say regardless of their practical competence. The Bramshill Scholarship Scheme (Bramshill being the then Police Staff College), gave officers at Inspector level the opportunity to take time out to study full time for an undergraduate degree, but I had not taken up that opportunity. I slowly began to realise, however, that things were moving towards a position where officers promoted to the superintending ranks, and certainly to chief officer posts, were almost invariably graduates, either having entered as such, or benefited from the scholarship scheme, or by way of some other voluntary and self-initiated external study programme.

I had, since an earlier stage in my career, been involved in organisational development activity, had worked full time on a project team, and was still involved on a part-time basis with things to which there was a theoretical perspective. This activity involved engagement with external consultants, researchers, and academics, as well as working closely with colleagues qualified in a number of management and related disciplines. Things had moved on from the time when the only higher education qualification valued in the service was a law degree. Bramshill scholars were by now studying sociology, psychology, systems science, and for business and management qualifications.

The result of all this was to produce the beginnings of a feeling that in order to compete on even terms in relation to career progression and to feel more comfortable on a more personal level in the company I was keeping, I might have to think about seizing the next opportunity for some sort of degree-level course that came along. To be honest, therefore, my motives were definitely extrinsic in the sense that they were mostly to do with my standing in others' eyes, rather than being driven by a conscious awareness that I personally needed developing or that the organisation would benefit in terms of performance as a result of my further learning. I had already been on staff college 'Command' courses and on internal and external leadership training of various sorts. Some of this had been at a fairly advanced level, but it hadn't been accredited in any particular way, so I still felt at a disadvantage compared to my graduate colleagues.

The Opportunity

In 1995, my Force instigated its own Master's-level programme for a number of police officers and some senior 'civilian' police staff. This was done in collaboration with a management school at a nearby university and should have involved a pre-MBA course, followed by a full MBA programme. We started the pre-MBA course, but it proved to be a disaster. The school and course were badly organised and eventually we abandoned ship. We then switched to another university and in 1996 started a 'management' MBA programme. One felt there that one was in the hands of honest, competent professionals, albeit the Programme Director appeared somewhat eccentric and not quite the sort of character I expected to encounter in that role. It might say something about the whole atmosphere that prevailed that I now found myself talking about 'participants' in the programme, as opposed to having felt like a 'student' during the earlier aborted course.

Programme Methodology and Assessment

We learned that the planned two-year management MBA programme would indeed not involve sufficient attended modules or events to be classified as part time, but would involve up to half a dozen attended two/three-day residential modules at conference centre venues. These would be to address individual components of the knowledge domains featuring in the programme, one of which, in the case of the police officers, was to be at our own HQ in connection with the policing focus. There were to be a number of one-day sessions at the business school marking the transitions between different stages of the programme. Additionally, as the approach to the programme was very action learning-orientated, we were all assigned to action learning sets, in each case comprising a cross-section of about six participants from different backgrounds and employment situations. In my case, the Programme Director was the learning set facilitator. Action learning set meetings were not planned in accordance with a fixed rota, but the general expectation was that there would be one every couple of months. The main focus of the programme was to be three work-based projects, each to be the subject of a 20,000 word report and assessment would be based on these project reports and a viva, so the learning was going to be very substantially workplace-based. There was, of course, an extensive reading list issued.

Barriers

To support the workplace projects, participants were required to identify an 'in-company' coach and the coaches attended a briefing session at the business school. My coach was my line manager, the Divisional Commander, who had been a Bramshill scholar and at that point was the holder of Bachelor's and Master's degrees and had been the Force's Head of Strategic and Corporate Planning (or whatever the post was called at the time). Given what he had done himself, his approach was pragmatic to say the least and was perhaps symptomatic of a gulf between the theory and practice of how the programme was meant to function. His view was, 'I don't fully understand what all this is about, I don't really have time to get involved, but I'm willing to help where I can, so tell me when I have to do something or say something and if it involves writing something, write it for me.'

Another issue about which, in my case, there was a gulf between the espoused approach to the programme and the reality was time. As far as the Force was concerned, the official position was that attended modules, day briefings and action learning set meetings could take place in 'duty time'. For some of my colleagues, junior in rank to me and with shift-based responsibilities, this was a distinct advantage. Their duties were rostered accordingly and they were struck off for the days needed to attend course commitments. In my case, the situation was altogether different. The nature of my job role (and of the other roles I moved on to during the course of the programme) was such that any work not done whilst I attended these same events was still waiting for me when I got back.

As well as the nature and volume of my workload, I always felt there was a tacit understanding based on how I was viewed personally and professionally by my bosses, that I would do what was needed without it diverting any time or effort from the 'day job'. Consequently, I worked long hours to make up for lost time and sometimes this involved working seven days a week. I also had on-call responsibilities and although I was generally able to organise things so as not to be called away from course commitments, I had to do additional hours on call at other times to compensate. I believe a few of my shift working colleagues even found some time for course-related reading and writing during the wee small hours of their night shifts. Needless to say, I don't think I read or wrote a word of coursework during any working day and all such activity was undertaken in what would otherwise have been my own time, some of it whilst on annual leave.

Cost and Payback

I didn't particularly resent those of my police colleagues who were able to do what was required with less cost to their private and family life, but I was aware that my situation was perhaps more akin to that of participants employed in the private sector and the professions, or engaged in business on their own behalf. The pressures, particularly during the periods when my three project reports were in preparation, were considerable. They resulted in my wife claiming to this day that she should have been awarded half an MBA. At the end of it all, aside from paying the course fees, the Force had done nothing to facilitate my studies. This, together with the fact that in my view the organisation had enjoyed the immediate benefit of my learning being applied through the implementation of my work-based projects was later of some significance. When, three years after completing the MBA, I decided to retire from the Police Service, I was entirely comfortable taking the position that the Force had had its money's worth out of me and I had no hesitation taking my MBA and the personal learning and development I had derived from it away with me to pastures new.

Disconnects

Given that the whole ethos of this particular MBA was about (to paraphrase) 'knowledge bearing fruit in works (Francis Bacon)', something that was clearly seen as being of great importance was the selection of work-based projects and their relevance to one's role and responsibilities in the workplace. Compared to some, perhaps then more conventional MBA programmes, there was some emphasis here on oneness of purpose between life, work and study. On occasions, the way some people talked about this aspect of things got almost too metaphysical for my liking. I didn't then and I don't now necessarily see the inevitability or necessity for one's whole life and being to be inextricably wrapped up with one's work. The fact that work and study more or less occupied my whole life for this period out of sheer necessity for the time and workload reasons I have described, was not a reflection of my active commitment to the principle being preached about oneness.

To compound this failure on my part to fall in line with one element of the connectivity my tutors would have liked me to have, realities to do with my personal career situation and organisational needs eventually conspired also to somewhat disconnect the studying bit from the day job. This occurred over time. Initially, the task was to define a first project connected with my day-to-day role. The attitude of my sponsors and coach to the programme seemed ambivalent in the sense that they had instigated the programme of which I had become part and agreed to support me in my endeavours, but in reality they were so busy that they didn't even have the time to participate in any discussion with me about what my work-based projects should be, what areas of theory were most relevant to them and, therefore, what options I should exercise over discretionary modules within the programme.

Whilst undertaking the abortive pre-MBA programme, I had been moved into the role of Divisional Operations Manager on a larger, urban division, leading something called the Operations Network Team (ONT). This team was composed of the middle-ranking operational managers of the division (mostly at inspector level) who, in addition to their immediate operational responsibilities, were also involved in developmental activity relating to building the division, recently created as a result of organisational and boundary changes, into a cohesive entity and preparing it for an auditing process concerned with its preparedness to implement an early incarnation of neighbourhood policing. I chose a project focusing on 'Change and Police Culture' related to the developmental tasks that were the responsibility of the ONT.

Another New Day Job

About halfway through what would have been expected to be the life of this first project, in the rather peremptory way that was usual for the Police Service, I got promoted and moved to a new job. This was to a HQ-based programme leadership role in relation to what went under a rather grand and symbolic (or embarrassing, depending on your point of view) name, which I won't reveal, as it might make other players in this story too readily identifiable. This was the high-tech/high-touch programme intended to embed neighbourhood policing in the Force and to help develop it for the wider British Police Service and export it under the auspices of 'UK Policing plc' (in pursuit of which I spent some time in the USA during this period). The move curtailed the action phase of the divisionally based project and meant it would have to be reported upon after my move and change of role. I was, nonetheless, able to produce some evidence of the way that my study and development of theory had been shared with the ONT in such a way that it had influenced, and would continue to influence, the way the change processes on what had become my old division were being led.

A Certain Lack of Direction

The nature of my new role lent itself perfectly to an MBA project related directly to the programme for which I now had responsibility. At this point, I was directly reporting to one of the two chief officer sponsors of the MBA programme, who was the Force's acknowledged change leader. Several other participants in the MBA programme were also in full or part-time roles supporting the programme. It therefore might have seemed reasonable to expect him and other senior colleagues to want to maximise any opportunity to better coordinate the MBA-related activities of the whole cohort of students (about eight of us, initially) and to see that the learning taking place at the theoretical level was being appropriately applied. Again, I received no direction or guidance from within the organisation, with it being signalled that the choice of what I focused on was entirely mine. I'd like to think this was testament to the trust reposed in me to make the optimum choices in relation to a second project, but in truth I think it was another case of people being distracted by other priorities and concerns. My old boss remained as my coach, on the same 'sleeping partner' basis as before.

In consultation with my tutor and action learning set colleagues I resolved that my second project would be about the very issues that were by then causing me some concern, and so the selected focus was 'Chaos, Complexity and Knowledge Creation'. As this project evolved it took the form of a critical examination of the organisation's, the chief officer teams', and my sponsor's own approach to organisational learning and to leading the sort of programmes in which I was involved, including his and the Force's management of our participation in the MBA programme itself.

The next period of the programme, during which the action part of my project was to progress the 'day job' policing project and the learning part was about the chaos, complexity and knowledge creation involved, was exciting for a number of reasons, most of which might be considered to be the wrong sort of reasons. I will have to be brief about a whole series of developments that occurred in fairly quick succession, but broadly the following is a summary of what happened.

Winds of Change

After a period during which my sponsor (also the policing project's very hands-on sponsor and the lead in relation to the Force and the MBA programme) headed the Force in an acting role, a new Chief Constable was appointed. He was hugely intelligent, with what I described in one of my project reports and to his face as 'an ego the size of a planet', and his own agenda. He was sceptical about the policing project, moderately sceptical about the MBA programme and at loggerheads with our original sponsor on a number of fronts. He subsequently rose to a position of national importance. Part of my day job role came to involve mediating between the two and their respective followers.

Day Job Number Four

For reasons that perhaps were part of an attempt to remove me from that role and deflect me from what might have been seen as a prurient interest in the machinations of chief officers, I was moved before completion of my second MBA project into a radically different role as Commander of the Force's Operational Support Division, responsible for things like the tactical firearms unit, Royalty and VIP protection, police dogs, air support, public order policing and emergency planning. I moved at short notice and set about writing the report of my second MBA project whilst the day job again was completely unrelated to anything connected with the project or anything subject of the report I was writing. I was, of course, by then also supposed to be planning my third and final project, but at this point I was having difficulty defining anything that made sense in that regard.

As part of setting the scene for the events about to unfold, I should mention that, notwithstanding all the turmoil, a decision had been made to feed a second cohort of people into the MBA Programme. They had set out about a year behind us in the first cohort and there were others in the pipeline. There seemed remarkably little HR department involvement in any of the arrangements for this. In fact, the HR Director at that time had an unusual relationship with the Chief Officer team, and appeared to be bypassed in relation to such matters. There was one individual in an 'HR Planning and Career Development' role within the HR set up who was involved and he acted as the 'Link Manager' between the Force and the university.

A Bit of a Catastrophe

We suddenly heard one day that the MBA Programme Director was to leave his post forthwith following a decision that the specific nature of the programme he was running was not one that the university wanted to continue supporting. He was to continue in his role as a tutor and learning set facilitator for the immediate future. It appeared that part of the issue was that somebody influential in a major local authority contributing students to the programme had taken against something or somebody.

Counselling

At this point my learning set meetings became more like mutual counselling sessions, particularly as the now sequestrated Programme Director was its facilitator, that two of our members worked for the local authority at the centre of the controversy, and one of our number worked for the university (in a role completely unconnected with MBA programmes). The politics of what was going on potentially affected all their careers. I suppose my part in all this was as the representative in the learning set of a participating organisation whose senior sponsor of the MBA programme was influential and supportive of the nature of the programme and the departed director. I felt, therefore, that I was somehow seen as part of the cavalry that was supposed to come riding to everybody's rescue.

I was indeed embroiled in working unofficially with my sponsor and our Link Manager in HR towards our organisation playing its part in negotiations to safeguard the interests of current participants in the MBA programme and influence future developments. As far as the remainder of my studies was concerned, those of us already participating in the MBA programme were being assured that we could complete as planned with the assessment criteria and so forth unchanged. It was clear, however, that the university did not want to continue with the type of MBA programme that had attracted us there in the first place. I think, too, at around this point, I was negotiating an extension on the original two-year timetable on the grounds that the three changes of job I had undergone since the beginning had presented difficulties with the orderly completion of projects. I didn't know at that stage that there was another move to come and I don't remember an actual time limit being put on completion of the programme, such was the chaos prevailing.

More Catastrophe (or Opportunity)

As an organisation we had to consider the fate of what would have been the third cohort to enter the MBA programme, now closed to new entrants. I, at least until now, had no official role in respect of any of this. I was a mere MBA student. Just as the Force was on the brink of entering into a consortium of employers minded to follow the Programme Director to another institution, (including at least two very large, well-known and well-respected private sector companies), two more completely unforeseen things happened. The second of these was probably more dramatic than any development in this story so far.

The first thing to happen was that our HR Planning Manager and MBA programme Link Manager announced his imminent departure for his own 'career development' reasons and he duly departed to work for a large international charity. I am sure his reasons had partly to do with the rather odd situation in HR that I have described, the postscript to which is that some time later, the HR Director crossed swords with the Chief Constable and resigned one weekend, never to be seen again. The second development,

I think within days of the announcement of the Link Manager's departure and only days before an important meeting to decide about our future participation in the successor programme to the MBA, was that my chief officer sponsor and the Force's main supporter of the programme was suspended from duty as a result of criminal allegations in respect of which he subsequently stood trial and was acquitted. He was not disciplined and thereafter he retired without ever returning to his post.

I think this departure came in the very week that the Link Manager was leaving and immediately prior to a planned meeting of the potential members of an employer consortium that were possibly going to take forward the idea of a new external degree programme based on the MBA one, but hosted by a different university. Nobody remaining in the HR Department had any knowledge of what was going on in this respect, neither at that point did any of the remaining Chief Officers, who were all busy dissociating themselves from anything in which their suspended colleague had been engaged. This left a complete vacuum in official circles in relation to the management of both the old and potential new study programmes. Once again, I had to step up as 'senior student' and point out that we had been, at least verbally, committed by our departed sponsor to participation in a new programme. This now got very fraught because it was probably the case that the viability of the new programme, as far as institutions that might host it were concerned, was dependent on consortium members committing to fund students/ participants.

Link Manager, Coach and Student

I have always thought that it was probably more for the preservation of honour than as a result of wholehearted commitment to the idea, that the decision was taken that we would join the consortium and the new programme at a new institution. Events unfolded rapidly. There was enough of a consortium to attract three possible new host institutions. One got the business and a new programme was arranged for what would have been the next cohort of participants in the MBA programme. They were now going to participate in what became a MSc. in Transformation Management, hosted by another well-known university. By default, I was appointed as Link Manager in respect of the new programme, a role obviously additional to and unrelated to my day job. Around this time, I also agreed to become the in-company coach to one of the remaining MBA students about to embark on his third project at the former institution. All the while, I remained a student on the same programme, where I was moving into my third (extra) year, so I now had a day job and was also a Link Manager, coach and student at the same time. For me, the taught elements and attended modules were pretty much completed by then but I still had my third and final project to undertake. Nobody seemed really interested in this. I kept the same coach on the now usual terms and in the circumstances I was fairly anxious to get it over and done with as soon as practicable as I didn't really want the student role any more.

The Final Phase (Nearly)

As well as a lot of day-to-day operational activity, my then day job involved me in massive planning tasks: for major changes of our external boundaries that were going to make the Force about a third larger than it had been; major internal reorganisation to cope with impending budget cuts; the run up to the Millennium, with its attendant concerns about Millennium bugs bringing about the end of the World; and a significant increase in the need for certain types of specialist operations. Several of these tasks involved painful change processes.

I decided my third MBA project would focus on what might best be described as intellectual capital management. In terms of the theory base, this was, I suppose, a logical extension to what I had studied during the two preceding projects. Along the way I had acquired knowledge and understanding of organisational culture, motivation, strategy and dynamics, chaos and complexity, organisational learning and knowledge creation. Notwithstanding the tribulations I have already described, I had arrived at the conclusion that my own organisation had considerable potential as a learning and knowledge creating one. I felt, though, that it still hadn't really mastered the management and development of its intellectual capital and had yet to realise much of its learning and knowledge creation potential.

I was certainly more than busy with the day job issues I have described and also at this time I underwent training and took on extra responsibilities in relation to the management of firearms operations, which involved a fair amount of out-of- hours responding. I like to think that the knowledge and insights I had so far gained during the whole MBA experience were being brought to bear, particularly in relation to the change processes to which I have alluded. My own ability to cope with paradox, ambiguity and uncertainty was much enhanced, but I was also more alert than I had been before to the need to try and provide psychological security to those affected by chaotic and destructive approaches to change. I was, I hope, imparting useful understanding of these things to others, but this was mostly the product of my two earlier projects rather than being directly related to the body of theory on which I was now focused, which was about looking beyond problem solving, at real action learning, positive appreciation and collective storytelling, and was moving me into areas like social anthropology.

I dabbled a little bit in not very successful efforts to galvanise the whole MBA/MSc. community within the Force into acting collectively as a knowledge resource for the wider organisation, but I was not involved in the kind of creative environment that I had been whilst associated with the neighbourhood policing project. I had therefore resigned myself to the fact that, in terms of the action directly related to its theoretical focus that the 'rules' required, this third project was going to be weak.

One Last Twist (and Another Job)

The final twist in the story of my workplace-based learning adventure was yet to come. A few months into the somewhat frustrating period I have just described, I was summoned to the Chief Constable (the one I had accused of having the ego the size of a planet) and was told he was launching a major programme intended to 'close the gap between the Force's espoused values and its behaviour, with particular reference to diversity and inclusiveness'. The programme was to be managed by a senior officer adjudged to have the requisite skills and abilities, reporting directly to the Chief Constable. That senior officer was me. In the nature of these things, the move was almost immediate and as far as my third project was concerned, I thought it would immediately open up the prospect of action relating to the theory, particularly if the new programme was really going to address diversity in the broadest sense and embrace the 'requisite variety' needing to be recognised and encouraged if the organisation was going to progress. Things were to start with more of an internal focus on the basis that we were attempting to put our own house in order before shifting to concentrate on service delivery and external partnership.

The Examiner

As it turned out, the new role involved a monumental struggle to keep the thrust of the diversity programme as broad as I would have wished, in the face of huge pressure from certain quarters and certain people to dwell on race, gender and sexual orientation issues at cost to anything else. I felt it came to be about what would later come to be known as 'political correctness' and was, in my view, a missed opportunity, but that's another story. As far as the MBA was concerned, it enabled me, after a fashion, to submit a third and final project report in which theory and action were linked. By the time it was all done and dusted and I had been examined by viva, the Chief Constable was moving on, the diversity programme was falling by the wayside and I was almost on my way to my next job. I was awarded 'The Degree of Master of Business Administration, with Distinction in Management'. By the time what turned out to be the first and only cohort of students from the Force completed their MSc. Programme at the 'new' university, I was present at their vivas, seated with the examiners in my role as Link Manager.

10 Case Study 3: A Supermarket Dotcom Training Manager and a Work-Based Degree

© Istockphoto / Catherine Yeulet

My Situation

I am a 45-year-old Supermarket Dotcom Training Manager, undertaking a work-based learning degree course in Occupational Road Risk, as an outreach student.

I have been involved in the driver training industry for over 23 years, developing from a sole trading independent driving instructor at my own cost, to a consultant to Supermarket Dotcom. During the time I have been undertaking the course, I have been employed by Supermarket full time as a Training Manager and subsequently have been placed in the position of the Companies Occupational Road Risk Manager. This was strongly influenced by the achievement of graduating with a first class Honours degree, Bachelor of Science in Occupational Road Risk and winning the Gerry Fowler Award for excellence.

My background is that I have been married for 23 years, with no children, to a technical author in the avionics industry, who fortunately has been totally supportive throughout my studies, being both a sounding board, confident to voice her opinion to whether my work was boring and nonsensical or interesting and informative. This usually resulted in many changes and rewrites.

This leads on to one of the most important facets of undertaking a course such as this: 'Be prepared to take constructive criticism'. Your peers may avoid offering advice, because they want to avoid causing offence, but this will do you no favours in the long run. You need people around you to tell it as it is; this may be hard to take at first but will help develop your research and your approach to study and work in the long term. Sleeping in the shed can have its advantages.

Why Did I Decide to Do Something Like This?

My motivation was driven, as it always has been, by the desire to be the best in the field that I am involved in. The changes in legislation in April 2008 brought the charges of Corporate Manslaughter and Corporate Killing that would lead inevitably to companies developing their staff and managers to take corporate responsibilities regarding their outreach workers and general road users more seriously. The point of the degree, and hopefully the acquisition of a doctorate which I am currently studying for, will be to create a cadre of potential senior managers that a company could approach with confidence to develop systems and processes to keep the company safe from prosecution and develop additional savings at the same time.

Although I am in control of my own diary, I was still expected by my employer, who has been fully supportive thoughout my studies, to still achieve my key performance indicators. This inevitably would lead to earlier starts to the day to join my fellow sufferers on the M25, creating time to collate information and data while at work, allowing some time in the evenings to input this into a readable fashion. The most useful time was 5am on a winter's Sunday morning, slightly mad but guaranteed no distractions, all apart from an over helpful cat.

My Line Manager and Operations Director were both very supportive and opened information doors for me, as and when required. This was a pleasant surprise for me bearing in mind that I had been with the company for a respectively short period of time. It was gratifying that such a large and fast-growing company held me in such high esteem.

What Were the Barriers to Learning?

I found it essential to build a constructive relationship with both the academic staff of the university and that of the background administration staff. There has been more than one occasion where the administration staff worked hard on my behalf to keep me on track, avoiding late payments for example, and avoiding missing important deadlines for project completions. They have always been useful allies at the end of a phone and my academic Professor Skip Basil has also been very supportive.

Unfortunately, it is all too easy to fall into the trap of considering them as your own personal advisors. I am used to a 24-7 Supermarket Dotcom working environment, the university, however, has a much more tailored working period, both length of day, days of the week and months in the year. I found it very useful to email my advisor three to four weeks prior to the date you require the response, allowing enough time to incorporate constructive feedback. One aspect of university life is the relatively long periods of inactivity from the university where you have to prepare for work yourself and the frantic short period where you have constructive access to your advisor. You have to plan your work schedule for the whole year, not just week to week; this added to the fact that it all takes twice as long to produce good work as you first think it will.

Initially, I was personally very suspicious of hosting my work on the university's website for the constructive comments of other students, suffering from the misapprehension that my thoughts and ideas would be copied by others. This is incorrect, as your work is virtually unique to your job role and the company that it is set within.

The more students that embrace the website, the more you realise that you are not alone in the problems that you are facing and most work-based learning students find the concept of university academia a very intimidating place to find yourself, in a voluntary position, at 5am on a wet and cold Sunday morning.

What Sort of Workplace Environment Was I Coming From?

My workplace environment was based in two Dotcom operations in the south-east, Croydon and Aylesford, Kent. In addition, I covered the south-east of the country in my role as a Crash and Serious Incident Investigation Assessor. On a UK level I have to be available to train and support training managers in developing them to become approved driving instructors and fleet trainers, as well as developing external relationships with external road safety organisations/charities and private companies with similar occupational road risk profiles.

An integral part of my job role is to identify and fix problems quickly, with a sustainable outcome. The result is everything. The underlying facet of my position within the company is to initiate the process of proactively working the system of Fault Identification, Fault Analysis and Remedial Action (Fix It). The ruthless prioritising of a perceived problem and working a resolution as soon as possible is what the company requires.

The university response to a typical problem would be to analyse and then reflect on that analysis to see what has been learnt and how I, as an individual, and the company have learnt from this process. This in reality is a timeline I would rarely have afforded to me during a normal working day.

Being the first person within my group to undertake this format of further education, I have had no support with regard to the process of undertaking study and research. The outcome of this has been favourable for me as it has forced me to be far more self-reliant on solving my own problems.

What Supplements and Tools Did I Use?

I had no preconceived ideas on what university life would be like. However I have been surprised in just how remotely you do end up working.

My research has been made up entirely of collating data as an at-work researcher or trawling the Internet for gems of information amongst the millions of articles and journals available.

Unfortunately I have been a very late starter to the world of computers and the Internet and the amount of information available at times has been totally bewildering, in the context of filtering through the old and the new. This, added to my basic level of IT literacy, led to a near vertical learning curve.

Did the Method of Capture of Workplace Experience Work?

Although the subject of my degree seemed to be of a finite nature as the various projects were worked on and subsequently completed, I found that what I was writing about was a situation that was developing and evolving in the workplace in real time.

It was admittedly sometime before the light bulb moment happened, but when it did, it allowed the research aspect of the project to flow in a more measured and controlled manner.

There was little or no need to force an issue to produce useful or credible information or data.

The subject of Occupational Road Risk was clear and present and as the van fleet had grown to some 8,000 drivers covering a combined distance of approximately 60 million miles, the chances of a serious injury or death of one of our staff or a member of the public had grown at an expediential rate.

The Method of Learning Assessment, Did it Work?

The programme for both the degree and the M.Phil. was clearly laid out by the university by means of workbooks, but understanding the workbooks was a different proposition.

My advice to future students would be to ensure you find some space at home where the majority of your studying is undertaken and format a wall planner clearly marking out objectives and timescales. Make these as realistic as possible, as family and work commitments combined can totally decimate a complicated plan.

Build in a two to three week buffer from final completion date to accommodate wholesale rewrites, which occur when you realise that you should have read the whole of the workbook several times before embarking on your module.

Copy the framework on to your wall chart, as all the answers to your questions will be in the workbook, just not in the order that you would expect.

Prior to delivering your work, ensure that you read both the workbook and your module many times, to ensure you deliver what is required of you, that is, how many copies are required, if you are delivering by hand where should you go, how should your work be bound and any additional forms required by the administration team: you don't want to blow it at this stage.

The quality of paper, font and how it is laid out is as important as what you have written; remember, the easier it is for someone to navigate their way through your work and understand what you have been attempting to achieve, logically, the more favourable the outcome will be.

Mentoring, or Tutoring?

On refection, the mentoring and tuition from my tutor was extremely good, although at times a little optimistic. Be prepared to ask questions and keep on asking questions until you feel confident that the work you are about to undertake is going to be in the right direction. I found that email was by far the best format of communication. Keep in contact with your tutor regularly but ensure you give them a reasonable time to reply.

The Time Commitment and Study Style, Balancing Conflicting Demands

The early drafting of work is essential, both for constructive feedback from your tutor and your fellow students. My innate enthusiasm (sometimes that of a mad March Hare), was fortunately matched by the pragmatic, but still enthusiastic, approach of my tutor. At times I felt completely lost but my tutor was able to drag out of the embers of a resent project.

The Outcome and Benefits to the Individual and Company

The outcome for the company is that they have a member of staff who is in a position to sustain and develop systems and processes that will continue to benefit the company and that of its staff. From my perspective, I feel considerably more confident at work, with the qualification I received giving me greater credibility in the workplace.

Costs, Who Pays the Balance Between Cash and Kind?

Initially I started paying for the course myself, but the company took over the payments as soon as I became a full-time member of staff and committed to continuing to pay until I finish my Doctorate.

More Reading/References

As I mentioned earlier, I found the Internet a revelation as far as helping with research. However, I found the keeping and upkeep of my bibliography a hard task.

Lessons Drawn from this Case

- How to access this type of learning opportunity?
I found this course by asking around and banging on doors. In hindsight it would have been more advantageous if universities advertised their courses on one main database, with a free phone number and for professionals to navigate you to and inform you of courses that may be useful to your own personal circumstances.

- What should the employer provide?
Personally, I think if an employer supplies funding and support, then that should suffice, as the qualification you finally receive is yours and not the company's.

- What should the awarding body provide?
The tutors themselves have been excellent, but some more practical classroom sessions in the initial stages, based on how the university works, the website and particularly the handbooks, would have been a great help.

• How to prepare yourself for this type of learning?
Nothing can properly prepare you for this type of learning. Planning and preparation is essential. Supporting yourself with good IT, a good laptop is worth its weight in gold, make sure you back it up on a separate drive. Software to help with your bibliography is helpful and if you're not a good typist, software such as Dragon 10 can help enormously (you speak into a microphone and it converts into text for you).

In summary, there will always be doubters around, my advice is to 'follow you dreams', plan to make sure it does not become a nightmare! With organisation, drive and commitment you will find your course achievable.

11 Case Study 4: A Senior Manager, Oil Company Vice President and a Ph.D

© Istockphoto / Tonylady

My Situation

This case study deals with the experience of a 55-year-old senior manager doing a part-time Ph.D. at the School of Management, Surrey University, whilst working full time as a Vice President of a major oil company.

The background to the case is that I had worked for the same company ever since leaving school and had achieved my undergraduate degree whilst an apprentice. In 35 years of full-time employment I had risen from being a technical assistant to working in commercial roles and finally to working in senior management roles. My current job, Vice President UK Region, meant I chaired the boards of the refining and marketing companies in the UK. I was also on the board of several third-party companies and institutions, including chairing the board of one of the first sector skills councils, Cogent.

In a sense I was lucky because I was the master of my own agenda and had a secretary and support staff who handled much of the daily grind. However, I was also in a very high public profile job and was on duty 24/7. This was not a job where you could say, 'I'm not available Monday afternoons' or indeed, 'I'm not available Sundays.' Also, my job involved a lot of travel and I did not work from a single office. My base was wherever I happened to be. In taking on a university course it was clear that this was something I had to fit into spare time, whenever and wherever that occurred, and that my availability to spend time on university study could change at very short notice. Also, I did not exactly have a lot of free time to spend. My wife was relatively relaxed about me taking on university study but did not expect it to encroach on our time. In taking on the workplace-learning commitment I somehow persuaded each person in my life that I could do the university study by cutting back on time I was giving to others.

Why Did I Decide to Do Something Like This?

The question 'why' is extremely important for anyone considering serious workplace learning. Taking on something like a Ph.D. is a large commitment and you need to be very honest with yourself about why you are doing it. It is the source of the motivation that sustains you through all the grind. I have never run a marathon but I imagine it is something similar to the motivation needed to get through all the training.

In my case there were several strands to the why question. Firstly, my undergraduate time had not been well spent. Being already employed by as an apprentice, I had viewed the time at university as a sabbatical. I had left university with an OK degree but always felt that maybe I had not really done justice to myself. Secondly, during my career I had learnt a great deal but had nothing to demonstrate what I had learnt. I had worked in many countries with different cultures and learnt so much about my own culture as a result. I had experienced a range of jobs from the very technical to the very political. I had done some excellent short courses at Harvard, Stanford and Cambridge but, even there, all I had to show for it was a fine collection of rather smart university-branded shoulder bags.

Maybe the biggest reason for going back to university was that I had grown up with a very hard-edged mathematical science education and was now working in the world of politics and perception. I was handling issues such as public outrage which made no sense to me at all and I felt I needed to know why the world behaved so irrationally. Also, somewhat naively, I thought my experiences were unique and that I had something that I could teach others. It felt right to go back to university and re-engage in a more informed and purposeful way.

What Were the Barriers to Learning?

The biggest barrier to going back into the world of education as a mature student is that you know all your friends will think you are bonkers. Doing an accredited programme with assessments at the end is a very risky business and your personal reputation is on the line. Also, for the programme to be worth doing it has to involve a serious commitment of thinking time and that is a scarce commodity for anyone in full-time employment. One's free time is supposed to be when the brain switches off and you relax. However, if you are doing a serious accredited programme, this has to be the time the brain switches up a gear.

Interestingly, my employer was absolutely fine about supporting me doing this and paying all the costs. I made the case that I would be studying how to do my job better and they readily (maybe too readily!) agreed that there was scope for investment here. I was also very surprised how supportive my colleagues at work were. I was doing a research degree that required me to interview them and make detailed notes of discussions with them. This could have been a major barrier but they took a positive interest in what I was doing. The important factor here was the fact I picked a research programme that integrated with my work environment and added value to it. Without this I think the conflict between my work and my study would have grown to become an insurmountable barrier.

Probably the biggest problems occurred in the home environment. The trouble with qualitative research, particularly qualitative research using ethnographic data collection, is that it is very time consuming. The quality of my time with the family definitely suffered.

What Sort of Workplace Environment Was I Coming From?

My workplace environment was several offices, plus my virtual office, plus a variety of other venues. To a large extent I worked on my own in my own time and in my own space. So in many regards it is a much more flexible environment than, say, manning a desk or a machine for a set shift. However, it is much less free in the sense you are always on call and work time extends heavily into non-work time. You cannot plan to be free at pre-arranged times. Thus, while there would be days where I could happily spend time in the office researching for my thesis, there were days when I was working round the clock and could not conceivably spend a minute thinking about academic work.

Another feature of my work environment was that it was all about analysing situations, presenting arguments and managing workload. This might sound very similar to academic study. However, my job was in the culture of a large international business corporation. It was all about ruthless prioritisation and cutting through issues quickly to get to the nub of an issue. A quick concise answer to a problem was all that was ever needed and debating options and arguments tended to get you classed as a dreamer. However, in the academic world, all people care about is exploring the options and arguments. The answer often appears to be irrelevant. Managing your brain so that it handles these very different thought processes is tricky.

Another important consideration is that the university programme I was engaged on was not a company-managed workplace development programme. There was no mentoring support in the workplace. So it was up to me to make sure that I did not let my academic work interfere with my employment and keep it low profile. This is in stark contrast to environments where people are on company-led programmes and are expected to progress along a path. However, I suspect that a lot of workplace learners will be in my situation and have to manage the interface between work and academia themselves. This is not a trivial task. It is vital that one stays on top of the work environment and this requires your work colleagues to feel that you are putting the job first. Equally, the university environment has routines and priorities that you are expected to observe. However, the key to workplace learning is that the job is the focus and the academic world adds value to the job.

Finally, my work environment was public. I did many public speeches and the occasional TV interview. I had meetings with government ministers and other public figures. In the office I was someone who everyone recognised. This requires one to be in a very different mindset to the average university student. Managing the identity conflict between one's business world and one's academic world is critical to being able to simultaneously be successful in both.

What Supplements and Tools Did I Use?

I had had this image that I would be working at the university, using the library, going to odd lectures and mingling with other academics. Nothing could be further from the truth. Very occasionally I received an email saying there was a lecture I might be interested in, but the diary never worked out. Apart from an hour with my tutor each month, I had virtually no contact with the university. I found myself diving in for the monthly tutorial and maybe grabbing a book from the library as I passed. My academic experience was nearly all online, on my own, at home.

The main tool in my research was the various electronic databases of journal papers. The first task was, of course, to work out how to use this tools and, for someone used to working with the IT systems of a leading oil company, wrestling with remote access to a university IT system proved depressing and frustrating. No wonder degrees take so long. Most of the time is spent trying to find your way round the university IT system, figure out how to log on the multiplicity of online databases, and then do it all over again because the data link has dropped out. University IT systems are definitely a barrier to learning!

The university library was fine for borrowing the more commonplace books. However, most of the books I needed were not stocked by the university library and I was encouraged to use the inter-library service and the British Library. But borrowing books and papers this way was very complicated and time consuming with paper dockets having to be countersigned and posted backwards and forwards. Most of the books I needed were not expensive and it was much quicker and easier to buy online from Amazon or drop into Waterstone's in Gower Street for a browse. I did sometimes wonder what the point was of having a university library. If you needed regular access to a book it was much better to buy it and have it at home, and any books you did not need regularly seemed to be too obscure to be stocked in the library anyway.

Did Capturing Workplace Experience Work?

My academic study was going nowhere until I found a work issue that I could use for my research project. Indeed, some people say that you should not consider doing any academic study until you have your research project in place. The breakthrough for me was this realisation that you have to use whatever is going on in your job. It is cannot be an artificial construct on the side. I had been on many courses where there had been an element of working through a workplace problem. Like many, I had always picked something safe and peripheral. However, this was not going to work for something as big as a Ph.D. I picked something that was neither safe nor peripheral. It was a major public relations problem where I was the key figure representing the company, and my research would involve interviewing people who were attacking the company in the press. This was not an artificial project but the core of my job.

Like all real-life experience, my project started at a point where there was a history, a current situation and a number of future scenarios. I started by doing a deep literature search of the history and interviewing people who had been involved in the history. This added depth of research immediately gave me insights I would never have achieved in my normal work process. I then proceeded with ethnographic capture of events as they unfolded over the next couple of years. I was an actor in my own research and this raised a number of ethical and procedural questions. All my data capture was checked by others who had been at the events I described and my interviews were checked by the interviewees. This provided a strong discipline in capturing the workplace experience. Colleagues and third parties became an integral part of the research project.

Another important feature was learning how to write academically. For more than 35 years I had lived in a world where the key skill was to generate clever ideas. In the academic world, is important to justify why your methods of data capture and analysis are reliable and verification is key. The first year of my work with the university was spent trying to discover what was actually needed in this area. I would read books on epistemologies and paradigms and regurgitate this stuff only to be told that this was not really adding value. The academic world has its structures and there are thought police who have to be appeased, and it is easy to think that this is all academic study is about. However, academics know how to work round the rules and concentrate on the real world. As with the internal world of a major oil company, presentation norms are everything. It was just a matter of learning the different set of presentation norms for the academic world.

Did the Method of Assessment Work?

The programme was structured as a normal part-time Ph.D. so the assessment process was by thesis and viva. Writing the thesis was an excellent way to structure the study work. The discipline of a literature research, followed by a methodology development, followed by data presentation and then analysis is a good framework. Of course one does not necessarily write it in that order and chapters tend to get reworked as one goes along. However, in the end document structured the learning extremely well.

A viva is also a very effective way of focusing the mind. After more than 35 years without sitting any kind of exam I found the experience quite frightening. I sat outside the interview room waiting to be called and thinking 'why on earth am I putting myself through this'. However I did two vivas, one to upgrade from M.Phil. to Ph.D. and one to gain the Ph.D., and on both occasions the experience added a lot of value to the research. In fact, each time I came out thinking that there was a lot more I should have discovered. More importantly I felt I had been properly tested and that gave me a sense of achievement.

Did the Tutoring Work?

As mentioned above I chose my tutor on the basis of his mentoring skill. In fact I had turned down the opportunity to go to a more prestigious university and study under an expert in the field because I recognised that I would need a lot of help with the basics. (I also rather arrogantly thought I already knew my subject.) The process was a monthly one-hour face-to-face meeting at a time we negotiated mutually on the basis of our diaries. The meeting was always at the university, the tutor's time being considered more precious than mine so I had to travel to him. He was an excellent mentor and guided me as I found my own way. He was infinitely encouraging; praising work that I later realised was rubbish, and giving me prods when I needed them.

I also had a process of emailing work-in-progress drafts to him which he would annotate and return. The relationship developed into something akin to a normal work relationship and we became close friends. This was quite key. The research and the thesis writing was just another part of my job and the tutor was part of my support team. Without this relationship I could never have completed the programme.

What Were the Time Commitment and Conflicts?

Physically, the time commitment seems quite light, just one hour per month plus a bit of travelling time. However, the research time was significant. In part this was because I had chosen a qualitative research approach and the data source was the events in my daily job. Every meeting I had which related to the research required me to write up notes. Typically the note writing would take twice as long as the meeting, which meant it was usually done each evening when I got home. When it came to data analysis I would sit for days pouring over documents and tabulating the content. In all I documented and manually analysed around 1,000 interactions! When you start a research project, qualitative analysis looks a soft option, just a compilation of fluffy anecdotes, but in reality it is at least twice as much work as quantitative analysis.

Finding reference documents, reading them and making notes for the thesis was not so bad. Once I had mastered the mechanics of getting hold of books and papers the rest was easy. I had developed a skill in my normal work which enabled me to quickly skim and condense sources. My thesis referred to some 400 books and papers and I must have read and rejected at least as many again. In total I must have spent a couple of hours per day of additional time working on the research and the thesis over a three-year period. However there would have been weeks when I did nothing and days when all waking hours were spent on the thesis.

The major time conflict was probably with my family life. As the family became more irritated by the time I was spending on the thesis, I reacted by putting more and more effort into getting the thing completed quickly, which was probably counterproductive! There were also ethical conflicts between my role as the face of a major oil company and my research role as an independent ethnographer of events involving the company. It was something that troubled me deeply and I was open with people that I was basing my research on things they were involved with. I dealt with this by letting people see what I was documenting and comment on its accuracy. I also used the MP representing the area in which the events occurred as an independent verifier. This is probably the most difficult conflict for someone doing a workplace research project. Your academic work inevitably ends up making judgements about your workplace and these judgements are going to be published in your thesis.

What Was the Outcome and What Were the Benefits?

The most important outcome was the sense of achievement and the depth of understanding this gave. The experience was much more worthwhile than my normal full-time undergraduate degree. I felt that the academic study had helped me see solutions to work problems that I would otherwise have missed. Indeed, I have now retired and have set up my own company based on the learning I achieved in the programme. The combination of work practice and academic discipline is very powerful. Either of them on their own gives a single viewpoint but having them together gives binocular vision. Things just jump out at you.

Was it important that the programme lead to a high-level qualification? I think that it was not important at the start and indeed I would not recommend doing something like this just to get the qualification. However, the discipline of accredited assessment was important to making the experience worthwhile. It made it harder to drop out mid-way. There is something important in setting real, publicly visible, challenges for yourself and then succeeding. Quite a different experience from the Harvard PMD I did 20 years ago. That was a social experience with some learning on the side. This was a much deeper and genuinely measurable learning experience. It was something I had achieved against the odds.

How Much does it Cost and Who Paid?

The course fee totalled around £4,000 for the three years and there was probably another £1,000 for books. This was paid for by my employer, but I would have paid it all myself if they had not.

More Reading References

The first thing I would recommend anyone to do is buy a recent compendium book of articles by leading researchers in your chosen subject area. They are usually quite cheap (because the authors are recycling what they already have) and it gives access to a range of opinions in the subject. It will test whether you are actually interested in the subject.

I would also recommend reading Khun, T. S. (1996) *The Structure of Scientific Revolutions*, Chicago, IL: University of Chicago. It's a short, easy to read, book that gives you a good perspective of what academic knowledge is all about and how it evolves over time.

For my actual research work, I made heavy use of Yin, R. K. (2003) *Case Study Research: Design and Methods*, Thousand Oaks, CA: Sage.; Bryman, A. and Bell, E. (2003) *Business Research Methods*, Oxford: Oxford University Press.; and Robson, C. (2002) *Real World Research* (2nd ed), Oxford: Blackwell. They are the most thumbed books in my bookcase and they are the books that helped me understand how academic research differs from the business world.

What are the Lessons Learned?

- The first lesson is that this was not an easy thing to get started. The opportunity only came together because I happened to know a university professor who was willing to take me on and I happened to find a workplace project that made sense. Both of these things came together by accident rather than design.

- The employer was very supportive, but the key was not the money but the moral support. Doing any research project inside a company is a pain for that company and for your work colleagues, because any workplace learning is going to involve doing some kind of research thesis about them. Having an environment where it is OK to do this type of thing is vital.
- The important thing from the perspective of the awarding university is flexibility and ease of access. The university in question was not that great in this regard. It was very much geared to students who were on campus all the time. Little things like having to go to the campus and queue to get your library card and not being able to log on to some research databases when off campus were an unnecessary nuisance. One gets the feeling that university administration departments do not think of students as customers. When you are an 18-year-old living off baked beans and beer you may accept this treatment, but as a 55-year-old company director used to managing a customer service operation, you realise that things could easily be so much better. That said the tutor was fantastic and did his utmost to hide the university wiring.
- In terms of preparation, the key thing is to be clear why you want to do go for a qualification while you are working full time, and make certain it is a motivation that will sustain you through the difficulties. Also, it is essential to view your full-time job as the subject of your learning and be prepared to package it for academic analysis. It requires a level of openness to scrutiny about your job that would not normally be the case. Also you have to pick your tutor carefully. He/she will be your lifeline and you have to be able to work together well.

12 Case Study 5: A Civil Servant, a Degree and Professional Qualifications

My Situation

This study relates to a 54-year-old Civil Servant, working full time, who decided to gain a degree and then professional qualifications to enhance career prospects and obtain greater job security.

After I joined the Civil Service in 1972, my job roles developed quickly from clerical to executive grades having entered the service with both GCE O and A levels. I spent the largest part of my career visiting businesses in Greater Manchester where I had to both educate traders in Excise and VAT tax procedures whilst also checking tax compliance. Computers entered the workplace in the 1980s and I graduated towards being a Computer Auditor where, in the early days of commercial computing, technical assurances were required to support colleagues who largely handled paper-based tax compliance interventions.

© Istockphoto / Tom Hall

In the early 1990s I recognised that I needed a formal degree in business/computing to assist my job role, by being better academically trained to carry out my computer audit role and let me stand out from the crowd of generalist Civil Servants. I therefore enrolled with the OU and commenced a long trail of studying job-related modules; mainly business and computer/systems related.

Currently, I am an Internal Audit Manager within HM Revenue and Customs, a role I moved into in 2001 and that required attainment of external professional qualifications. These qualifications entailed a mix of private and official time (two weeks) to attend the National School of Government and subsequently to study for about 16 weeks per exam at home to prepare for examinations. The exams consist of a Practitioner level comprising 5 examined modules at Diploma level and a higher-level range of exams at Post Diploma level that, when passed (four examined modules), entitles the student to become a full member of the Institute of Internal Audit.

To supplement these formal examinations, students have to keep a formal log of work done to evidence the use of those examined skills operationally. This log is examined by the Institute of Internal Audit (IIA) before professional recognition is given. Failure to achieve the fully qualified status could result in the student being removed from the job role. This was a constant, and to an extent, destabilising threat. The pressure was definitely on. Students were aware of the cost being borne by the employer. Repeated exam failure also had the threat of the student having to pay for their own re-sits. I was never aware of any student being 'removed' from the job, but plenty left voluntarily.

Why Did I do it?

For my OU degree, I was partly motivated by casting sideways glances at my colleagues in a computer audit team who mostly had degrees. When I left Grammar School at 17, my choice was, upon completing my A levels, to take a job. University education was far more limited in the early 1970s and my parents would not have been easily able to afford to support my further education.

Whilst the Civil Service is looked upon externally as a 'secure job', I have had six offices close under my feet and the consequence of each closure is that hard-earned reputations and personal achievements are lost when moves are made to new managers in new locations. You have to start again. I moved from Manchester to Liverpool to Southend and back to Manchester as a result of a combination of choice and office closure. Therefore, I had a need to climb out of generalist grades into more technical roles and eventually professional ones.

There were no promises of success from achieving further academic or professional qualifications, but sitting back guaranteed no success. I took a risk and it paid great results.

Barriers to Overcome

Taking on a degree course when my children were young was hard. My wife worked part time and we had to also look after aging parents. Further, I had to link my academic study into formal work-based personal developments plans where I had a line manager who commenced to measure my degree achievement.

I felt that this was an unwarranted intrusion, particularly due to the fact that my line manger had little or no academic ability and he was passing unqualified judgement on my efforts. I felt that the benefit I gained from subsidised study was far outweighed by employer interference in my private life study. I therefore continued degree study at my own cost.

Subsequently, my professional study for audit qualifications was entirely different. This was wholly funded by my employer who was generous in providing for the entire cost of the study to include both time off work for college-based training, and paid time off work for revision study. This amounted to about two weeks per exam. The balance of the study took about 16 weeks per exam and this was all carried out at home. Study at work during official time was not allowed. Indeed it was frowned upon and this did annoy students. It was OK to be idle at times but to use that time productively to study was not allowed.

Normal audit duties had to fulfilled at the same time. This was tough but my OU experience had given me the self-study skills I needed to dedicate myself to long and largely unaided private study. My children were by then teenagers and as a family we had the demands of aiding their education by supporting and assisting them in their homework and so on.

The Workplace Environment

At the time of commencing the professional study (2001), the department had a better organisational structure and governance. Strategic policies existed for training and senior managers made the decisions to drive policy.

Professional training routes were few but they were clear. Public spending cuts were beginning to bite and there was a veiled threat of expulsion from the team if you failed exams. Re-sits were not automatically paid for and official study time was not always allocated. Those staff who failed tended to leave by their own volition.

The Supplements to Workplace Experience Used

Professional Study was effectively distance learning – there was an allocated telephone/email-based tutor but these were rarely used. Students tended to form their own self-help groups and did find time to meet sometimes by travelling hundreds of miles for short meetings.

The IIA do offer students assistance by a range of means. There is a web-based knowledge centre where students can access a library of technical topics, audit position statements and current thinking on a wide range of the exam topics. There is also a forum where questions can be asked and a range of auditors and students respond to give a wider view of the issue.

Nationally, the IIA has a range of committees that provide four or five half-day presentations a year to assist professional auditors to maintain their development whilst also providing low-cost admittance to students where they can build upon their training and create further networks.

At the OU, large emphasis is placed upon the student using online first-class web forums. Indeed, parts of the assignment question and marking requires the student to contribute towards online discussions to try to develop their ability to read and consider other students postings to develop their own arguments. Study is entirely at home supplemented by three or four Saturday tutorials. There were many times that I was the only attendee. I had one-to-one tuition which was great. I was able to really discuss my personal study problems and for the assignments I was able to obtain a better understanding of the questions. I did occasionally attend summer school where I decamped from home to York University for seven full days of tuition. I was amazed at the stamina of some of the students as they were able to drink all night, study for a full nine hours during the day and survive for a full seven days. I wasn't that dedicated.

The Method of Capture of Workplace Experience

For the Diploma level examination, the award of the PIIA is not given until both the examinations are passed and supplemented by a work-based log. This log is a comprehensive record that is based upon IIA directed milestones; the student has to maintain this to prove the practical application of core skills. The student has to provide evidence of when and where they developed their skills and this has to be supported by an audit team lead and finally signed off by a senior manager within audit. The log was a thorough document that could easily fill 50 pages of work. This log had to be approved by a central training manager before being sent to the PIIA where they also scrutinised the work record.

A log for the post-degree qualification had also to be maintained and submitted. This log was far more discursive and the student had to be more reflective upon what was learned, the benefits achieved rather than evidence of having done this or that.

The Method of Mentoring or Tutoring

Mentoring for the professional training has developed over the last eight years. Originally it was a named person within the audit unit who could be approached and asked for assistance. This was rarely done. The mentor also rarely asked about study issues.

Today, mentoring is far better organised, but it is still really up to the individual mentor to go out of their way to assist the student. The role is partly one of 'how is it going' and 'make sure that you are keeping up with the study'. It is not formal. There is no guidance. There is no training or evaluation of the quality of mentoring. In many ways this is an area for improvement. But overall, students pass exams if they study.

Tutoring can either be at a formal college or by distance learning. College-based tutoring is established and is provided by qualified professional auditors who know the subject matter well. The course syllabus is well established and daily college study is by a brief discussion of the subject matter supported by break out groups to answer sample questions. This can be rushed. The real study is at home!

At the OU, I considered that my tutors really did not have a great understanding of the subject matter; they discussed the subjects but really did not have a great in-depth knowledge. It was again more of an introduction to the module subject matter. Students were of vastly differing levels, from mature students who had not written anything academic in 40 years, down to foreign language students who struggled with basic English. Tutors were available in the evenings for assistance and advice; the use of email also assisted. But again, students were largely on their own. I always saw a lot of course drop-outs and I personally thought that any student who made it to the examination room and signed their name on the paper had virtually passed by virtue of having completed the study aspect of the course they would have the skills necessary to succeed.

The Time Commitment and Study Style

I did not study for both my OU Degree and professional qualifications at the same time. That would have been too much. My day-to-day job requires me to manage an audit and to perform a large part of it and this means travelling to anywhere in the UK to meet managers and operational staff to discuss systems.

If I travelled by train, then I could read my course texts. At evening in hotels I had time to also read the same texts, but after a long day and working with colleagues there was more pressure on socialising or discussing the day's work. I did work on the bus coming into work in the morning when I decided to travel by that mode of transport. Lunchtimes became 20 minute sessions of reading, early evening was an hour here or there, in short, whenever I could find time, and had the will, I opened my books.

The big danger was looking forwards and thinking 'there are four months to the exam, plenty of time' and there never was. When I fell into this trap, I had to make risk-based decisions on which parts of the text I could afford to leave out. I found lots of duplication of coursework where a particular point was identified for learning and then many examples to re-enforce knowledge was given. I ignored the wider examples.

The Outcome and Benefits

I commenced study for my degree before I moved into my current job role which required a commitment to training and passing exams. I put my degree on hold and dedicated myself to five-years professional study. This was a period of two years to pass PIIA, a year when I applied for permission from my employer to study and take the higher-level exams, and then a further two years to pass those. I then restarted my OU degree study but I had managed via the PIIA and the OU to have my professional exams scored and a credit transfer to be allowed towards my science degree. This credit transfer agreement will be of benefit for all auditors in the UK. The benefits to my employers in respect of my study is that the internal audit profession with HMRC is 'professionally qualified' to perform its role. This is recognised not only by the Treasury within Government but also worldwide. My science degree was modular and based upon systems, business and technology (computing) subjects and this is central to my audit work.

Personally, I have made myself a marketable commodity. I have transposed myself from a generalist Civil Servant with a wide range of skills to an individual that has professional and academic qualifications aligned to skills acquired in Government; indeed some of those skills are hard to obtain as I have worked at the centre of Government as well as working undercover for parts of my Civil Service life when carrying out covert investigations. I have also worked in EU countries where I have assisted in training their auditors in the skills and attitudes they require to perform quality IT audits.

Costs, Who Pays and Balance Between Cash and Kind

My employer initially paid 50 per cent of the course fees, but as the years passed this reduced to 25 per cent as new managers took over with differing views on the financing of further education. In those days there was an absence of departmental strategic policy and local managers were able to set their own policy that overruled previous approaches. This did both annoy and demotivate me. It is interesting that there is now recognition of the need for a more highly qualified Civil Service with relevant skills to enable the job to be done better.

13 Case Study 6: A Care Commission Officer with the Scottish Commission for the Regulation of Care (Care Commission) and a Graduate Certificate

© Istockphoto / Dean Mitchell

My Particular Learner Situation

I am 53 and employed full time as a Care Commission Officer with the Scottish Commission for the Regulation of Care (Care Commission). These are my personal reflections on my year of work-based study and don't necessarily represent the views and experiences of my employer or fellow students!

The Regulation of Care Award (ROCA) was a one-year work-based distant-learning graduate certificate course with the Anglia Ruskin University. This bespoke course had been designed by the university together with the Care Commission and another regulator, the Scottish Social Services Council, whose job is to regulate the social services workforce in Scotland.

My family of six sons are all grown-up and living away from home and, for the year of my studies, I was the fifth card-carrying student in my family! My wife is employed full time as a learning support teacher and frequently comes home feeling emotionally and physically drained and in need of moral support; quality time as a couple is therefore important. Despite the boys having flown the nest the void has very quickly filled with other responsibilities and, long before starting the course, I intimated that some of my voluntary roles would be curtailed in the coming year.

I have a home-working contract and work some 33 miles from the nearest Care Commission local office and usually on my own. I am based in a large rural area in south-west Scotland where I regulate the standards of care in a variety of different types of care service. I usually undertake field work at least two days a week and frequently have other appointments to keep and drive approximately 10,000 work miles every year. This demands considerable self-discipline combined with a willingness to respond flexibly to changing priorities. This prepared me well for my student year as I added one more set of very real demands to my weekly schedule. The course came at a time of significant change in the Care Commission with new methodology having just been introduced, and I had some pretty challenging cases too, so had to learn to manage my time even more carefully.

Why Did I Decide to Do Something Like This?

The decision to study was made for me! As a Care Commission Officer (CCO) I was required to join a new professional register for social services workers. The register is qualification-based and despite having qualified 30 years previously and completed a post-qualifying degree nine years later, I was now required to complete a new qualification in the regulation of health and social care. However, I generally enjoy work-based learning and have appreciated the many short courses I've been able to attend over the years. The prospect of a new course which had to be combined with a full-time job nevertheless filled me with ambivalence. More than 20 years after my last graduation, I wondered if I still had the necessary skills and discipline, let alone the time to study at a graduate award level. The prospect of being part of this programme leading to a recognised qualification in care regulation was, however, very attractive.

What Were the Barriers to Learning?

Time and other commitments, at work, at home and in the community were all very real barriers. Tiredness and other distractions would conspire to prevent me from getting on with study and especially hindered my reading. Many times I put down a book after realising I had been staring at the same page for half an hour! My employers gave me a day a week for study purposes, and a commensurate reduction in workload. However, this time allocation was sometimes swallowed-up through attendance at the 'Learning Set' with my tutor and other students at our regional office 90 miles away. I also had to attend a number of practice-based workshops at another office a similar distance away. Each involved approximately five hours return travel making these very long days with an early start.

The need to be competent with IT was crucial and, despite being conversant with basic word processing and use of my work IT systems, I was at first hindered by my limited IT skills. Support was provided with a pre-course workshop to introduce us to web-CT; nevertheless, I found myself on a steep IT learning curve as I progressed with the course. For example, I learned to make the most of the Internet and how to create tables and diagrams that would really work for me.

Last time I was a student I had use of a very large university library and my employer also had an excellent library service. To begin with I worried that the lack of such a facility on my doorstep would be a major barrier to learning but this particular fear proved unfounded. More of that later!

At one point in the year I had a minor health scare which set me back two weeks. This was compounded by my professional workload as I tried to get back in to stride. The university granted me an extension for one of my assignments which, in the event, I didn't need. It was nevertheless an important 'safety-net' which destressed the situation for me, so I would advise students to seek extensions in such circumstances if only to remove some of the stress.

What Sort of Workplace Environment Was I Coming From?

As already noted, I have a home-based contract and work mostly on my own although I am part of a ten-person team linked to the local Care Commission office which also provides administrative support. Two other colleagues were undertaking the course at the same time as me and another two had already completed it so there was a lot of empathy with the demands of the course. As a small and well-established team, despite working alone so much of the time, there are good support mechanisms with monthly team meetings, six-weekly professional supervision with my team manager and a lot of informal support by telephone and email. Elsewhere, other ROCA students from other regional and local offices were also working their way through the course and were another important source of support.

I have a lot of professional autonomy and am responsible for managing my own time. Although my workload was reduced for the year it was nevertheless sometimes difficult to manage; whilst my core activities can be planned in advance it is hard to plan for new work coming in, sometimes time that is set aside for report writing or preparation is eroded through the need to respond to unplanned work demands. At other times such unplanned work, for example, if a complaint is received about a care service, has to take priority over scheduled work. Similarly, incoming telephone calls or emails can lead to planned work having to be put aside until a more pressing task is completed.

What Supplements and Tools Did I Use?

In many respects the university and my employer spoon-fed us! One morning a large parcel arrived with information about the university, its library and other resources together with work books, reading resources and study guides. In addition, my employer had provided me with the key text book that would be used throughout the course. For the first semester especially it would have been possible to complete the necessary modules without reference to any other reading! However, a little bit of study whets the taste buds and very quickly I had an appetite for reading. Professional journals, books I already owned and others bought from Internet sites all supplemented my reading and helped me to relate the core reading to my areas of professional activity.

Above all, the Internet took the place of the university library I had got so used to in my previous student days. Although the university had its own library, it was approximately

400 miles away and I never did work out how to access it online and locate the resources I wanted! I have to admit, I gave up fairly quickly as my employers have a subscription for IDOX, a business library service, which provided a more user-friendly and very prompt service. I could do Internet searches, identify journal articles of interest and they would be emailed to me in a matter of minutes. No more standing at a library photo-copier with a pile of 10 pence pieces! IDOX also provided a very fast lending service for books and, provided they were in stock, they would drop through the letter box just a couple of days later. Due to return dates I tended to use IDOX to check books out before buying my own copy; I discovered just how easy it is to get cheap second-hand books, even quite new editions, via the Internet which I could then cover in pencil marks and post-it notes to my heart's content. Occasionally I did need to fork out a little more and get a new copy.

The other fantastic thing about the Internet is the creation of a virtual tutorial group where we could have discussions and share our experiences from the comfort of our own home. Sometimes these discussions were instigated by our tutors but often by us as students. This was very useful although its benefit was lessened by some students not playing a full part. This was probably symptomatic of their other responsibilities rather than any lack of commitment to the course. It was disappointing though when contributions to Web-CT discussions were met with little or no response. One course requirement was that we submit our work to our tutors and peers for comment before finalising it and submitting it to the university. This worked really well when fellow students gave their time to it and were prepared to respond critically. Many, however, were ill-at-ease with this approach which therefore had only limited mileage falling far short of its potential. One important incentive was that tutors only added their feedback once the student had given feedback to at least one other student!

Did Capturing Workplace Experience Work?

The course included both academic and work-based practical modules, although both felt very pertinent to the work situation. Undertaking the written submissions provided very good opportunities to apply theory to the real-life everyday situations with which I was so familiar. An unexpected revelation was that I could learn from the regulation of other industries quite different to my own. I discovered too that this professional discipline of regulation has a wealth of literature and research outside my area of previous experience. Traits that I had experienced in my work for years had, not only been recognised by others, but had their own nomenclature! (Words such as 'nomenclature' instead of 'professional vocabulary' begin to trip off the tongue very freely after reading a few academic books!) This was quite defining for me as I began to view myself far less as a social care professional who regulates and much more as a regulator with a toolbox of specific skills and methods.

As well as the more academically focused assignments, there were practical work-based assessments where each of our core areas of professional activity was looked at alongside the relevant national occupational standards (NOS). This demanded that we use examples of our own work to demonstrate our competencies in relation to the NOS. We were required to produce a portfolio or 'folder' on the cases selected from our workload. As work-based learning, this took full account of my employer's values, policies and procedures and methodology as well as professional codes and the theoretical framework presented by the course. Despite being the 'bread and butter' of my professional life, I sometimes found this more challenging than the more academic written assignments. This was where I felt the need to prove my worth! I sighed an especially big sigh of relief when a direct observation by my Practice Learning Assessor (PLA) had been completed!

My work involves four core areas of activity one of which, 'enforcement' is used sparingly. Previous years' students had therefore found this too hypothetical to produce a credible folder. I was fortunate therefore that, this year, the 'Enforcement Folder' was replaced by a Web-CT quiz. I have to admit that the prospect of undertaking such a quiz, even with a generous time constraint, filled me with anxiety. It sounded much too much like the exams I had always dreaded! However, undertaking this remotely, at a time of my own choosing, with the capacity to consult relevant documents and guidance as I did the quiz, proved to be a very fruitful learning experience.

Did the Method of Assessment Work?

The course was continuously assessed with marks given for each of the written assignments and work-based 'folders' being assessed as either a pass or a fail. The course had been designed very sympathetically with many opportunities for feedback along the way and very clear pointers as to whether we were on the right track. The pass mark was set relatively low at 40 per cent which I think encouraged most students to believe in the possibility of a pass.

The course adopted a 'patch-work' approach where the two major academic assignments were divided in to two or three 'patches'. As already noted, we had to submit our patches for peer comment via Web-CT. This was a new experience for me but one which I feel gives opportunity both for constructive feedback and support of fellow students. Our tutors also commented and this gave us further opportunity to develop our patches before combining them to form a final written assignment to submit to the university for marking.

It was clear from the course design that the hope of the university and my employer was for everybody to maximise this opportunity for learning to the full and that nobody should fail. Nevertheless, the system of assessment was designed to satisfy the appropriate academic criteria and invigilated externally to maintain standards.

Did the Tutoring Work?

The role of my tutor was to support me through the course, to provide teaching input at the 'learning set' and provide feedback on the standard and content of my work before submitting it. There was also a PLA whose role was to steer students in a similar way through the work-based units. This approach was well-considered and very supportive. Students were under no pressure to meet with tutors or PLAs one-to-one but opportunities were provided for that for those who wished it. Part-way into the first term my tutor arranged to meet me to touch base and satisfy herself that I was on track.

Tutors also participated in Web-CT discussions and provided feedback on patches. It was also possible and actively encouraged to email tutors individually with specific queries.

What Were the Time Commitment and Conflicts?

As already indicated, time could be a significant barrier to making a success of the course. I recall being told that there needed to be a commitment equal to one working day per week (seven hours) plus the same of our own time. This was probably how it averaged out over the year but there were weeks when it was considerably more. An unusual feature of ROCA is that it runs from January to December and, by planning my work carefully at the start of the year, and arranging my direct observation before the summer, I was able to spend much less time on it through the summer school holidays. This needed good planning on my part as one of the modules ran throughout the year culminating in an assignment on professional values at the end of the year. By anticipating this and doing some groundwork earlier in the year, it was possible to put it on the back-burner through the summer.

This was important for me as, quite apart from ensuring I had a summer holiday and some rest and relaxation with my wife, I was also to pick up more responsibilities in my church during the summer while other leaders were away.

My biggest grouse throughout the course in respect of time was the inordinate amounts of time taken to reference my assignments correctly and to carry out a word-count and the attendant editing process. This was a good discipline and undoubtedly resulted in a crisper more cogent assignment but it is very important not to underestimate the time this needs. Referencing is greatly helped by ensuring a running list is maintained of any references used, including page numbers, throughout the course; this can then be used to cut and paste. However, even then, my marker picked up several times on missing references!

What Was the Outcome and What Were the Benefits?

The most important outcome was that I passed and fulfilled the condition placed upon me for joining the professional register. There was never any sense, however, of the course being a necessary evil or of jumping through hoops for the sake of it. The course had been designed to ensure learning that would equip me better for the job. A particular benefit was that the underlying principles of the theoretical models provided by the training were very much in accord with new developments in the Care Commission. Not only that, but an external review of the future of the regulation of care was published during my study year and its recommendations also had great resonance with our models. This led to a strong sense that, not only was the course meeting the criteria for registration, but also equipping me for the changes soon to take place in my sector.

How Much Does it Cost and Who Paid?

The course costs were met by my employers and, although I did spend out a little on books over the year, all the essential reading material was provided and it would have been possible to complete the year without any personal outlay.

More Reading

Prior to starting the course we were all lent a copy of Northedge, A. (2005) *The Good Study Guide,* Milton Keynes, UK: Open University Worldwide. This is a large volume and I didn't read it from end to end. However, it was very useful to dip into and provided a lot of solid advice and case examples helpful to somebody preparing to study. The chapter on IT skills and use of Internet resources was especially helpful in introducing me to the twenty-first century world of study.

What are the Lessons Learned?

I am not sure if there is anything that I would wish to change about the course other than perhaps the university's rigid approach to word counts. This is not because I can't see the benefits, but due to the disproportionate amount of time consumed by staying within the word count.

I feel that I was very fortunate to be in the fourth cohort of students for ROCA and my employers and the university had taken on board very well a lot of points raised by previous cohorts.

The main lessons I learned for myself in relation to work-based training were to plan my time carefully but to be prepared to be flexible and make full use of the range of support available. I had a definite sense that all involved with the course had an investment in it being a successful learning experience which made it completely safe to voice any fears and apprehension as the course progressed.

14 *Case Study 7: A Learning Architect, Designing Programmes that Engage and a Doctoral Research Programme*

© Istockphoto / Chris Schmidt

About 20 years ago I woke up one morning and found myself dead. This was particularly frustrating as it turned out that brain death had occurred some 10 years earlier and nobody had had the good manners to tell me. Fortunately a cure was at hand, my brain was catapulted back into life not by some *Star Trek*-style cortical stimulator device but by the simple, yet elegant, act of learning. In my case the process involved taking a year's sabbatical at the age of 40 and returning to university to do a full-time Master's programme. I am pleased to report that I am now very much alive and learn something new every single day. At the end of a day or week I reflect on the period that has just passed and I ask myself – not 'what have I learned' but rather 'what new ways have I found to learn'. Learning is the difference between being a member of the waking dead and doing something worthwhile. In our organisations it is the difference between success and falling well short of achieving our collective goals.

I am now a lifelong learner, but also a passionate champion for the academic recognition of learning that takes place in the workplace as part of doing your job, whatever that job may be. My personal quest for continued learning led me to Middlesex University and the Institute of Work Based Learning. Here I have recently completed a Doctorate in professional studies and in the following pages I will explain why I found the process so stimulating and provide an insight to the advantages and sacrifices involved with this style of study.

My Situation

When I started this programme I was employed as Director of Learning for one of Europe's largest commercial training organisations. As such I was responsible for the design, development and deployment of our entire standard curriculum and in addition worked closely with large global organisations to design learning solutions to their specific requirements. Not surprisingly this was a high-pressure environment and the pace of identifying, bidding, winning and delivering business was at times relentless. In such circumstances, the challenge is to provide solutions fit for purpose that incrementally build upon previous developments. Whilst these are often imaginative and demanding they are necessarily always just enough, just in time. There is little time to consolidate insight within and across programmes and the emphasis is very much on taking what appeared to work well and repeating it many times in differing environments. Although I was paid to guide and reflect, I increasingly found that my own opportunities for reading, refection and constructive dialogue were limited and I was starting to feel that my own professional knowledge was aging and that in many cases I was trading on past achievements rather than creating new professional knowledge. It was for this reason that I started to look for opportunities for postgraduate study.

I looked at several part-time programmes offered by UK universities but failed to find a match between the topics of study offered and my interests, also I felt that the demands of my job were probably incompatible with the structured nature of a traditional part-time university qualification. What I needed was a course of study that I could shape both in terms of the curriculum and pattern of work.

Why Did I Need Another Qualification?

In the later part of the 1990s I had spent four very happy years as a Professor of Systems Management in the Information Resources Management College of the National Defence University in Washington DC. My main role was as a tutor on their Advanced Management programme, a 14-week full-time programme that was equivalent to half a Master's degree. On first joining the college I had attended the programme as a participant and subsequently I assumed overall design responsibility for two of the four core modules and I also taught on the policy module. The programme was aimed at senior personnel from all US Government departments and prepared them for leadership roles in information resources management. The combination of rapidly evolving US Government legislation and equally rapidly evolving technology capabilities (at this time the World Wide Web was in its infancy) provided lots of challenge in terms of keeping pace with developments and I was routinely reading two business books per week and several professional journals. It was a time of rapid and continuous personal growth, a time when I should really have completed a Doctorate but somehow never made the time. When I came back to the UK I looked back with some regret that I had missed a golden opportunity to gain the Doctorate. As time passed and I became immersed in the day-to-day challenge of managing a dynamic and growing business, I read less and felt that my knowledge was becoming dated and sterile. Worse still, I felt for the first time in 15 years that my commitment to personal learning and development was very much taking second place to that of developing others. I gain great satisfaction from developing others but I recognised that unless I could reaffirm my own commitment to ongoing intellectual growth it would ultimately degrade my ability to add value to those who looked to me for guidance. So the scene was set for me to return to academic study and I renewed my search for an appropriate vehicle with some vigour.

Linking Learning to Working

For me the barriers to getting back into higher education were that:

- I wanted a qualification structured around what I wanted to learn about, not what someone else deemed that a professional in my career space should be learning.
- I wanted a qualification that started when I wanted it to start and ended when I had done the work. I wanted as few rigid attendance dates as possible and preferably little or no commitment to attend formal lectures or courses.
- I wanted a qualification that could be woven into the fabric of my day-to-day work so that the things I studied had direct bearing and relevance to the challenges I faced and the products of my study could be fed seamlessly back into my everyday engagements and hence be of direct benefit to my clients and peers.

At this point I had a stroke of luck; by chance I met a Professor at Middlesex University. He reviewed some work I was doing for a client and asked me if I had considered expanding upon the work as part of a work-based qualification. He outlined the structure of work-based learning as pioneered by Middlesex and invited me to the university to talk to staff in the institute and meet current doctoral students. I was fascinated by their approach and now realise that what they have is a well-hidden gem. Basically they have two core capabilities; they have developed key techniques in:

- recognising and providing accreditation for prior learning achieved as part of doing your job;
- a robust and academically sound mechanism of awarding academic credits for project work conducted in the workplace.

The whole process starts with a review of prior learning, this takes the form of a reflective essay with supporting materials and samples of the products that your learning gave rise to. The university then assesses your application both in terms of academic depth and quality of thought and, if appropriate, awards APEL points at level 3, 4 or 5. Level 3 is equivalent to final year undergraduate study, level 4 Master's and level 5 Doctorate. Once this process is complete the next step is to construct a 'learning agreement' that sets out how the remaining credits will be achieved through essays and project work. The learning agreement is a three-way agreement between the learner, their employer and the university, in this way we ensure that the learner is likely to get support in the workplace because the learning has direct applicability to the industry and is relevant to current business challenges. At the same time the university needs to be satisfied that this is a project that will contribute to the body of professional knowledge and is structured in a manner that is commensurate with the level of award sought.

I obtained maximum credit for prior learning and structured a learning agreement around a project to be conducted in multiple industries aimed at determining how organisations can show that they have achieved an appropriate return for their investment in training and development initiatives. This is a knotty problem and one that was of direct interest and relevance to all our clients. It was also an area where there is significant dissatisfaction with existing techniques.

The university assigned an advisor to guide me through the process and engagement with them and a supervisor to act as first point of reference on all matters relating to the academic content of my study. The only compulsory element of the programme was a research methods unit that entailed regular half-day modules at the university during the first term after my registration. The research module was assessed by means of essays and reports.

Combining Study and Work

With the learning agreement approved and the research methods module completed I was pretty much a self-directed learning agent. My contact with the university was in the form of:

- regular phone and email contact with my supervisor;
- attendance (not compulsory) at university research seminars where participants in the programme would present their work for feedback and sharing;
- desk research using library, inter-library and web-based resources;
- dialogue with fellow professionals and engagement with professional bodies and forums.

In scoping the project work, three huge questions present themselves and these need to be answered early and honestly. These questions are:

- What question are you trying to answer? Here the key is how do you scope it so that it has sufficient depth to sustain you through the months or years that you will engage on the problem and how do you ensure that the question will still be of relevance to your industry when you have completed your study?
- How are you intending to research this domain? The choice of research technique will influence what you can discover and how you will discover it.
- Where are you going to look for evidence and most importantly how can you get appropriate access?

In my case the first question was simple, there was and still is wide professional interest in my chosen field and a real desire for a new approach. Also my company could see an opportunity to transfer my emerging thinking into new consulting offerings and to upskill our learning consultants with these ideas and techniques as they emerged. The third question was also in my case pretty straightforward; because of my role and wide personal network I had access to Learning Directors in a wide range of companies and industries – before I started the work I gained agreement from a number of these colleagues to allow me access to their senior staff to conduct interviews and data gathering.

For me the trickiest question centred on choice of research technique. Over the years my world view had been moulded and shaped by a range of learning experiences each of which explored a new domain of knowledge and new ways of bringing order to chaos with new models of enquiry. As an engineer and scientist I was schooled in the quantitative paradigm of scientific enquiry and although I was well versed in techniques of qualitative research, my only direct experience was in my Master's dissertation and this had employed a series of mini-case studies. However, the nature of this domain of knowledge appeared to lend itself to the development of theory from the data and although I had never attempted such a grounded theory approach I launched myself into the method with gusto but some trepidation.

Initial Lessons Learned and Key Advice to People Who Tread This Path

Any programme of part-time study is always going to be challenging and in the world of education self-guided learning is an extreme sport. You are on the edge and the support mechanisms are often tenuous, as a result this can leave you feeling very alone and exposed. Work-based learning is the most extreme form of this particular form of masochism, you have no routine or spoon-fed content and exercises to fall back on. The subject matter, mode of enquiry, research design and problem specification are all in your own hands. Yes, you get advice and help but ultimately the buck stops with you. What became obvious to me as a result of attending research seminars with other students was that it was all too easy to become becalmed, like the ancient mariner adrift in a flat sea with no direction and no land fall in sight. Some were a long way into their studies but were questioning the nature of their research question, others were casting around hopefully for somewhere to conduct their data gathering. I now unhesitatingly give these three nuggets of advice:

- Sort out access to data sources before you do anything else.
- Quickly build a deep and trusting relationship with your supervisor. Choose your supervisor, don't have one appointed to you.
- Don't build your research around someone else's problem or one that appears to be convenient. Pick something that you care deeply about because you still need to care about it in three years time.

Capturing Insight, Synthesising Knowledge

As with all endeavours, time spent in planning and preparation pays dividends later. I briefed all the organisations I would deal with, gave them an information pack setting out what I was doing and how they would contribute and benefit. I set out for them how I would deal with confidentiality and other ethical concerns and then I put the design into action. The grounded theory approach requires extensive information gathering.

I used semi-structured interviews mostly face-to-face but where this proved impossible for geographic reasons I resorted to telephone interview. All interviewed were taped and I made personal notes and mind-maps during the interviews. The data gathering went smoothly, as did the micro-analysis and line by line coding of the interview transcripts. What I had not anticipated was the manner in which theory was to emerge from the data. At one stage I thought the analysis complete but remained uncomfortable that the insights and relationships appeared to be disjointed and limiting. It was only through the process of writing that I was to engage in further development and sense making. I had previously thought of the writing process as a means of setting down for posterity thinking that had already emerged whole from the data, I could previously not have conceived of writing as being an integral part of the theorising process itself. As I grappled with a variety of models and conceptual schema through which to convey my findings, I found that the internal debate was producing new insights and new connections. I had always accepted that new knowledge was created both through socialisation and personal reflection, but I had previously never been so consciously aware of engaging in the process.

Throughout the whole process I had regular contact and meetings with my supervisor and this was particularly useful in providing impartial challenge to my thinking but more importantly my supervisor was an invaluable resource in guiding me through the design and conduct of a grounded theory-style research programme.

My research produced a new understanding of how companies value learning initiatives. That understanding is already starting to impact the conduct of professional practice and has the potential to significantly enhance an organisation's awareness of the progress and impact of its learning initiatives. But most importantly, it has caused me to evaluate what I do and why I do it. I have once again opened my mental toolkit for inspection and found it lacking.

Assessment and Award

The award of the Doctorate in Professional Studies requires the accumulation of a predetermined number of level 4 and 5 academic credits. In my case, the bulk of the level 5 credits were attained through one large learning project as described. This involved the submissions of a 35,000 word dissertation backed up by sample products of techniques and methods that I had developed for my company. As part of the process I had also published in refereed journals, professional journals and presented at conferences. The university put together an examining committee for my dissertation including external examiners with an interest in the subject. Finally, some months after submission, I was invited to defend my dissertation in front of the examiners, this involved detailed debate around both the theory and the outcomes of the project. I found the whole process to be stimulating and rewarding.

How Much Time Did I Spend on This?

I confess that I did not keep a log of the time I devoted to this course of study – partially because the work-based nature of the learning makes it difficult to distinguish between when you are working to produce outcomes for your organisation and when you are working on the same questions from a research perspective. What I can say is that doing a Doctorate is no simple matter, it involves sacrifices, lots of reading, lots of writing and most importantly lots of quality thinking and reflection time. When it came to write up time I asked my company chairman if I could drop to a four day week for around three months so that I could do the writing – fortunately for me he understood the challenge and said NO. What he advised was that I go away and not come back until I had finished. This was great advice, I made a plan of action and locked myself in my study for ten days, my target was to write 4,000 words per day. At the end of ten days I had my dissertation done all but final polishing. I am blessedly a quick reader and a quick writer but I am convinced that the discipline of focusing exclusively on the challenge at hand paid huge dividends.

Lasting Outcomes

Learning has been an integral part of my life for most of the last 20 years and in my current role I have the privilege and honour to be entrusted with guiding and mentoring the development of some of my organisation's best young professionals. It is a rich and rewarding experience to see others grow in capability and confidence; it is even more rewarding to experience such growth in oneself. It is all too easy to become complacent and tread old familiar paths, this programme has set my foot firmly on the pathway to further self-discovery. I look forward with interest and wonder at where it may take me next.

15 Case Study 8: IT Operations Manager and a Foundation Degree in Business Management

My Particular Learner Situation

This case study examines the experience of a 47-year-old IT Operations Manager who undertook a three-year Foundation degree in Business Management, starting in 2005, whilst working full time for Sussex Health Informatics Service.

Prior to working for the National Health Service I worked in the private sector as the company's IT Manager for the UK. I joined the NHS in January 2004

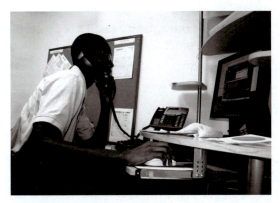

© Istockphoto / Marje Cannon

working for the Royal West Sussex Trust in Chichester and moved over to the Health Informatics Service (HIS) when it was first set up in July 2004. The Sussex HIS was formed from the IT departments of 19 separate NHS trusts, which were merged to form a single organisation that would deliver IT products and services throughout the whole county. It currently covers more than 280 sites and employs over 500 staff. My role as the IT Operations Manager means that I am responsible for the day-to-day technical support of all desktop computers and IT infrastructure for all of our customers across Sussex. I currently manage 150 staff through six direct reports who are based each at different locations enabling them to cover the whole of the county.

Before undertaking the Foundation degree I had a business IT qualification at HNC level along with other technical qualifications that were related to my previous role in the private sector. However, prior to attaining these qualifications, I had left school at the age of 16 and went straight into employment; I did not have the chance to explore further education immediately after school as my parents were keen for me to find employment at the earliest opportunity and it did not seem important to me at the time.

In 2005 I decided to look into the prospect of higher education and the Foundation degree in Business Management was exactly what I was looking for. The course was part time and suggested the required amount of study time would be two hours per week plus one compulsory residential weekend per year. The study weekends involved attending lectures and workshops, giving and receiving presentations and participating in group discussions. The degree ran over three years and was delivered through Chichester College of Technology in association with Portsmouth University and, at the time, it seemed that it would fit in well with my lifestyle as it appeared that the relatively short amount of study required each week was unlikely to encroach seriously on my home life or on my work commitments.

Why Did I Decide to Do Something Like This?

There were two main reasons that I decided to go ahead with workplace learning. Firstly, I was very aware that IT positions within the public sector generally require a qualification at degree level and as such, regardless of experience, candidates without a degree were unlikely to even reach the interview stage. My lack of degree therefore put an invisible but very real ceiling on my career.

More importantly, on a personal level, I felt that without a degree I had not achieved my academic potential which was something that I was determined to change. I wanted to test myself and stretch myself academically.

What Were the Barriers to Learning?

The biggest barrier, for me, was definitely time and to be honest the amount of studying that was required far exceeded the recommended study time advertised by the college. One has to wonder whether this was a deliberate advertising strategy. I would estimate that at least 12 hours were required each week and whilst I did take some study leave when I was working to a tight deadline, the majority of studying took place in my own time, usually on a Sunday. As the course progressed my home life did begin to suffer as I replaced enjoyment of virtually anything else with studying which, of course, had a massive impact on my family life.

Another difficulty was the way in which I was expected to write my assignments: I've always written in 'black and white', so to speak, but here I was in an academic environment expected to produce work in 'uni-speak' and to back my research and reasoning up with various theories that, until now, I had been completely unfamiliar with. One particular module that I struggled with was economics, a concept that was totally alien to me that was supported by theories that, at the time, were equally difficult to comprehend; I did pass but only by 2 per cent which I found rather disappointing. In retrospect the low score was largely because I simply did not put the amount of work into the module as I could, or should, have done. I did, however, manage to attain 83 per cent in my final module where I produced a project around work-based learning that focused on a mobile working presentation. I even received a letter of recognition from the university for this!

A further obstacle was the dramatic drop-out rate. Initially 23 students embarked on the degree course. However, only three of us completed it. This had a huge impact on the dynamics of the group; where initially there were sufficient people to evoke lively discussions, as the course progressed and the numbers dwindled, there simply were not enough students to work through issues and problems with. You cannot have the same supportive group work environment with three people as with 23. There were various reasons as to why students abandoned their studies, for instance, a large number dropped out over the Christmas period in the first year as family commitments took priority, others moved away and some struggled with the coursework because English was not their first language. I have to admit that I questioned the college's initial judgement in enrolling some of these students as the course was extremely demanding for those whose first language was English let alone those who were struggling with a language barrier on top of comprehending complicated theories and concepts around business management.

What Sort of Workplace Environment Was I Coming From?

My employer, the Sussex HIS, provides IT services for the NHS across the whole of Sussex for in excess of 35,000 users. As I have been with the Sussex HIS ever since its inception I feel very much part of the organisation and feel myself to be well supported at work. When I started the course, three years ago, I was the Sussex HIS Unit Lead for St Richard's Hospital and was based in Chichester. About 18 months ago I was promoted to Regional IT Manager for the whole of West Sussex which involved considerably more travel across the county for meetings. The extra travelling time meant that I was unable to study during the working day and when I returned to the office at St Richard's Hospital it would generally be very noisy and the environment was not conducive to learning at all.

When I started my new role I definitely prioritised work above studying as I was working through new issues and work situations and was keen to prove myself worthy of the position. Also my staff increased from eight direct reports with whom I worked closely in the office in Chichester, to 45 staff based across a number of sites such as Worthing, Haywards Heath and Crawley, so line management became another major priority above my studies. In hindsight, I should, and could, have taken more study leave in order to concentrate on my coursework.

What Supplements and Tools Did I Use?

The university utilised an online system called Athens which gave me access to subject databases and electronic journals and papers. The way in which Athens works is that the databases and journals are purchased by the university library and made available to students via their library website. I used Athens extensively as it allowed me to log in and access these resources from anywhere that allowed access to the Internet which was very convenient.

The university also had Virtual Learning Environment (VLE) called Victory which was an online teaching platform that acted as a tool where you could post questions for tutors and other students as well as actively take part in online forums. The system was linked to other universities who were running the same course and therefore gave me access to a much broader range of knowledge than just that which was within my study group.

Along with the electronic resources which were available to me I also read a lot of text books that I borrowed from the college and university libraries. I visited the libraries frequently as my course required me to refer constantly to the relevant text books but I often found that the books I needed were either not available or were not part of the library catalogue and so I had to buy quite a few of the key books for myself. In retrospect,

I now realise that my employer would happily have paid for the books and kept them after my studies were finished as part of our Education, Training and Development library but as my degree had been fully funded I had not realised that they would also have paid for any additional training materials that I required, and I did not think to ask at the time.

I was supported by tutors throughout each aspect of the training, with different tutors assigned for each module and a separate one who oversaw the whole course. I would have liked to have had a personal tutor who worked with me throughout the course – somebody with whom I could have built a relationship and worked through my ongoing study issues – however this was not available. Overall, however, I felt that the teaching provision was well placed by the university and college.

In terms of support for learning from my employers, the Sussex HIS has a study leave policy which allows staff to take time away from the office to concentrate on their studies. Although my study leave was approved by the organisation I only really took a handful of days throughout the three years that I was studying and these were generally during the lead up to an exam or when I had needed to complete an assignment in a short period of time. On reflection, if I were to undertake this type of study again I would ensure that I included more time for study leave into my work schedule.

Did Capturing Work Place Experience Work?

Some of the modules worked better than others in terms of work-based learning and reflecting on real-life experience to support my research and assignments. For instance, my experience of line managing a reasonably large team of staff and dealing with the various issues that crop up within the team allowed me to translate my workplace experience into my assignments and research around the human resources module. This module was the first one on the Foundation degree and concentrated on people management; as a manager of people I saw this as a pivotal module within the whole course and I was able to reflect on the experience of my involvement in a disciplinary action within my team which I felt really helped to put the whole assignment in perspective and bring it alive for me. As it was so relevant to my work I felt much more involved with this module and benefited directly and immediately from my studies.

There were certainly elements of work-based learning in the majority of my assignments and presentations throughout the whole three-year period and I did refer to the culture of my work organisation in many of my study assignments. However, I did struggle to grasp a lot of the theories that were referred to and how they translated back to my real-life workplace experiences. I found that many of the theories merged into one another whilst some seemed to contradict others which made comprehending them a challenge. On the other hand, some of the theories that we referred to seemed to be more a case of common sense rather than an actual theory per se and referring to them in my work was also somewhat challenging.

Whilst I was able to reflect on my experience in a lot of my coursework there were some modules where it was just not feasible to do so. For instance, at that time I had no experience of any aspect of marketing and therefore when we came to writing about that area of business management I had nothing tangible on which to base my work.

How Did the Method of Assessment Work?

The degree was assessed through a combination of exams and coursework assignments such as written papers and formal presentations.

The main problem with the assessment was that, unlike in a standard Bachelor's degree, the only options were pass or fail. This meant there was no opportunity to excel or reason to challenge yourself to achieve a higher class of degree. As a result I felt that there was no real incentive to work harder than was necessary to just achieve the 40 per cent pass mark, other than personal pride, which was not always enough in the circumstances.

This was particularly an issue with the coursework and assignments, the exams were slightly different as you had to give it your best shot so as not to risk failure. With the coursework assessments they were very good at explicitly defining the marking criteria so you knew exactly what you had to do to pass. This was good in that students had a clear understanding of what was required and there was little risk of failure. However, on the down side there was no motivation to do more than the bare minimum needed to pass. I did feel afterwards that I could have done myself better justice, but extra marks meant extra hours put into it with no significant benefit and by the end of the course I was keen to retain as much free time for myself and my family as I could.

In respect of the exams, some were multiple choice whilst others were written papers. The multiple choice papers were not too difficult but the best advice I could give with a multiple choice paper is to stick with your first answer. I made a rule never to go back and change my original answer as apparently more often than not people change a correct answer to an incorrect answer.

The written papers were more stressful and arduous. Aside from the anxiety of time constraints and not having any notes to refer to, the hardest challenge for me was that they had to be written by hand. It seems so old-fashioned to handwrite in the modern world that we live in today and to be honest, my hand and wrist muscles just aren't used to it. Ten minutes into the exam I would feel as if I had got repetitive strain injury in my wrist which made writing extremely painful and difficult. I really don't know how they managed to read my handwriting towards the end of some of the papers.

What Was the Method of Mentoring or Tutoring?

As I mentioned previously, I didn't have a personal tutor or mentor at the university. Much to my disappointment personal tutoring is not a teaching method is that is used at Portsmouth University, instead we had different tutors for each module and a tutor in overall charge of the course. The quality or effectiveness of the university tutors varied hugely, some were very good and their teaching was clear, informative and in some cases inspiring whilst others were pretty poor. Indeed, in one case the whole group actually put in a complaint about a tutor because his teaching was so poor, it was a stressful time as we all had grave concerns as to how we were going to pass the module when the level of teaching being provided was of such poor quality. Fortunately, the university listened to our concerns and they did agree to provide an alternative tutor for the remainder of the module; regrettably the change didn't take place until approximately halfway through the module but I did manage to pass the assessment and so felt lucky that the experience didn't have too detrimental an effect.

Most of the tutors came from an industrial background and so they had lots of real, hands-on work experience. This proved to be extremely useful as they were able to relate theories to real world examples which, in turn, helped me to translate theory into my own real-life experiences which was required for some of my assignments. Some of the other lecturers at the university seemed to have all been borne out of the same mould – the classic portrayal of fusty old professors who are all beards and sandals! You could tell they'd never been in a business environment but lived in 'ivory towers' and were rather out of touch with what we like to call the 'real world'. I feel that it is extremely important for work-based learning courses to have lecturers who have come into academia only after a business career, so that they can bridge the gap between theory and reality. If this bridge is not provided I think that work-based learning would be very difficult to pursue, especially for people who have been in work and out of education for some time.

At work my boss was my mentor, although I didn't use him very much in this capacity. He was very supportive of my studying though, having identified it through my personal development plan as a way to progress my career and he had signed off the funding for the course. He always gave me study leave when I asked for it and would have given me more had I needed it. I found it was very important to have this sort of flexibility when coursework deadlines loomed large. More than this, I felt I had his moral support and this was very important to me as it made me feel valued and also gave credence to the efforts I was putting into my studies.

Did You Find it Difficult to Make the Time Commitment Needed for Study?

I spent around 12 hours per week reading and studying and, yes, sometimes it was extremely difficult to find this time. I did all my studying outside of work hours, so I would spend time on it most evenings and pretty much all day on Sundays. Obviously this had a massive impact on my home life, leaving me little time for leisure activities, relaxing and seeing my family.

I did get a bit of a hard time at home about the time I spent on studying – particularly from my wife. My children don't live at home so although it impacted on my time with them at weekends they were OK with that. I think that I was more concerned about missing out on time with them than they were, but it was a choice I had made when I decided to take the course and I stood by my study commitments.

The main conflict was with my wife. Although we had discussed the course before I committed to it, I do not think she realised how much work was involved, how important it was to me or how much of my spare time it would take over. Because of this lack of a clear understanding prior to me starting the course I ended up feeling that she wasn't giving me the support that I had hoped for and expected. Having said that, I think towards the end of the course she was at least resigned to my distraction.

At the start of the course I was very keen, doing a lot of reading around the subject and getting busy with my assignments as soon as they were set, determined to give myself plenty of time and do a good job. Towards the end of the course I found it more and more difficult to keep focused. I found myself leaving assignments until the last minute, ignoring deadlines until they crept up on me and then hastily dashing them off. Three years is a long time to maintain concentration and, as previously mentioned, thanks to the clarity of the marking system I knew what I could get away with on coursework and still pass.

What Was the Outcome and What Were the Benefits?

Well, the key outcome for me was that I attained a Foundation degree and I would say there were three significant benefits that came out of this.

Firstly, I felt a strong sense of personal satisfaction and pride from my achievement.

Secondly, the addition of a degree to my CV will definitely open up far broader career opportunities for me. Throughout my career I learned that no matter how experienced I may be at my job, without degree-level qualifications, many doors would always remain closed to me.

Finally, my boss said that he believed that this course has helped develop me as a manager and in all modesty I agree with him – I certainly have a better understanding now of the business processes applicable to the Sussex HIS than I had before I undertook this course.

So, as you can see, there were benefits to me on a personal level, to me on a professional level and to the Sussex HIS as my employer.

Furthermore, this Foundation degree has become the first step towards undertaking further learning, although that was not my original purpose. The Foundation degree has given me both the entry qualification and the confidence to get on to the Chartered Management Institute for Strategic Management Level 7. This is the highest professional (as opposed to academic) qualification available and I was very pleased when the Sussex HIS agreed to fund this course for me as well.

To be honest, when I first started the Foundation degree I merely wanted to improve my CV, I felt it would open up further career opportunities for me, but I had no intention of going on to study any further. However, halfway through the course I started seeing it as a possible stepping stone to further training. I'm not sure if I'll progress any further academically after this as it is just so time consuming and I do think that I would benefit from a break, at least for a year or two.

How Much Did it Cost and Who Paid?

I'm not entirely sure of the total cost of the course as this was organised through the Education, Training and Development department but the course was fully funded by my employer, Sussex HIS. I did pay for my own books but was told afterwards that the organisation would have paid for these had I asked and would have been retained by them for other staff to use.

More Reading

You can read all about the course on the Portsmouth University website under the business section.

What Lessons Did You Draw from Your Experiences?

I would advise anyone who is thinking of doing a similar course to make sure both that both themselves and their families are fully aware of the time commitments. It can cause quite a lot of tension in the family and stress to individuals. One of my staff did the same course but dropped out four months before he would have completed the course as he found the time commitment too much of a strain which was a great pity.

I'd also suggest reading up on how to write university assignments. It's very different from anything I had done in the past and although you learn as you go, I think it would be beneficial to crack this nut right at the beginning so that you can then focus on the more important aspects of the course. When you're used to cutting to the chase and driving towards conclusions as quickly as possible in a business environment it can take a while to get used to the academic way of theorizing and arguing every case. Also the Harvard referencing system is a nightmare – it would help to get your head around it as early as possible so that you don't waste time learning it whilst you're writing assignments.

I felt I was very well supported by both my employer and the university which was important. Certainly anybody studying and working full time needs to feel supported at work. The only improvement that could have been made is if my employer had made me aware that they would have paid for my books but that is a bit of a chicken and egg situation as I never approached them and they were unaware that I was purchasing books. So a lesson for other work-based learners is to ask about this, rather than just assuming you have to pay for your own course materials.

16 *Case Study 9: A Local Authority Manager and a Work-Based Master's Degree*

My Background

© Jonathan Norman

I am 40 years old and live in Manchester with my partner and eight-year-old son. My time at school was not as great as it could have been and I did not achieve many qualifications on leaving. It took me until I was 20 years old to pluck up the courage to go to university, where I undertook a youth and community work degree. I think the social life took over from my learning and I came out with an average grade, although during my time at university I did begin to enjoy study, which had not been the experience for me previously.

My career began in the voluntary and community sector and I remained there until after my son was born. It wasn't until I started work that I begin to realise that I did have potential and that I could better myself bit by bit. After around four years I moved into a local authority as a manager and it was then that I began to think about taking on some form of further education. I had always wanted to undertake a Master's degree but felt that this may be a challenge that was unobtainable.

Why I Did the Course?

I came across the Masters degree at Lancaster through a friend, who was thinking of undertaking the course, but didn't get the necessary backing from their employer in the end. I think the initial reason for me being attracted to this particular course was the 'vocational' feel it had to it. That is, its focus was around how you could apply your theoretical learning into your workplace and vice versa. My degree had been a very similar vocational format. I began to feel that this could possibly be something I could undertake. My learning styles have never been based around pure theory, I have always had to apply the learning to real situations to help me understand and make sense of it.

What Were the Barriers?

I suppose the main barrier for me was around my self-confidence and returning back to formal study and writing essays after so long away from any kind of learning. I saw the Masters degree as a real opportunity to challenge myself and achieve something that I had previously thought could possibly be unobtainable. Although the thought of walking back into a classroom for the first time and meeting students who were all undertaking an Masters degree was frightening!

The second barrier for me was finance. At the time, I managed a short-term funded programme in Oldham Local Authority, and I gained permission to finance the Masters degree through the training budget as the benefits of me undertaking this study and what I would bring back into the workplace as a result were obvious. I also had a very understanding and committed boss!

Both my partner and I worked full time and we had a son, so the biggest barrier was around the unknown time commitment of undertaking two years of study and how this would impact on my family life. As it turned out, due to the area of work I chose for my dissertation in the second year, I was able to carry out most of the research during work time which lessened the impact on my family life. The first year was harder, as I would have to wait until my son was in bed before I could start work on the pressing essay of the term.

I found it really helpful that the university attendance days were spread across the terms and only one day at a time, which meant that I did not have to take much time out of work, therefore lessening the impact on my day-to-day workload.

My Workplace

My employer was Oldham Council and I worked as a manager within children's services. My substantive area of work was managing a children's fund programme, which was set up to develop preventative measures for children and young people around issues such as health, crime, poverty and community cohesion. Following on from the launch of the Every Child Matters Agenda, my role widened to develop a partnership working within the children's trust and embedding the Every Child Matters Agenda. This widening role gave me the freedom and flexibilities to follow a path of learning that directly related to my workplace. As part of this new role I worked with a virtual team, and we were afforded the opportunity to undertake some visioning around the new agenda. Things fell into place at the right time really around my study, as we were looking at change management as part of the MA and one of the biggest changes in children's services was also being implemented at the same time.

Tools to Support My Learning

There was some real innovative thinking by the university around supplementing our learning opportunities, mainly because we were all in full-time employment and only in university around one day every half term. One of the main areas of learning was the 'virtual learning network'. This was an online network where lecturers could post questions or areas for us to think about and there were discussion groups set up between the students to discuss particular aspects of the topics we were studying. I found the virtual network really useful as a reader, and learnt a lot from other people, but I felt it took a bit of confidence to actually engage and post thoughts and ideas for all the other students to see! Daft really as I felt I got a lot out of it, but didn't put as much back into it as I should. There were a group of students on the course that would always be posting messages, thoughts and comments up on the network and others of us that would only do this periodically.

It was also a good way for us to have some ongoing communication with tutors and to check we were on the right track with our thoughts. I found it very useful when somebody put a reference on the network for an interesting piece of reading they had found relating to the relevant topic. The tutors also put copies of the handouts and presentations on the network for us to refer back to and extra information as they came across it.

I found the booklist very scary when we received it in our first year, but as I became more familiar with the reading, the books became easier to navigate. Again, I think this was more about preconception of my abilities than my actual ability to 'handle' a text book. I found the Internet invaluable, especially when searching for other books I may have wanted to purchase. I found a great secondhand book site, which listed stock and linked you to a host of secondhand bookshops (abebooks.com). It saved me a fortune!

As part of our days in university, we were formed into action learning sets. The group I was a member of morphed the group into something more flexible. We would, on some days, work well as an action learning group, with members bringing topics, issues and problems to the group for us to discuss. On other days, the group felt it more important to spend the afternoon in the university library (especially for those who lived far away from Lancaster!). We also shared drafts of our essays together to gain constructive feedback and to share our ideas and different ways of viewing the same question. Sometimes the action learning set just became a 'mutual appreciation club' where we just built up each others' confidence when we were feeling low and that it was all getting a bit too hard for us!

The students on the course came from very different work backgrounds including health, private companies, self-employed, voluntary sector and education. Roles ranged from managing director through to project workers. This really helped as we were able to learn about other organisations and companies and how they approached their employees' learning as well as how they implemented change. The wide variety of students on the course provided a lively wealth of knowledge and expertise in different areas for us all to learn from, and, in some cases, led us to thank our lucky stars for the organisations we worked in!

One of the best tools for my learning was one particular tutor on the course, who supported me at the beginning of my study and then supported me through my dissertation. I could send drafts of my essays via email and get some really useful feedback and detailed comments for me to rework the drafts. It also helps to know you are on the right track and not gone completely off the rails with the subject! It is fair to say that different tutors had differing ways of supporting fellow students on the course and to differing levels of detail.

In terms of my workplace, although the funding had come from here, during my actual two-year study period, there was no access to support and the balance between my day-to-day work and my MA study is something that I had to ensure worked. On reflection, I think, particularly in local authorities, academic research and work-based practice do not go hand in hand. The health services are more au fait with research-based practice as I am discovering in my new job.

My Work-Based Dissertation

When choosing your dissertation for the second year of study, it is vital that you are passionate about the topic and research you choose for your dissertation. If you aren't that passionate, you will be sick to the back teeth of it by the end and completely lose interest! This will come out in your writing up and analysing of the work.

I have always been passionate about the involvement and participation of children and young people in the development of services to meet their needs and felt that this would be a great area to base my dissertation around. This was a real opportunity for me to find the capacity to undertake a large piece of research involving a large amount of children and young people, to drive change in the way we deliver those services and to develop a more sustainable culture of participation in service development and delivery.

The dissertation also afforded me the opportunity of looking at the various theories behind the participation of children and young people, and critically, reflecting on some of the work I had undertaken in the past around participation.

I had the great advantage of having a budget to undertake this research, as this was research that had to be undertaken for the children's services directorate I was working in, that I could underpin clearly with theory.

My research focused on the five outcomes within the Every Child Matters Agenda: health, staying safe, enjoying and achieving, making a positive contribution and achieving economic well-being. My task was to speak to and record the thoughts, ideas and experiences of children and young people in Oldham as to how they thought they could achieve these five outcomes, and how they thought services that were delivered in Oldham could be improved.

To ascertain and record feedback, I utilised age-based focus groups, interviews, questionnaires and the medium of film to raise awareness about the research and to demonstrate that children and young people do have a voice and want to use it.

My Experience of Assessment

We all are different types of learners, with different styles. For me this course really worked, as there was a lot of self-reflection that had to be input into the essays, focusing on you as an employee in your day-to-day work but also on you as a learner. Some people find this critical self-analysis quite challenging. For me, this area was much easier to write about than the more clinical theory-based work around change management.

As the study, and therefore the essays, were very much based around your own experience within your workplace, I feel that the tutors found it hard to fully assess some of the analysis requested, as this was so personal to the student. There may at times have been misunderstanding about some of the context discussed, again because of the unique experiences of the student within the workplace.

An area that I did find very interesting was that of having to use 'academic speak', where it was necessary to utilise longer words to put your point across in an elaborated language. This took a bit of getting used to and I think I probably dropped points in my initial essays due to the lack of practice at this. The way we use words and express ourselves within our workplace differs greatly from the academic world. Referencing was also very difficult at first, but like anything, after lots of practice, this became easier. Interestingly, I use referencing continuously now in the papers I am writing in my workplace and would never had done this before my Masters degree.

In the first year of the course, the tutoring was classroom-based learning around change management and, at times, I did feel that, through essays, we were asked to critically analyse information that was given to us or we had read, but during the classroom-based sessions, this was sometimes discouraged, especially from visiting tutors who did not actually work on the programme.

It was the first year the Masters degree had run and we did feel that we were the guinea pigs! I think we were quite a vocal group and therefore we were quite forthright with the tutors on the course about our views. There were a lot of changes in the tutors on the course and the expectations and guidelines given around essays and marks. I think that because we were all in full-time employment and giving up our time at work in addition to paying for the courses (the majority of students out of their own pockets), there were some feelings of unhappiness around the management of the course as a whole, but on reflection, this was probably necessary as this was the first year of the course and therefore a learning experience for all.

I really enjoyed the second year of study, because it was predominantly about your dissertation and analysis of your own learning as a student. It was difficult to gain constructive feedback on your topic of dissertation as this was very personal to your experience in your workplace. The feedback gained from the tutors was around the academic application of research, the tools you deployed and your levels of understanding around the theory and how you have applied it.

Time Commitment

As mentioned earlier, it is hard if you have a family and work full time to engage on any study course. I found the amount of days at university to be really helpful as they were not in blocks but odd days spread throughout the year. It is vital that you have an employer who can clearly see the benefits of your study to the job and the organisation you work within, this in turn means they will be more supportive as they can see what they are getting out of it.

Finding time for study, work and family does become a juggling act, but I do think we were all expert jugglers by the end of the course. As the course was only over a two-year period, the end was always in sight and it didn't feel as though it was a never-ending journey. I think it is vital to be able to undertake some of the research and writing up in work time if possible, if this is supposed to be a partnership between your academic study and work-based learning and practice. This will mean one less ball to juggle continuously. There does have to be quiet time found in the house, whether that means grabbing a couple of hours after the children have gone to bed and foregoing that glass of wine with dinner or putting whole days aside at weekends to do some focused work whilst my partner took the kids out (which I know some students found useful to do, but this didn't suit me). For me, it was definitely worth the juggling and sacrifice over the two-year period as the end result was gaining the Masters degree as an individual, not being a mother, partner or daughter, but something I did for myself by myself!

What are Some of the Benefits to Doing This?

One of the biggest benefits for me was around my self-confidence and sense of achievement. It was a challenge that I put up for myself, faced by myself and achieved. When I initially walked into the classroom of strangers on the first day, I automatically thought I shouldn't be there, that everyone was more able than me. I eventually graduated with a first!

I made a new community of friends and we still meet once a year to have a meal and see what everyone is up to. Others keep in contact through email and support each other through similar work-based problems that arise.

The area of research I chose for my dissertation was really interesting to me and I learnt a lot that I now apply in my day-to-day work. I do feel that, through time and research on my chosen topic, I am more of an 'expert' and can speak with some authority on the subject.

I am confident about my own self-reflection and the critical analysis of others' work. I recommended this course to one of my colleagues who is now a student and I support her periodically.

As a direct impact of me gaining an Masters degree to add to my CV, and my confidence boost through my achievement in not only passing but gaining a first, I have now moved to another local authority to take a up a job with much larger responsibilities. Taking part in this course had a huge impact on me personally and professionally and I think it would not be an easy task to quantify this.

In terms of benefits to the employer, the research and findings that I published were used to examine current service provision and develop a vision for some service change. It broke down barriers around how we can engage children and young people in a meaningful way. I do know that my work is still being used to influence change.

The film that was made as part of the research was shortlisted for the National Children and Young People Now Awards and I took a group of young people to London for the awards ceremony; some of these young people had not been to London before.

More Reading

I suppose the further reading to take from this would be my dissertation and my reflective journals that we had to keep.

Lessons Learnt

The first lesson would be not to take this on lightly; it is something that has to be right for you and your employer. There are some times through the two years when you do feel as through the Masters degree is taking over your life and to some extent you have to let it, especially when the dissertation is due!

The employer needs to also have some commitment to you as an employee and your learning. If this is not payment for the course, it has to be about flexibility around time allowed to undertake the study. For me it was definitely advantageous to choose an area of study that was vital for the employer to carry out, as the employer is likely to give more time, support and investment in extra capacity to aid you in the research area, plus financial input into research or time for you to carry the research out and write it up.

The awarding body needs to be aware of your working context and provide flexible support around this context. There also needs to be consistency in terms of expectation of students and good notice around essay subjects and deadlines for submission. The feedback on draft submissions needs to be timely to enable the student to complete the submission. It should always be in the back of the awarding bodies' mind that each student has full-time work commitments and possibly family commitments. If possible, I think it would be more advantageous to have the same tutor throughout your time on the MA, where a solid relationship can be formed (as attendance at university is sporadic) and an expert in your chosen field brought in to support you in your dissertation alongside your tutor.

How Do You Prepare Yourself for This Learning?

As talked about earlier, this is a time-consuming commitment over a two-year period, but worth the effort. I would not recommend embarking on a course like this if the drive has come from your employer rather than yourself as the student, as to succeed on this course or similar you need to be very self-motivated and know that you can direct and manage your own learning. It is never too early to start thinking about areas to concentrate the dissertation around so that earlier relevant essays can be used to undertake preliminary feasibility and preparation work which can be drawn on in the second year.

As long as you are motivated and can find the time to study then I would recommend this method of learning to anyone. It is challenging, satisfying, and hard work but opens up so many doors. I think there were two main areas for me that really helped me in my learning and they were a supportive and knowledgeable tutor and a close group of fellow students with whom I could comfortably share fears, anxieties, findings, discoveries and a beer with!

Resources

Northedge, A. (2005). *The Good Study Guide*. Milton Keynes UK: Open University Worldwide.

17 *Case Study 10: Working With Children and Learning Recognition*

© Istockphoto / Ekaterina Monakhova

My Learner Situation

Working with children was something that I had never thought of until I became a wife and a mother to twin boys. Being a mother opened up a fantastic opportunity for me to change. I gave up working to stay at home with my children and soon realised that working with young children was something that I was passionate about.

That was the best decision of my life and I am now doing a job that I love, getting up everyday not knowing what the day will bring; it may not be the best-paid job in the world but the satisfaction of seeing the children growing in confidence and moving on to their new settings fills me with pride knowing that I was part of their journey.

I have worked at the playgroup for 16 years; part of that time as an assistant, then a Deputy Leader and then finally the Playgroup Leader. I run a private playgroup within a local church. As a leader my role has many aspects to it, as well as being there for the children I have a huge amount of paperwork which has to be done out of hours; this includes record keeping, wages, tax returns and keeping up-to-date policies and procedures. Although I work part-time hours at the playgroup, the extent of the work means that I find it takes up full-time hours and sometimes more.

Before starting work at the playgroup I had worked in offices doing a variety of duties such as filing, computers, wages, telephone and reception duties, which I feel has helped me in all aspects of running the playgroup as you never know from one minute to the next what problems or challenges you will come across.

Training courses have played a big part of my Early Years career and more so when I received an invitation from the Early Years and Childcare team who are part of the Newcastle City Council. I was invited along to a training conference to encourage childcare practitioners to expand on their qualifications. The conference is when my life changed!

My family have been very supportive in my decision to attend Northumbria University and help to make my studying easier. Although my sons are themselves attending university, they are still on hand to keep me going, giving advice, listening to my moans and groans, even helping me with my mathematics when I had to attend a course.

What Was My Motivation?

During the 16 years I have worked at the playgroup I have seen many changes in the way we work, for example in legislation, and part of these changes are the required qualifications that need to be addressed. When I first started in the group it was a requirement that you completed a Certificate in Childcare course, it then changed to staff having to complete an NVQ at level three qualification and then, most recently, the announcement that all Early Years settings must have a graduate in place by the year 2015.

I attended meetings and conferences in my role as Playgroup Leader and the more information that I found out; the more I said to myself, 'Why can't that be me?' At the same time I was preparing myself for a huge change in my family, my two sons were in the process of completing their A levels and going to university themselves and therefore would be living away from home. I do not know whether it was a combination of supporting my sons or the information I had been given, but I suddenly started thinking, 'It can be me.'

On a professional level, a small private group would not be able to support a graduate's wage and therefore there was the possibility of the group having to close once the legislation came in that the group had to have a graduate in place by 2015. This would be a sad loss as the playgroup has been running for 20 years and all the staff would like to see it run for a lot longer (another 20 years would be nice). Weighing up both sides made it easier for me to make the decision as I had personally decided that I wanted to at least try and then, if I did fail, at least I would have tried rather than not try at all.

What Were the Barriers to Learning?

My biggest barrier was the fact that as a woman of 47, I had left school with a handful of CSEs which are now obsolete and having no other higher education, only working, experience, how could I attend university? I had watched and supported my own sons and seen all the hard work they had needed to get through their A levels to enable them to go on to university.

Fortunately at Northumbria University there are access courses linked to the work-based learning courses which enabled me to gain Level 3 English Language and Quantitative Mathematics. Both courses ran from March through to December. They were hard work at times, as I was not only attending university for two courses, but my work-based course was started in the April of that first year. This meant that I was attending university for two nights a week with the added pressure of attending a third course every fortnight.

I have to admit that in that first year it was hard to fit in the courses, work every day and have some sort of home life, but the excellent support from my family and work colleagues got me through this hard time. I am very fortunate that funding was never an issue as the course is funded through Newcastle City Council. The only problem I did have was time. It is hard to juggle your time to give family, study, and work the time they each deserve, and have time to yourself.

What Sort of Workplace Do I Come From?

The playgroup is based in a local Church and is a privately-run playgroup. We work as a group of five with me, as Leader, a Deputy and three Assistants. The group is registered for 24 children per session opening five mornings per week. All of the staff are very supportive of each other, which makes it a pleasure going to work. My role as the Leader means that I have to make sure all paperwork is kept up to date, as well as being the front line for any queries. As I like to spend most of my time with the children and not get bogged down with all of the paperwork, I spend long hours at home keeping everything up to date, this means that I that I am never far away from my work.

What Supplements and Tools Did I Use?

The course is work based and all of the work is done away from the university (keeping the motivation is something that I found hard at first). But, by attending the regular sessions and tutorials, it made it easier to stick to deadlines. As a Northumbria University student I have been making full use of the university library, and I find it useful to take my laptop and make use of the study rooms. As my home number is given out to everyone connected to the playgroup I often don't get time to study without any interruptions. Using the quiet rooms enables time to complete my assignments whilst having all the library resources around for information and reference.

As yet I don't think I have fully discovered all the resources that the library has to offer; this is something that I would like to explore further as I continue my university education. By this I mean that the library has many online services which I am gradually learning about, for example, accessing the library catalogue to find the books or journals that are relevant to your thesis. This service can be accessed from your home computer to save you trawling through the many books. In addition to making use of the university library I am building up a stock of books in my own personal collection. I have chosen to buy some books rather that borrow them from the library as they are not only a source of information for my course, but can be used as a long-term resource for the setting.

One advantage of the work-based learning is the close relationship between my colleagues and myself, in particular my chosen work-based advisor. Careful consideration has to be taken when choosing your work-based advisor as you want someone that will support you and also tell you when you are going wrong. This can be a difficult task! Another good source of information that I have used is the Internet. I had a good knowledge of ICT before starting the course and this has definitely supported my learning, making it quicker and easier to find out information.

Did Capturing Workplace Experience Work?

Working in an Early Years setting brings in the need for change. No matter how good your planning is there always has to be room for change, to meet the needs of the children. It is easy to get caught up in choosing a project that you think is relevant and you think the children will need or want, but to fully succeed the children need to help choose what they want. So for my first year I chose an easy option of ICT. Although the research and knowledge I gained covered the theory and legalities, which was valuable for my work as well as the group, I felt that the knowledge I already had prevented me from fully embracing my personal and professional learning.

For my second year I chose a subject that I felt, through observing the children, could be looked at and improved upon. Selecting an area in which I felt I was lacking knowledge and experience has been a valuable learning experience: I chose to make a sensory area/dark den but needed the knowledge to go with it. I therefore chose to complete a course in Special Educational Needs; this has not only fully expanded my own professional development but is helping the group to be fully inclusive.

The two very different work-based projects that I have chosen so far have not only been highly popular with the children but have proved an asset to the group. I definitely feel, from a learning point of view, that choosing something I knew little about made me push to learn as much as I could about it to enable the group to make full use of our new resource as well as giving me the confidence to face any new challenges.

Did the Method of Learning Assessment Work?

The work-based learning course follows a more flexible approach to learning, the portfolio is built up of four different modules. I found that the flexibility of work was right for me. I like to do the research, make notes and then, when I have all the information and resources that I need, I can then complete the module. The flexibility of the course enabled me to work at a pace I could cope with, using my time wisely, but also taking time off for commitments or unplanned events.

Starting studying after so long can be daunting, but what I did find extremely useful was the formative feedback the tutors gave. Each time a piece of work is handed in you receive written feedback. The reason I find this helpful is because if you are on the right lines it reinforces the fact you are heading the right way, but it can also steer you in the right direction or suggest ways to improve you work.

Did the Method of Tutoring Work?

At Northumbria University the course is run on an evening and was therefore easier for me to attend without having problems getting away from work. The course is run on a fortnightly basis and run by two tutors. Throughout the course there has been a good mix of class activities, taught lessons, discussion groups and tutorials and access to lectures. I can only speak on behalf of the course I am attending, but I definitely attribute my enthusiasm for completing the course to the relationships with the tutors and fellow students and the regular emails the tutors send (just letting you know they are around, passing on any relevant information and even to have a moan to). I do feel as though there is a good support network.

What Were the Time Commitments and Balancing Conflicts?

Attending university is not a problem for me as my classes take place in the evening; the only problem I sometimes have is finding the time to do reading and research. As I have previously only worked in the morning, I have made time to go to the university library to have some quiet time to get some study done with no interruptions. The following years are going to be a bit harder as the group is extending the opening hours and I will therefore have to ensure that I tighten up my schedule for learning. Although the course has an amount of flexibility there are still deadlines to keep and the work has to be finished and handed in on time, but I still think it will be comfortably achievable as the understanding of the course does get easier in time, it is just fitting in the research and reading that takes up the time.

One of the valuable skills I have learned is that everyone has a learning skill and to make full use of this you need to find out what kind of learner you are. Sometimes it can be a curse but on the whole building on your skills will improve learning. I have discovered that I am a reflective learner, which means that I learn like someone completing a jigsaw puzzle. I like to find all the pieces and gather them together and then complete the jigsaw. I have found this the most successful way that I work. It does have its disadvantages as it can make it harder to complete within the deadlines if I don't give myself plenty of time to write the module.

Completing the portfolio has presented problems in the sense that most of the learning comes from working with young children, their families or other staff members, and it is vital therefore that the ethics of each situation should be considered. This is especially important when children are involved as adults such as staff or parents can give informed consent to participate, but children can't.

What Were the Outcomes and What Were the Benefits?

At the moment I have just started level 5 of the BA Honour's course and feel a huge sense of achievement at the progress I have made so far. At the time of making the decision to undertake higher education I had a handful of CSEs, and already I have achieved distinctions in both English Language and Quantitative Mathematics, which are both far beyond my own personal expectations. At school my nightmare subject was mathematics and I could not believe when the result was confirmed as a distinction. It just goes to show that with hard work anything can be achieved.

When I look back at the English course I feel that it was a great benefit to not only achieve the right qualification to enable me to attend university, but the work covered during the course has helped me with my writing skills. As it was an access course it covered essays, reports, discursive, reviewing to name a few, these are all writing styles that I have used within my portfolio. I definitely feel that, being out of the office atmosphere for all these years, it was easy to forget how to write as we live in a world of technology where writing skills are not always necessary.

At the beginning of BA Honour's course I still remember being asked to write my goal, what I wanted to achieve from the course. At that time I wrote 'just take one step at a time'. I have taken small steps that have led me further up the ladder and have spurred me on to take bigger steps, and I have reached the point in my learning where instead of saying to myself, 'Why can't that be me?' and, 'It can be me,' I can now say out loud, 'It will be me.'

As a practitioner I now have the confidence that I will achieve my ultimate goal of qualifying as an Early Years Professional within the specified time and therefore ensuring the future of the playgroup way beyond our 21st birthday.

As I now move into another new academic year I feel as though the whole learning experience so far has given me the confidence to accept and adapt to any changes that will come along in the future, whether it is in my professional capacity or my personal goals.

How Much Does it Cost and Who Paid?

I have been very fortunate that the course has been funded through Newcastle City Council as part of an initiative to qualify as an Early Years Professional. This has enabled me to enrol on the course as the playgroup is too small to fund the cost of this training.

More Reading References

Accessing the university library has proven not just valuable to my degree, it has also given me the opportunity to access up-to-date journals and professional magazines, which are relevant to me as a practitioner. This is especially important in childcare as frequent changes are made to legislations and policies. Alongside the library services, the tutors are excellent at keeping you up to date with new ideas and information that comes out on a regular basis as well as giving out well-informed advice.

What are the Lessons Learned?

As an Early Years practitioner I feel that I have not only improved my own knowledge and built on my experience, I have become a more reflective practitioner, I am very aware of the way I observe and reflect on the child's learning, which enables me to fully embrace the Early Years Foundation Stage.

As my own employer, it is sometimes difficult to choose a work-based project, but as I have an excellent support team, we work together to ensure the best outcome for the group and the best for the children.

Being aware of my own learning style enables me to know how I need to work and what information I need to know. I find it helps me to have all of the information in my learning portfolio and this enables me to start collecting and researching from the beginning. I have found that information used in the modules also transfers into the others, which is why I like all of the information from the beginning.

It is vital to prepare yourself for completing a university course, the most important aspect being a good solid support network – by this I mean family, friends, colleagues, fellow students and tutors – with their support anything can be achieved.

18 *Case Study 11: A Wife, Mother, Employee and a Part-time Degree*

My Situation

© Istockphoto / Oleg Prikhodko

This is an autobiographical case study focusing on my experiences of balancing the demands of study for a part-time Masters at Lancaster University with life as a wife, mother and full-time employee.

My qualifications and expertise have been developed over the last 20 years commencing in the Black Country in 1990. During that particular economic downturn I managed to launch my professional career by splitting my week between two unrelated, part-time, temporary contracts of employment. One job was in careers guidance based in Walsall, the other in further education teaching in Dudley. After a few years this led into full-time employment within the Careers Service and my first real opportunity to be supported by my employer to undertake work-based qualifications.

Since those early days I have gone on to achieve many qualifications, some being purely vocational, others are a blend of academic and work-based study. In 1997 my husband, our daughter and I relocated for his employment to the north-west of England. Here I continued to climb the promotional ladder within the Careers Service rising to Senior Manager responsible for staff development. In 2003, I took up my current post at Lancaster University where my main duties involve designing, developing and managing undergraduate programmes of work-based learning. I would describe the job as fairly senior, working within a fast-paced, medium to high-pressure environment.

Whilst I have a wealth of experience as a lifelong learner, given the textbook subject matter I have chosen to focus this case study on my Master of Arts (MA) award. I feel it is important to point out that the university I work for (Lancaster) was also where I undertook my Master's study. Not only that, but it was also delivered by the department I work for (CETAD).

Why I Did it?

Why did I do it? Why did I choose to be in the first cohort of MA students delivered by my own colleagues within my own department? Well, you have to see this as I did, as an opportunity. I had always wanted to gain a Masters, partly because I felt many employers would not recognise my existing qualifications for what they were. I had an Further Education teaching qualification, a postgraduate-level diploma in Careers Guidance, an National Vocational Qualification 4, a certificate in management and a postgraduate certificate in Higher Education teaching; but I still felt that something was missing, something that would give me a really big badge that everyone would understand.

I had been asking my previous employers at various points in my career to support me on a distance-learning Masters and getting nowhere. Suddenly here was an employer willing to provide partial funding and some time off for attendance.

Therefore I guess the motivation was purely personal, to complete what was for me perhaps, unfinished business. I wanted a full Masters, a higher degree. Fortunately for me, my family were willing to support my ambitions and I had finally found an employer who would too.

Would I have undertaken this qualification without the support of my employer? Given that I had been interested for a number of years without putting my ambitions into action, the answer is clearly no. For me there is something about the time and effort being worth it in terms of recognition within the workplace, which is why a work-based Masters particularly appealed to me.

Barriers to Overcome and Access to the Learning Opportunity

In my experience barriers are a matter of perspective; you need to identify them and find ways to either overcome them or get around them. A lot of the time the barriers are self-perceived rather than real. I found that the key things for me in combating such barriers were determination and creative thinking on my part, together with seeking support from others.

If my employer had not partially supported me financially I would not have been able to afford the study. I also needed them to allow me to take 13 days out of the workplace to attend the class-based inputs. As the programme was mainly distance learning I was already donating all of my spare time to the self-study.

In order to negotiate my support package with my employer I firstly established what was involved in the programme, what I would be contributing in terms of my own time, effort and finances and therefore what I would ideally like my employer to contribute. I had also given considerable thought as to the business benefits my employer would be likely to gain from supporting me within the process and ultimately from my achievement of the award. Naturally I needed to persuade them that there was something in this for them as well as for me.

I strongly believe family come first and therefore I had to gain the support of my husband and daughter before I would even consider undertaking any further study. They had after all supported my ongoing study over many years and I would have understood if they had not been willing to give up some of their valuable time with me. So how did I get them onboard? Over the years I had shared my frustrations of not having the opportunity to undertake a Masters; of feeling that I had the ability but not the confidence to progress; feeling I had reached my career ceiling; just wanting the 'big badge' for my own personal goal. They did understand and they were excited for me, they wanted me to achieve my goal even though this meant further sacrifices for them.

Once on the programme there were days when I desperately wanted to throw in the towel; when I worried about putting in lots of hard work and still not achieving my goal; when I was scared of failure; when I was tired and just wanted it all to be over. My support networks of family, work colleagues and my peer group of fellow students all helped to keep me going through those lonely days of uncertainty and self-doubt. These are times when your gut determination and the want of your personal goal need to kick in; I found that this together with support from my network enabled me to plod on.

The Workplace Environment

My employer, Lancaster University, is a large campus-based university ranked very highly within the UK. It is undeniably a lovely place to work, with modern buildings with views of the countryside. Colleagues are generally fair minded, supportive and helpful. The pace of my job is rapid and the pressure is fairly high and there is no downtime or slack periods of the year; therefore all of the study for the MA other than the class attendance had to be to be undertaken in my own time.

Whilst I had easy access to the library and computer facilities, the downside to my work location is the nine hours of weekly motorway commuting, which frequently gets extended by traffic issues on the M6.

The Supplements to Workplace Experience Used

The Masters that I undertook was work-based blended learning. Blended learning involved undertaking a mixture of distance learning, self-study and class-based attendance. The class-based days consisted of action learning sessions where the tutor would give us a short input and then we would discuss our learning within our student peer group. There was also a 30–40 minute time allocation to meet with your personal tutor on a one-to-one basis to discuss your progress and your personal learning needs. The majority of the learning content was delivered via distance e-learning inputs including a student/tutor discussion forum. In addition to this, as with most courses, you were expected to read and research around the topic area in preparation for your class-based day.

This method of delivery had mixed blessings, on the one hand it allowed me to access the programme as class-based attendance was minimal. However, it could be frustrating if your peer group had not done their homework prior to the delivery day, as this limited their input and therefore it consequently limited your outcomes from the day. The e-learning discussion forum was also a lonely, isolated place, viewed from a distance by all but rarely entered for discussion.

My own peer group decided to meet separately one evening per month in addition to class attendance. This was invaluable to me as it allowed me access to a learning environment outside of work, away from my department and my working colleagues. The camaraderie from my peer group also kept me going at times when the going was tough, they helped me to see the alternative perspectives that very often minimised the perceived problem.

The Method of Capture of Workplace Experience (for example, Project Dissertation)

Assessment was wholly via written coursework, mainly consisting of essay-based assignments plus a 30,000 word dissertation. The essays considered how particular theories and concepts applied to your own workplace. In practice this involved taking an in-depth look at various aspects of work, deconstructing the situation, analysing it against theory and vice versa. The final stage was then suggesting how you might use your new learning to resolve particular scenarios or to develop new areas of practice.

The thought of attempting the 30,000 word dissertation was scary and the limited timescale within which it had to be done was terrifying. Not only that but I was in the first cohort so this was new territory to my department, CETAD. This meant there was no one I could talk to who had gone before and could say how it might be done or even to say that it could be done. The dissertation was based on establishing a project at work and then undertaking research and evaluation around it including researching and evaluating the research methods themselves. We were allocated a research project supervisor to support us in this piece of work. Each student could access their supervisor for a set number of one-hour sessions, I can't recall how many sessions but I certainly used up my allocation. It helped my morale tremendously to hear that my supervisor thought my plans for undertaking the work were feasible and that I was on track to meet the deadline.

The Method of Learning Assessment, Did it Work?

For me, the methods of assessment worked particularly well as they allowed me to explore new insights and perspectives on existing problems that occurred within my job. Not only could I work through them to resolve them but it gave me more confidence in tackling such problems. So unexpectedly for me, the job didn't seem as stressful anymore.

For the dissertation I undertook a project that directly involved volunteers from CETAD staff and also mature students from the study programmes that I am responsible for. I did at times feel guilty that I might be using up too much of their valuable time to further my own interests and goals. However, in reality what I found was that they wanted to help me, they wanted to be involved and the students particularly enjoyed being part of my research. I did have concerns that I was in a position of authority and influence over my students and therefore ethical consent had to be gained prior to the launch of the research project. Within this I had to reassure the university and the students that the opportunity to be involved was purely voluntary and that opting in or out at any stage of the process would have no prejudicial consequences for the students.

The timing of the research project was problematic as this coincided with a particularly busy period at work; however, other than taking a year out of study to combat this issue, there was nothing else that I could do. So for me, I decided to ride the storm and battle on. This was stressful because balancing the demands of the project, my study, life and work was difficult and as a result time got squeezed from the project. Now when I look back this didn't really matter as the effects did not jeopardise the project nor my study, it was just very frustrating at the time.

The Method of Mentoring or Tutoring

I'm not sure that there was any mentoring, however, the project supervision may be close to that. As a method of support it was excellent and allowed me one-to-one time with my supervisor to consider the issues, concerns and questions I had in relation to my project. My supervisor also checked chapters of my final dissertation to ensure that she felt I was covering the learning outcomes as I went along.

The Time Commitment and Study Style of the Individual, Balancing Conflicting Demands

Balancing conflicting demands for me was a matter of self-discipline, creative thinking, artful negotiation and prioritising with precision. Time was the biggest issue, therefore, before I commenced each stage of my Masters study I found myself thinking carefully about how I spent my time and where and when I had unused pockets of time. This included negotiating with others to change the way in which they approached tasks in order to free time up for myself which I could then use to study. Also breaking down all my tasks including study, housework, exercise and so on into bite-sized chunks in order to keep progressing on each task no matter how slowly. The final trick was to closely monitor all tasks, reprioritising as I went in order to avoid imminent meltdown when the unexpected inevitably cropped up. The concept may sound technical but in reality it is about making simple adjustments, for example, I persuaded my husband to order the shopping online whilst I stood in the same room doing the ironing; that way we were together getting two jobs done in less time. Also when he watched something on TV that I did not like, I didn't complain, I just got my books out and did some reading. I also blended my study into my life, for me I do not like spending long hours studying and in reality I only had the weekends to undertake the distance learning. Therefore I settled into a routine breaking my study into short blocks of two–four hours each, interspersed around set times for family, exercise and housework and so on The self-discipline came in when I was perhaps into a part of my essay or study that required more time, but when my study allocation was up I had to pack my things away.

The Outcome and Benefits

There have definitely been many benefits, more than I first imagined there would be. CETAD and the university gained immediate feedback on the rollout of their new MA and as a result made a few adjustments to the programme as they went along. I am more confident and therefore more able to take on greater challenges within my work. I have been able to put a lot of my learning directly into practice within my team utilising my knowledge to shape our BA and Foundation degree programmes. Through items like this case study my work is helping to raise the profile of my department, highlighting our role in developing and gaining recognition for work-based learning.

Costs, Who Pays and Balance Between Cash and Kind

The cost was split between myself and my employer, with them paying about two-thirds of the overall cost. Time off was given for the 13 full-day workshops and I was also allowed a few days out of work time to undertake the research project.

Lessons Drawn from the Case in Terms of:

How to access this type of learning opportunity?
After many years of trying to access this type of provision I found that building a business case and presenting it to my employer certainly helped them to understand what they would potentially gain from supporting my study.

What should the employer provide?
The minimum requirement for work-based learning is that your employer or voluntary placement is able and willing to provide you with relevant work experience to enable you to undertake the study. Other than this what they and you agree to provide is entirely negotiable between you and them, the final decision comes down to what you are prepared to accept.

What should the awarding body provide?
The awarding body, in my case the university, need to be clear over which particular work-based experiences and contexts you will need to be operating in, in order to support your study. For example, experience of managing a work-based change was important on the programme I undertook. However, as I had not previously been involved in designing a change process this aspect was new to me, but my employer provided me with the opportunity to undertake this.

How to Prepare Yourself for this Type of Learning

There are four things that I feel are important when preparing for this type of learning:

- Establish who your allies are and work with them in partnership to establish what kinds of support they can and will offer you. This includes members of your family, your employer, your colleagues at work, your friends and so on. Then when you need some help and support make sure you ask for it, don't wait to get stressed out.
- Time management is essential and, therefore, work out in advance where your spare pockets of time are and how you might want to use them. Also work with your allies to establish how you can release more time by allowing them to help you. I had a plan for the week, everyone was clear on how it would work and I (we) stuck to it.

- Find a study place and set it up ready to go. Mine was a large plastic box by the side of the settee where I kept my textbooks, pens and paper. I also had a foldaway desk in the spare room where I kept my old laptop computer and printer. You really do not need to spend lots of money on equipment and books, use your student discount card, buy reliable second-hand, borrow where you can and also maximise your use of the library. You might find that you employer may lend you an old computer or contribute to the cost of purchasing textbooks.
- Commitment is also required, when you feel tired and like giving up, just dig your heels in and get on with it. Believe me, when you have achieved your target qualification you will feel great.

More Reading/References

A few of the texts that I accessed which helped to develop my understanding and skills within higher education Masters level, work-based learning are:

Higher Level Learning

Kolb, D. A. (1984) *Experiential Learning*. New Jersey: Prentice Hall PTR.
Schon, D. A. (1991) *The Reflective Practitioner How Professionals Think in Action*. Aldershot: Ashgate.
Symes, C and McIntyre, J. (eds). (2000) *Working Knowledge, The New Vocationalism and Higher Education*. Buckingham: SRHE and Open University Press.

Undertaking Research Projects

Bell, J. (1999) *Doing Your Research Project, 3rd Ed*. Maidenhead: Open University.
Robson, C. (2000) *Small-Scale Evaluation Principles and Practice*, London: Sage.

19 *Case Study 12: McDonalds and Achieving a Foundation Degree*

Learner Situation

© Istockphoto / Bonnie Schupp

My situation is that I am 37 and married with two children. I started working at McDonalds in 1989 when I was 16. It was just a part-time job to earn money while I was at school doing A levels. My A levels were OK and got me into Leeds University to study chemical engineering. I was very interested in chemical engineering but I found the theory side of the university course very hard. I like doing practical things and the university course really didn't suit me. So I decided to drop out at the end of the first year. I had kept in touch with McDonalds and went back to them on a full-time basis. The idea was I would stay with them for a short period while I looked for a proper job. The job with McDonalds worked very well and I got promoted again and again. In about a year I was earning as much money as I would have done as a graduate chemical engineer. So I just decided to stay there.

I stayed with McDonalds, working part time for a couple of years when I had children, but about 3 years ago I went back to being full time and got promoted to Store Manager. McDonalds has a very extensive programme of staff training courses and a large training department. I had been on a number of company courses as part of the career progression to step up to each new level but the McDonalds degree was something completely different.

Motivation for Doing the Course

My regional manager basically selected me to take part in the trial of the McDonalds degree course and I thought this was a brilliant idea. I had dropped out of university when I was younger and this was a chance to go back. If I didn't take this chance I would probably never get another opportunity. Working full time, it is not often you get the chance to do something like getting a degree. I had felt bad about dropping out of university – it was like I was a reject – and I had thought about getting back to university. I had looked at OU courses but somehow I had never got round to it. I had always enjoyed learning and going on courses, and I had been reading books on management styles. So this opportunity was right up my street.

Looking back, I don't think I was ready for university when I first went. I had maths and chemistry A level but they weren't strong enough to help me cope with the theory side of the course. It was all books and theory but I am more of a practical hands-on learner. The course gave me the opportunity to study at higher education-level based on my practical experience in the workplace.

McDonalds gave me the opportunity to learn things in the real world, like stock control, managing people, health and safety, payroll, staff training, human resource management and so on. You do have to have quite a broad knowledge base as a business manager but you also learn a lot about yourself through work. When I started working I thought that managing people was just about telling them what to do. I now know how to involve people in decision making. When there is a problem and we need to change the way we are doing something I get my managers together and we brainstorm the possibilities. If they come up with the answers then they will believe them and get behind what needs to be done in store. I always find the best ideas come from group discussions. This is how you build up your skills. You don't get this by working on your own with books.

Course Structure

The course was run by McDonalds staff with a couple of Manchester Metropolitan University (MMU) staff there to monitor what was going on. They were really just there to check and didn't do any teaching.

The course started with a launch at the university where we all registered as students. We were all given our student cards and library passes, and we had lectures on how to use the learning resources. This was very helpful because using the online library and resources was something new. The event was managed by McDonalds and it went extremely well. It was a very smooth and easy introduction to the university.

A lot of the course was done through e-learning. This was very easy as the materials were very visual. Things like screenshots of schedules followed by questions about how things should work. This format was good because it kept your interest. We also had work books that guided you through exercises to find out things about your business and gather data. We then analysed the data, drew conclusions and wrote up an action plan. The workbooks were the practical application exercises while the e-learning dealt more with theory.

We had an assigned tutor from the McDonalds training department, and there were conference calls every four weeks. McDonalds were always asking for feedback on how things were working. The tutor was always available to answer questions and you could email him if you were having problems. We didn't have any contact with university teaching staff or any university tutor but there were two university staff who sat in when we were doing group exercises or presenting our workbook exercises. However, they were there to check that the McDonalds' trainers were marking our work to the correct standard. They had all spent some time in store understanding what we did and I think that was very helpful for them in their role.

We did have development weekends when we would work on case studies for a theoretical store. It was quite funny at one point because in the middle of an exercise where we were ranking staff for 'in selections' process, suddenly there was an urgent request from the boss to do something quite different. The university staff thought this was very unfair and were saying to the McDonalds' trainers – 'You can't do that! You can't throw in another task while they are in the middle of the first task.' But we told them that this is what life in the business world is like. You get situations like this every hour. You have to cope with doing two things at once and having priorities that change. The university assessors thought McDonalds were being very harsh but we thought it was just what we do day to day.

Peer Support

Four of us knew each other quite well and we helped each other quite a lot. We compared notes and so on. Then, when we had the eight days of intensive study, all the people on the course stayed together in an environment like the 'big brother house'. We all made good friends with each other and it really helped the learning. There were staff from franchise stores as well as company stores which gave a different perspective. The eight days were to help us complete our reports and do the presentations and it really worked well having everyone together working to a deadline.

Time Commitment

Some of the coursework was done in company time, for example, the data collection in stores and the assessment exercises, but a lot was done in personal time – maybe six hours per week. We also had two residential training periods- one of three days and one of eight days. We were doing the course in just five months as opposed to the normal 14 months, so it is possible that when the course is run next time the time commitment will be more spread out.

It was a bit difficult balancing family time with the coursework, sometimes it required using 'middle of the night' time! Because I do different shift times it was relatively easy to fit the coursework in without the family time suffering. However, there were times when you were rushing to finish a piece of work and things became difficult. I think I got much better at time management as a result of the course.

Assessment

We started the course with an APEL exercise which covered much of the level 4 work. This was a bit nerve racking. It's not easy to write about your experience. We had to do a power point presentation and provide notes to go with the presentation. It was rather daunting standing up and presenting. Then there were questions from the examiner. But actually it was quite informal and was OK. All in all it took about one working day to prepare the

APEL report and present it and I think it accounted for 30 per cent of the course. So it was a worthwhile exercise.

The assessment of the coursework was mainly through reports on the workbook exercises. Normally, a couple of the modules were combined into one assessment report. The report contained references to the source documents, the data and the conclusions of the analysis. They were like small research projects where we were collecting and presenting evidence and conclusions. It took two or three days to do each report. I found this quite a good way to do the assessment, particularly when the conclusions were presented as action plans and the evidence could be put as bullet points. However, I would have benefited from going on a report-writing course first.

Learnings From the Course

I found that a lot of the things we learnt in the modules confirmed what I already knew. I had been making decisions based on experience and intuition but when I worked through the modules I found they led me to the same decisions. You look at each store as a business and gather all your data about the store and analyse the data to see what the outcomes are. Nine times out of ten the analysis gave the same conclusion I would have reached through experience. I felt that the level 4 stuff we did was a bit below the level we were already operating at. However, the level 5 stuff was more challenging and introduced new stuff like corporate responsibility, business planning and marketing. I had never thought about these areas before and they gave me a new perspective on the business. It was like I was looking at the business from the outside, which is something I had never done before. I really enjoyed what I was learning. I had always thought that customers just turned up, so thinking about marketing and what you need to do to get customers to turn up was really interesting.

Part way through the course I moved to a new store so had the opportunity to apply all the things I have learned. I used to go into a new store and just accept things as they were, maybe changing one or two things. This time I decided I would observe what was going on and understand how everything was working before making a decision on anything. McDonalds is a very fast-paced business so normally you just dive in as fast as you can. The course taught me to stand back and reflect on what was happening, and then analyse what I should do. It's definitely a new skill that the course has taught me.

Benefits

The most obvious benefit from the course is that my business results have improved which has helped me out in my career. When I had my performance review at the year-end I was rated highly and hopefully I will more on to a higher-profile store. I also feel more confident in my business decisions and I seem to prioritise and manage time better. My management of staff has improved. I now feel I'm their leader rather than being their boss.

I also feel very proud at completing the course. It's quite a challenge to go back to learning after so many years. If I am honest felt a bit of a reject for having dropped out of university when all my friends had gone on and completed. My parents were very supportive when I dropped out of university and encouraged me to follow whatever career worked for me. They are so proud of the fact I have gone back and got the degree. People at McDonalds are all asking about the course and it is exciting to be in the first group that has done this.

Final Thoughts

Looking back there were difficulties balancing family commitments but I would not change a thing. If you had told me how much effort it was going to be at the start I would still have done it. It was well worth the effort. I enjoyed the challenge and it was challenging enough without being too challenging. I'm now thinking about topping this off by going on to get an Honour's degree.

I don't think we missed out by not being at the university campus. The first day when we went to the university we felt so out of place. I don't think the university could have offered us much that we couldn't have got from McDonalds anyway. All the e-resources were available through McDonalds and at least you could use the photocopier without hassle!

20 *Case Study Lessons*

JOHN MUMFORD

The purpose of the case studies is to explore work-based learning by discovering what those in employment experienced when they attempted to gain a higher education qualification. The case studies are individual narratives with minimum guidance on the issues discussed. This chapter extracts from the narrative the important observations grouped into issues. These are then discussed in the summary and conclusion.

Background and Motivation

The main motivation for undertaking an accredited university programme appears to be the status of a qualification:

- 'I had already been on staff college 'Command' courses and on internal and external leadership training of various sorts. Some of this had been at a fairly advanced level, but it hadn't been accredited in any particular way, so I still felt at a disadvantage compared to my graduate colleagues.' (case 2)
- 'I recognised that I needed a formal degree in business/computing to assist my job role by being better academically trained to carry out my computer audit role... I had a need to climb out of generalist grades into more technical roles and eventually professional ones... I took a risk and it paid great results.' (case 5)
- 'I had always wanted to gain a Masters partly because I felt many employers would not recognise my existing qualifications for what they were.' (case 11)

However for some the personal challenge was equally important:

- 'I was very aware that IT positions within the public sector generally require a qualification at degree level and as such, regardless of experience, candidates without a degree were unlikely to even reach the interview stage. My lack of degree therefore put an invisible but very real ceiling on my career. More importantly, on a personal level, I felt that without a degree I had not achieved my academic potential which was something that I was determined to change. I wanted to test myself and stretch myself academically.' (case 8)
- 'Not being a graduate has not concerned me and has not knowingly affected my career adversely, but I was keen to underpin the knowledge and practical experience I had gained over the years by obtaining formal qualifications which would also assist in my personal development.' (case 1)
- I had left school with a hand full of CSEs which are now obsolete and having no other higher education, only working experience, how could I attend university... but I suddenly started thinking 'It can be me.' (case 10)
- 'Working full time it is not often you get the chance to do something like getting a degree.' (case 12)

Some regarded the qualification as less significant and were motivated by academic challenge:

- 'I was starting to feel that my own professional knowledge was aging and that in many cases I was trading on past achievements rather than creating new professional knowledge. It was for this reason that I started to look for opportunities for postgraduate study.' (case 7)
- 'I was handling issues such as public outrage which made no sense to me at all and I felt I needed to know why the world behaved so irrationally.' (case 4)
- 'I wanted to extend my knowledge base further and use the terminology used by senior industry professionals.' (case 1)

In three cases the driver was business need:

- 'I intend to grow my business. To enable me to do this, I felt that whilst I could buy business expertise in most areas it would beneficial both to the business and to myself if I broadened my own abilities.' (case 1)
- 'The decision to study was made for me! I was required to join a new professional register for social services workers. The register is qualification-based and despite having qualified 30 years previously and completed a post-qualifying degree nine years later, I was now required to complete a new qualification in the regulation of health and social care.' (case 6)
- 'My regional manager basically selected me.' (case 12)

In summary, the motivation in these cases seems to be related to feelings of self-worth and a desire to advance ones existing career path. There is no evidence of workplace learning being used as a vehicle for 'job-hopping' which is a concern for employers. This matters because so many employers fear that staff returning to academic study is a sign they are preparing to exit. The message that may be derived from this is that employers can increase staff motivation and job performance by creating a working environment that encourages and recognises workplace learning.

The Barriers Faced and the Level of Commitment Needed

One of the most striking aspects of the cases is the level of commitment by the learners, family support and the sacrifice of personal time. All the individuals remarked that the study took over their lives:

- 'I used to think I was very good at time management but I have progressed several levels further.' (case 1)
- 'I used to get up at 5am and do a couple of hours study before going in to work.' (case 1)
- 'I worked long hours to make up for lost time and sometimes this involved working seven days a week.' (case 2)
- 'The most useful time was 5am on a winters' Sunday morning, slightly mad but guaranteed no distractions, all apart from an over helpful cat.' (case 3)

- 'Time and other commitments, at work, at home and in the community were all very real barriers... I did work on the bus coming into work in the morning when I decided to travel by that mode of transport. Lunchtimes became 20 minute sessions of reading, early evening was an hour here or there, in short, whenever I could find time, and had the will, I opened my books.' (case 5)
- Tiredness and other distractions would conspire to prevent me from getting on with study and especially hindered my reading. Many times I put down a book after realising I had been staring at the same page for half an hour!' (case 6)
- Fortunately for me my family were willing to support my ambitions and I had finally found an employer who would too... I persuaded my husband to order the shopping online whilst I stood in the same room doing the ironing; that way we were together getting two jobs done in less time.' (case 11)

This commitment was seen by many as a serious barrier:

- 'The biggest barrier was around the unknown time commitment to undertake the study over two years and how this would impact on my family life... I would have to wait until my son was in bed before I could start work on the pressing essay of the term!' (case 9)
- 'The biggest barrier, for me, was definitely time and to be honest the amount of studying that was required far exceeded the recommended study time advertised by the college.' (case 8)
- 'The pressures, particularly during the periods when my three project reports were in preparation, were considerable. They resulted in my wife claiming to this day that she should have been awarded half an MBA.' (case 2)
- 'I have to admit that in that first year it was hard to fit in the courses, work every day and have some sort of home life, but the excellent support from my family and work colleagues got me through this hard time.' (case 10)
- 'I found that the key things for me in combating such barriers were determination and creative thinking on my part, together with seeking support from others... Time management is essential and, therefore, work out in advance where your spare pockets of time are and how you might want to use them.' (case 11)

There were also comments about the practicalities of scheduling work and academic requirements:

- 'One aspect of university life is the relatively long periods of inactivity from the university where you have to prepare for work yourself and the frantic short period where you have constructive access to your advisor.' (case 3)
- 'You cannot plan to be free at pre-arranged times. Thus, while there would be days where I could happily spend time in the office researching for my thesis, there were days when I was working round the clock and could not conceivably spend a minute thinking about academic work.' (case 4)
- 'The minimum requirement for work-based learning is that your employer or voluntary placement is able and willing to provide you with relevant work experience to enable you to undertake the study.' (case 11)

The over-riding message is that accredited work-based learning is an 'extreme' commitment:

- 'Work-based learning is the most extreme form of this particular form of masochism, you have no routine or spoon-fed content and exercises to fall back on. The subject matter, mode of enquiry, research design, and problem specification are all in your own hands. Yes you get advice and help but ultimately the buck stops with you.' (case 7)
- 'This had a massive impact on my home life, leaving me little time for leisure activities, relaxing, and seeing my family.' (case 8)
- 'I would advise anyone who is thinking of doing a similar course to make sure that both they and their families are fully aware of the time commitments.' (case 8)
- 'The first lesson would be not to take this on lightly; it is something that has to be right for you and your employer.' (case 9)
- 'One's free time is supposed to be when the brain switches off and you relax. However, if you are doing a serious accredited programme this has to be the time the brain switches up a gear.' (case 4)
- 'When you feel tired and like giving up, just dig your heels in and get on with it. Believe me, when you have achieved your target qualification you will feel great.' (case 11)

However there was one case where the time commitment was not viewed as onerous and this was the case with the most proactive employer involvement:

- 'It was relatively easy to fit the coursework in without the family time suffering.' (case 12)

Work-based learners are in a very different situation to full-time students is the immediate message. Everyone mentioned time pressure as a major constraint but no one mentioned money as an issue. These learners are cash rich and time poor (the reverse of a normal student population) and this means their needs are very different as we see below. There is a risk however that university regard these part-time students as second class and employers see them as 'shirkers'. The evidence suggests these are people battling against the odds and both employers and universities need to recognise the magnitude of the commitment they make. It demonstrates high levels of personal management, organisational ability, independence, self-motivation and determination, the ideal characteristics of a higher education student. There is also the hint that proactive employer engagement is a potential solution.

Support from Tutors and Mentors

All chosen cases mention the importance of mentoring and the empathy with lecturers and tutors:

- 'Most of the tutors came from an industrial background and so they had lots of real, hands-on work experience. This proved to be extremely useful as they were able to relate theories to real world examples... I feel that it is extremely important for work-based learning courses to have lecturers who have come into academia only after a business career, so that they can bridge the gap between theory and reality.' (case 8)

- 'One of the best tools for my learning was one particular tutor on the course... I could give drafts of my essays via email and get some really useful feedback and detailed comments for me to rework the drafts.' (case 9)
- 'At times I felt completely lost but my tutor was able to drag out of the embers of a resent [resubmitted] project.' (case 3)
- 'He was an excellent mentor and guided me as I found my own way. He was infinitely encouraging; praising work that I later realised was rubbish, and giving me prods when I needed them.' (case 4)
- 'It helped my morale tremendously to hear that my supervisor thought my plans for undertaking the work were feasible and that I was on track to meet the deadline.' (case 11)
- '[The academic staff] had all spent some time in store understanding what we did and I think that was very helpful for them in their role.' (case 12)
-

However, for some the tutors and lecturers failed to meet expectations:

- 'Another obstacle...was the lack of practical business experience shown by some of the lecturers. Some had never worked outside academia and although most were great whilst imparting academic knowledge some seemed unable to relate academic information to a business environment in a practical context..' (case 1)
- 'When you have already spent 12 hours that day working as a managing director you don't want to sit in a room being lectured by someone who doesn't know how the business world functions.' (case 1)
- 'At the OU, I considered that my tutors really did not have a great understanding of the subject matter; they discussed the subjects but really did not have a great in-depth knowledge.' (case 5)
- 'In one case the whole group actually put in a complaint about a tutor because his teaching was so poor.' (case 8)

Even when the academic support was judged good, there were issues of continuity:

- 'It would have been very good to have had a university tutor to guide me all the way through the course.' (case 1)
- 'I would have liked to have had a personal tutor who worked with me throughout the course – somebody with whom I could have built a relationship and worked through my ongoing study issues – however this was not available.' (case 8)

There were mixed messages about workplace tutors and support:

- 'There was no mentoring support in the workplace. So it was up to me to make sure that I did not let my academic work interfere with my employment and keep it low profile.' (case 4)
- 'The [workplace tutor] role is partly one of "how is it going" and "make sure that you are keeping up with the study". It is not formal. There is no guidance. There is no

training or evaluation of the quality of mentoring. In many ways this is an area for improvement.' (case 5)

- '[The tutor's] view was, "I don't fully understand what all this is about, I don't really have time to get involved, but I'm willing to help where I can, so tell me when I have to do something or say something and if it involves writing something, write it for me."' (case 2)
- 'We had an assigned tutor, from the McDonalds training department and there were conference calls every four weeks. The tutor was always available to answer questions and you could email him if you were having problems.' (case 12)

Several cases emphasise the importance of the learner being able to choose their own tutor:

- 'I chose my tutor on the basis of his mentoring skill. In fact I had turned down the opportunity to go to a more prestigious university and study under an expert in the field because I recognised that I would need a lot of help with the basics.' (case 4)
- 'Choose your supervisor; don't have one appointed to you.' (case 7)
- 'One advantage to the work-based learning is the close relationship between my colleagues and myself, in particular my chosen work-based advisor.' (case 10)

This highlights the importance of tutors and the choice of tutor is often personal. Tutors must be familiar with the workplace, have continuity of relationship, emphasise with the learner, and take their role seriously. Mentoring is equally important in terms of balancing work and study as well as providing unaligned support and advice. These issues are explored in Chapter 6.

Support From Peers and Networks

One of the most positive experiences reported by all learners was the support provided by peers on the programme:

- 'One of the things I really gained from the programme was having a group of peers that I could discuss my business problems with… I needed the regular physical contact with the class.' (case 1)
- 'Establish who your allies are and work with them in partnership to establish what kinds of support they can and will offer you.' (case 11)
- 'Sometimes the action learning set just became a 'mutual appreciation club!' where we just built up each others' confidence when we were feeling low and that it was all getting a bit too hard for us.' (case 9)
- 'My own peer group decided to meet separately one evening per month in addition to class attendance. This was invaluable to me as it allowed me access to a learning environment outside of work, away from my department and my working colleagues. The camaraderie from my peer group also kept me going at times when the going was tough, they helped me to see the alternative perspectives that very often minimised the perceived problem.' (case 11)

- 'I needed to build a network of friends and other work contacts who could act as advisers and mentors.' (case 1)
- 'Be prepared to take constructive criticism. Your peers may avoid offering advice, because they want to avoid causing offence, but this will do you no favours in the long run.' (case 3)
- 'All the people on the course stayed together in an environment like the 'big brother house'.... it really helped the learning.' (case 12)

There were diverse views about e-based alternatives to physical face-time:

- 'The e-learning discussion forum was also a lonely, isolated place, viewed from a distance by all but rarely entered for discussion.' (case 11)
- 'The other fantastic thing about the Internet is the creation of a virtual tutorial group where we could have discussions and share our experiences from the comfort of our own home. Sometimes these discussions were instigated by our tutors but often by us as students.' (case 6)

Many of the case studies highlight the learning that can be achieved through interaction with peers with different backgrounds:

- 'The programme was very action learning-orientated, we were all assigned to action learning sets, in each case comprising a cross-section of about six participants from different backgrounds and employment situations.' (case 2)
- 'I found it very helpful to compare experiences with others who had different jobs. It really broadened my business understanding.' (case 1)
- 'The wide variety of students on the course provided a lively wealth of knowledge and expertise in different areas for us all to learn from, and in some cases led us to thank our lucky stars for the organisations we worked in!' (case 9)

It is clear from the observations of the case study learners that a physical engagement in a community is vital to the learning experience. In some cases it was nurtured as a classroom interaction, but others achieved it through Internet chat groups. However, all cases found it important to cultivate a group of peers both formal and informal, who could support and criticise – critical friends.

Support From the University Administration and Facilities

All the cases are positive about the overall learner experience but the administration and facility support area is consistently criticised:

- 'I personally felt that there was little consideration given to part time students. Most of us were working full time in addition to our studies and therefore the need to manage time effectively was critical.' (case 1)
- 'The school and course were badly organised and eventually we abandoned ship.' (case 2)

Some of the case study learners recognised the problem but put a more constructive gloss on the situation:

- 'I found it essential to build a constructive relationship with both the academic staff of the university and that of the background administration staff. There has been more than one occasion where the administration staff worked hard on my behalf to keep me on track.' (case 3)

The level of resources provided by the university seemed to generally disappoint, particularly the library facilities:

- 'I had had this image that I would be working at the university, using the library, going to odd lectures and mingling with other academics. Nothing could be further from the truth.' (case 4)
- 'Although the university had its own library, it was approximately 400 miles away and I never did work out how to access it online and locate the resources I wanted! I have to admit, I gave up fairly quickly as my employers have a subscription for IDOX, a business library service, which provided a more user-friendly and very prompt service.' (case 6)
- 'I visited the libraries frequently as my course required me to refer constantly to the relevant text books but I often found that the books I needed were either not available or were not part of the library catalogue and so I had to buy quite a few of the key books for myself.' (case 8)
- 'Most of the books I needed were not stocked by the university library and I was encouraged to use the inter-library service and the British Library. But borrowing books and papers this way was very complicated and time consuming with paper dockets having to be countersigned and posted backwards and forwards.' (case 4)
- 'I don't think the university could have offered us anything we couldn't have got from McDonalds anyway.' (case 12)

There was a contrast drawn between universities and some professional bodies or employers:

- 'The Institute of Internal Audit do offer student assistance by a range of means. There is a web-based knowledge centre where students can access a library of technical topics, audit position statements and current thinking on a wide range of the exam topics. There is also a forum where questions can be asked and a range of auditors and students respond to give a wider view of the issue.' (case 5)
- 'The (induction) event was managed by McDonalds and it went extremely well. It was a very smooth an easy introduction to the university.' (case 12)

Often the university administration is not sufficiently adequate for the needs of those in full-time employment, the work-based learner:

- 'The stated aim of the course was to be able to communicate at a business level but many aspects of the way the courses were run did not function at that level of professionalism.' (case 1)

- 'No wonder degrees take so long. Most of the time is spent trying to find your way round the university IT system, figure out how to log on the multiplicity of online databases, and then do it all over again because the data link has dropped out. University IT systems are definitely a barrier to learning!' (case 4)

The lesson from these comments is that work-based learners are often in high-pressure jobs and are used to having support systems that work efficiently. What's more they are willing to pay for these systems. Systems which may be adequate for full-time three-year undergraduate courses are clearly not designed to recognise the needs of a learner balancing work, study and social life where time is at a premium – the time poor, cash rich syndrome. It seems that professional bodies may be better attuned to these requirements and, when properly equipped to do so, employers can provide much help in this area.

Engaging with the Learning Style

Most of the case studies make reference to the challenge of getting used to the academic style of learning, writing, and assessment:

- 'I had no experience of higher education and didn't have any idea how to do research or academic study. I had to learn this at the start of the course.' (case 1)
- 'An area I found interesting was having to use 'academic speak', where it was necessary to utilise longer words to put your point across in an elaborated language.' (case 9)

The cases highlighted that those in full-time employment need help learning how to study:

- 'The lecturers seem to presume experience in academic study, which implied they knew little about the student attending their lectures!.' (case 1)
- 'I received no direction or guidance from within the organisation, with it being signalled that the choice of what I focused on was entirely mine.' (case 2)
- 'As it was so relevant to my work I felt much more involved with this module and benefited directly and immediately from my studies... However, I did struggle to grasp a lot of the theories that were referred to and how they translated back to my real-life workplace experiences.' (case 8)

There is a fundamental issue of academic thought prioritisation which many find hard to reconcile:

- 'When you're used to cutting to the chase and driving towards conclusions as quickly as possible in a business environment it can take a while to get used to the academic way of theorizing and arguing every case.' (case 8)
- 'The ruthless prioritising of a perceived problem and working a resolution as soon as possible is what the company requires. The university response to a typical problem would be to analyse and then reflect on that analysis to see what has been learnt and how I as an individual and the company have learnt from this process. This in

reality is a timeline I would rarely have afforded to me during a normal working day.' (case 3)
- 'My job was in the culture of a large international business corporation. It was all about ruthless prioritisation and cutting through issues quickly to get to the nub of an issue. A quick concise answer to a problem was all that was ever needed and debating options and arguments tended to get you classed as a dreamer. However, in the academic world all people care about is exploring the options and arguments. The answer often appears to be irrelevant. Managing your brain so that it handles these very different thought processes is tricky.' (case 4)

The situation is mirrored when academic staff found themselves working with learning processes designed by employers:

- 'The university staff thought this was very unfair and were saying to the McDonalds' trainers – "You can't do that! You can't throw in another task while they are in the middle of the first task." But we told them that this is what life in the business world is like.' (case 12)

This style conflict is perhaps epitomised by the different meanings of 'academic' in the workplace and the university. In the university world it is concerned with a well-structured and argued analysis while in the workplace it dismisses an idea as an irrelevant daydream. The lesson here is that learners in full-time employment have been trained in a type of problem solving which is very different to academic thought and support in understanding the academic approach is needed from the outset for any work-based learner undertaking a higher education qualification. Personal development planning modules are available in some universities which are designed to address this issue.

Linking Back to the Workplace

Several cases highlight the importance of a constructive relationship between employer and employee:

- 'My Line Manager and Operations Director were both very supportive and opened information doors for me, as and when required.' (case 3)
- 'It is vital that you have an employer who can clearly see the benefits of your study to the job and the organisation you work within, this in turn means they will be more supportive as they can see what they are getting out of it.' (case 9)
- 'Managing the identity conflict between one's business world and one's academic world is critical to being able to simultaneously be successful in both... It is vital that one stays on top of the work environment and this requires your work colleagues to feel that you are putting the job first.' (case 4)

There were cases where this relationship had clearly broken down:

- 'The attitude of my sponsors and coach to the programme seemed ambivalent in the sense that they had instigated the programme of which I had become part and agreed to support me in my endeavours, but in reality they were so busy that they didn't even have the time to participate in any discussion with me about what my work-based projects should be, what areas of theory were most relevant to them and therefore what options I should exercise over discretionary modules within the programme.' (case 2)

- 'I felt that this was an unwarranted intrusion particularly due to the fact that my line manger had little or no academic ability and he was passing unqualified judgement on my efforts. I felt that the benefit I gained from subsidised study was far outweighed by employer interference in my private life study.' (case 5)

There were also cases of over-zealous and ineffective integration:

- 'In many respects the university and my employer spoon-fed us! One morning a large parcel arrived with information about the university, its library and other resources together with work books, reading resources and study guides. In addition my employer had provided me with the key text book that would be used throughout the course.' (case 6)
- 'I had to link my academic study into formal work-based personal developments plans where I had a line manager who commenced to measure my degree achievement.' (case 5)

However in some cases integration worked well:

- 'I had been on a number of company courses as part of the career progression to step up to each new level but the McDonalds degree was something completely different... McDonalds gave me the opportunity to learn things in the real world... You don't get this by working on your own with books.' (case 12)

Project work provides the most constructive interaction between the workplace and the university:

- 'I found that what I was writing about was a situation that was developing and evolving in the workplace in real time.' (case 3)
- 'The breakthrough for me was this realisation that you have to use whatever is going on in your job. It is cannot be an artificial construct on the side... Like all real-life experience my project started at a point where there was a history, a current situation, and a number of future scenarios.' (case 4)
- 'I definitely feel from a learning point of view that choosing something I had a small knowledge about made me push to learn as much as I could about it to enable the group to make full use of our new resource as well as giving me the confidence to face any new challenges.' (case 10)

What can be observed, is that the workplace has a dynamic of its own and, as many of the cases show, the learner is pulled in different directions. The key is to locate an area of constructive interaction between the workplace and the university environment and project work offers the best solution so far. It is a mutually common concept which is flexible enough to encompass real-time work issues and academic requirements thus spanning both cultures.

Did the Assessment Method Work?

Surprisingly, views about assessment in the case studies were generally positive, as it is usually a point of contention and concern:

- 'It was clear from the course design that the hope of the university and my employer was for everybody to maximise this opportunity for learning to the full and that nobody should fail. Nevertheless, the system of assessment was designed to satisfy the appropriate academic criteria and invigilated externally to maintain standards.' (case 6)
- 'We started the course with an APEL exercise which covered much of the level 4 work... it was quite informal and was OK. All in all it took about one working day to prepare the APEL report and present it and I think it accounted for 30 per cent of the course.' (case 12)

There was particular support for reports and theses as an assessment method, providing the assessors are familiar with the work context:

- 'These were assessed as written reports and there were also assessed presentations. I felt these gave a good assessment of knowledge as they allowed you time to develop what you knew.' (case 1)
- 'Writing the thesis was an excellent way to structure the study work. The discipline of a literature research, followed by a methodology development, followed by data presentation and then analysis is a good framework. A viva is also a very effective way of focusing the mind. More importantly I felt I had been properly tested and that gave me a sense of achievement.' (case 4)
- 'One course requirement was that we submit our work to our tutors and peers for comment before finalising it and submitting it to the university. This worked really well.' (case 6)
- 'As the study, and therefore the essays, were very much based around your own experience within your workplace, I feel that the tutors found it hard to fully assess some of the analysis requested, as this was so personal to the student.' (case 9)
- 'For me the methods of assessment worked particularly well as they allowed me to explore new insights and perspectives on existing problems that occurred within my job.' (case 11)
- 'I found this quite a good way to do the assessment, particularly when the conclusions were presented as action plans.' (case 12)

However, for some the writing conventions were difficult to justify or make sense of particularly coming from a world of short problem-solving bulleted report writing:

- 'My biggest grouse throughout the course in respect of time was the inordinate amounts of time taken to reference my assignments correctly and to carry out a word-count and the attendant editing process. This was a good discipline and undoubtedly resulted in a crisper more cogent assignment but it is very important not to underestimate the time this needs.' (case 6)

- 'Another difficulty was the way in which I was expected to write my assignments: I've always written in 'black and white', so to speak, but here I was in an academic environment expected to produce work in "uni-speak".' (case 8)
- 'The timing of the research project was problematic as this coincided with a particularly busy period at work; however other than taking a year out of study to combat this issue, there was nothing else that I could do.' (case 11)

Noticeably, there was some serious criticism of the universities that used a formal examination system:

- 'We also have exams; two exams of three hours each covering three subjects. These were fine as a test of how you coped with pressure. In the real world you don't often find yourself having to solve complex business problem in extremely short timescales and without references. You have time to think and explore and consult others.' (case 1)
- 'It seems so old-fashioned to hand write in the modern world that we live in today and to be honest, my hand and wrist muscles just aren't used to it. Ten minutes into the exam I would feel as if I had got repetitive strain injury in my wrist which made writing extremely painful and difficult. I really don't know how they managed to read my handwriting towards the end of some of the papers.' (case 8)

Assessment can be described as the 'elephant in the room' of work-based learning. There is a university perception that those in full-time employment don't like to be assessed academically, but they are used to continuous assessment at work by peers and line managers, and actually the case studies were positive about the need for and experience of assessment. However, the key observation from the cases suggests that learners want to be assessed thoroughly, not least because it adds credibility to the qualification awarded, however, assessment is required to be in a form that mimics workplace challenges.

Outcomes and Benefits

There are many assertions that effectiveness in the current job role has improved as a result of the learning programme:

- 'The experience has certainly boosted my business skills.' (case 1)
- 'The benefits to my employers, in respect of my study, is that the internal audit profession with HMRC is "professionally qualified" to perform its role. This is recognised not only by the Treasury within Government but also worldwide. My Science degree was modular and based upon systems, business and technology (computing) subjects and this is central to my audit work.' (case 5)
- 'My boss said that he believed that this course has helped develop me as a manager.' (case 8)

- 'My business results have improved which has helped me out in my career... I also feel more confident in my business decisions.' (case 12)

It seems that the personal benefit to learners far outweighs other returns, which is not a surprise given the high levels of personal commitment, particularly of time, required to carry out and complete the learning programme:

- 'I have made myself a marketable commodity. I have transposed myself from a generalist civil servant with a wide range of skills to an individual that has professional and academic qualifications aligned to skills acquired in government.' (case 5)
- 'This was quite defining for me as I began to view myself far less as a social care professional who regulates and much more as a regulator with a toolbox of specific skills and methods.' (case 6)
- 'The main lessons I learned for myself in relation to work-based training were to plan my time carefully but to be prepared to be flexible and make full use of the range of support available.' (case 6)
- 'My research produced a new understanding of how companies value learning initiatives. That understanding is already starting to impact the conduct of professional practice and has the potential to significantly enhance an organisation's awareness of the progress and impact of its learning initiatives. But most importantly it has caused me to evaluate what I do and why I do it. I have once again opened my mental toolkit for inspection and found it lacking.' (case 7)
- 'I had never thought about these areas before and they gave me a new perspective on the business.' (case 12)

These personal benefits went beyond 'skills' and expressed themselves in feelings of self-worth and personal motivation:

- 'From my perspective I feel considerably more confident at work; with the qualification I received giving me greater credibility in the workplace.' (case 3)
- 'One of the biggest benefits for me was around my self-confidence and sense of achievement.' (case 9)
- 'I am now a lifelong learner, but also a passionate champion for the academic recognition of learning that takes place in the workplace as part of doing your job, whatever that job may be.' (case 6)
- '[I have] a huge sense of achievement at the progress I have made.' (case 10)
- 'I have achieved distinctions in both English Language and Quantitative Mathematics which are both far beyond my own personal expectations. At school my nightmare subject was mathematics and I could not believe when the result was confirmed as the distinction.' (case 10)
- 'One of the valuable skills I have learned is that everyone has a learning skill and to make full use of this you need to find out what kind of learner you are.' (case 10)
- 'One of the biggest benefits for me was around my self-confidence and sense of achievement.' (case 9)
- 'I feel very proud at completing the course... I [had] felt a bit of a reject for having [previously] dropped out of university when all my friends had gone on and

completed... It's quite a challenge to go back to learning after so many years.' (case 12)

Reassuringly, most cases reported that the learning from the university experience had been applied in the workplace:

- 'I found myself thinking about the theories I had learned and seeing where I could use them... For me the ability to adapt what I learnt in the classroom so that it works in a particular business situation is the most important thing I gained.' (case 1)
- 'I like to think that the knowledge and insights I had so far gained during the whole MBA experience were being brought to bear, particularly in relation to the change processes to which I have alluded... looking beyond problem solving, at real action learning, positive appreciation, and collective storytelling, and was moving me into areas like social anthropology.' (case 2)
- 'I have also applied a lot of what I have learned directly to business situation.' (case 1)
- 'The course taught me to stand back and reflect on what was happening.' (case 12)

The articulated benefits are found on several levels. Firstly there is the practical transfer of techniques and knowledge from university to workplace, then there is the acquisition of 'new' relevant skills to the individual and finally there is self-development. Reassuringly, the benefits generally resonate with the motivation to enter the programme, which suggests that individual expectations were met.

Summary and Conclusion

From the learner perspective, the strongest messages seem to be about the importance of the mentor relationship and the integration of business as well as the workplace. In most cases the mentoring comes from the university but where employers put effort into supporting the learner, the mentoring can be successfully supplied by a workplace trainer. However, the overarching message is that the mentor is the most important support for the learner and the learner must choose a mentor that he/she can relate to well.

The workplace integration comes usually through the learner making a careful choice of project work which unites the work and academic objectives. However, where the employer has developed the programme with the university, this unification is already designed into the course and the learner does not have to make a judgement. Where the employer is not engaged, there can be a genuine conflict that the learner has to manage. Consequently, it is important that the learner continually relates what they are doing in the university to the current workplace objectives.

It is also necessary for the learner to be realistic about time commitments and impact on work/life balance. Many stressed the extent to which the support of family and peers is key to managing these conflicts. They also highlighted the different language and way of thinking in the academic world. The learner has to lead a double life where they simultaneously identify with conflicting worlds with differing behavioural norms and have to be committed to both worlds.

For the employer, the key message is that the experience will make the employee more confident and effective in their current job role and as a result the business will benefit. Employees doing these types of programmes are usually highly motivated towards their careers and willing to make great sacrifices to improve their job performance. If the programme is university delivered, they will need support to manage the interfaces between their work and the academic programme, but this support needs to complement, rather than compete with university delivery. A workplace mentor can add great value if the role is formalised, properly understood and given adequate priority, but it can be a detrimental if half hearted. In some cases, course delivery by a company training department can also work well, but it is a major commitment by a company.

The relevance of the academic project to the workplace is of mutual interest and it is worth employers using this as a research source. It is of course helpful if employers contribute to the cost but this is not the biggest issue. Helping employees remain connected with the workplace and making what they are doing in the university relevant to work colleagues is probably more significant.

For the higher education institution, the key pointers seem to be around the provision of an efficient, responsive, administrative support system, as well as the choice of tutors and mentors with relevant workplace experience. The capabilities and needs of learners in full-time employment is clearly different to the capability and needs of normal full-time students. Therefore the higher education institution needs to ensure it provides what is actually required, not what it is used to delivering. Many learners from the workplace are used to 'state of the art' IT systems, database access and office services. What they usually lack is involvement in an academic learning community. All the case studies stress how much is learnt from interaction with other learners, but the normal campus approach is inappropriate, nor does the workplace necessarily provide the necessary learning community. It is an area where a university can add huge value.

It is also interesting that there was a clear message that learners wanted rigorous assessment and independent validation of their learning. However, there were concerns about the forced use of 'academic speak', and formal examination tests which do not replicate the way knowledge is applied in the workplace. Processes like APEL and presentation of team project work seem to be better methods of assessing learning as it relates to the workplace.

What is perhaps most striking about the case studies is that they generally reflect the model of the early universities. The learners all had a wealth of experience and wanted the university to help them express this learning. In some cases they simply wanted their capabilities assessed and validated; in others help with the intellectual challenge of putting their knowledge together was required. They were all individuals who had taken charge of their learning and knew what they needed in terms of gaining skills and knowledge to deepen their vocation or technical skill base to enhance their career.

This is a very different view to that normally promulgated by business leaders that 'the job of universities is to prepare students for the world of work' (CBI report – Future Fit, 2009). It perhaps suggests how universities and employers can become partners in lifelong learning. It also counters the popular view in the press that vocational degrees are somehow 'dumbed down'. It is clear from the case studies that skills acquired in the workplace provide a progression to high-level academic achievement.

The overriding observation from the case studies is the way a university engages with work-based learners has to be different to the way it provides for full-time students. There are, however, elements of the full-time educational model which are even more relevant to work-based learners and other not. The most important feature is a process to foster a learning community and mentor work-based learners in understanding what they are learning. Traditional teaching methods, designed to expose a student to new knowledge and experience, may be counterproductive but exercises that stimulate reflective thought are essential. The physical buildings, administrative systems and campus life of a traditional university may not impress a work-based learner. Indeed, they may serve to emphasise that work-based learners are outsiders to the 'real' university. Work-based learners already have a locus for their learning. It is the workplace. What they need is help to reflect on the learning they are already doing and have that learning validated.

PART III

The Rights of the Learner

21 *The Informed Learner*

The individual entering the world of employment transfers from a context which focuses on the needs of the individual to an environment focused on group requirements. The individual becomes a specialist contributing to a group working together on a common task(s), and does so by making their knowledge productive for the group as a whole (Drucker, 1993). The individual in this work context accumulates personal knowledge because it is of value to the group. Possession of this knowledge also becomes a source of personal competitive advantage (Nonaka and Takeuchi, 1995). Immediately then a tension emerges between the needs of the individual and the group. But these knowledge workers cannot be bullied into sharing their knowledge (von Krogh, Ichijo and Nonaka, 2000). Consequently, organisational or group learning requires a process whereby individuals are enticed to share their specialist knowledge.

These behavioural organisational learning models characterise organisations as socio-technical systems comprising collective participation by individuals and groups (Argyris, 1992). They presume that stability of shared understanding is important for organisational efficiency and survival (March, 1999). However, organisations compete for survival and this competition manifests itself as a drive for innovation resulting in new products and services. Leaders in organisations are exhorted to have new ideas and induce change however most new ideas are bad ones (March, 1999). Thus this form of innovation creates conflict and resistance to change and may itself be caused by conflict (West, 2000).

Theories of organisation emanating from the Tavistock Institute tradition, for example, open system theory (Miller, 1993), propose that behaviour within organisations can be interpreted as a manifestation of tensions between groups in a system of interacting groups. Organisations respond to threats by defensive repertoires such as protection of task and technical rationalism (Argyris and Schon, 1978). They create secret knowledge which defines membership of the group and excludes outsiders. Mechanisms predicted by both organisation systems and organisation learning theories for an organisation under stress (Schon, 1983; Miller, 1993), lead to what Argyris and Schon (1978) describe as Model I behaviour where actors have to justify their actions with technical rationality. Protective mechanisms encourage people to keep their views private (Argyris and Schon, 1978). The expected impact of such behaviour is that ideas which cannot be expressed as logical extensions of existing knowledge are quickly 'filtered out'; this phenomenon is often referred to as 'institutional lock'. Once decisions are formed they cannot be reconsidered even though new information may challenge the decision (Gregory, 1988).

The legitimate push for rational thinking in an organisation can thus become a major obstacle to creativity and innovation. So the need to constantly justify ones belief in front of others inhibits knowledge creation (Von Krogh, Ichijo, and Nonaka 2000). In addition, individuals dread incompetence and behave according to organisation defence routines, not as individual personalities (Argyris, 1992). Knowledge creation thus requires an enabling context which overcomes these defence routines. Knowledge creation in the workplace beyond the individual needs a micro-community of knowledge which develops its own rituals, language, norms and values (Von Krogh, Ichijo, and Nonaka 2000).). This phenomenon is cited in many of the case studies when referring to learning support arrangements. Networks and learning communities are highlighted as key components of knowledge exchange.

It is therefore not surprising that the major part of any organisations formal training budget is spent on behavioural alignment and change management. Organisations frequently use their training function as a means of intervening in the learning of their staff in order to break this institutional 'lock', introduce and embed change as well as encourage innovation. In addition, there are often company 'entry to work' training programmes (for example, apprenticeships) which teach some basic skills. However, for those already in work the interventions tend to be stimulations to learning rather than teaching, in the traditional university sense. They also are focused as much on getting the individual to share his/her own learning with others as they are on enabling the individual to learn from others. The learner in full-time employment participates in a process designed to promote organisational learning, not a process engaged to promote individual learning. It is thus not at all surprising that the case study learners in this book felt they were personally 'locked' in group learning situations in their workplace and needed a learning experience that would free this lock.

However, Government policy seems quite oblivious to all of this. The upskilling of the UK workforce envisioned in the Leitch Report referred to earlier is firmly labelled for employers to tackle. It should also be noted that university funding models focus primarily on the needs of full-time students and, as the case studies show, those who return to part-time university learning face considerable challenges. In this respect there is a clear presumption that the state will fund full-time learning to the age of 21 and employers take over the burden thereafter. As a result, Government rhetoric lambasts employers for failing to upskill their workers but simultaneously promotes a system where skills can only be recognised through engagement with an academic infrastructure that is not designed to meet the needs of those in employment. Also, Government initiatives like Sector Skills Councils go some way to addressing this issue but their mission is to facilitate the development of generic programmes that meet business training needs. The forgoing discussion suggests that this can only be a partial solution, at best.

So there is a situation where the employee is engaged in a learning process which is defined by an organisational learning requirement which may be at variance to his/her own needs, and is faced with the alternative of re-entering a Government-funded academic system which appears generally equally unsympathetic to the working person. There is clearly a market failure. The notion of continuous professional development then seems to be denied to a large sector of the population, those in work. A solution is to empower the learner so that he/she can demand a better service from universities. We need 'informed' learners who know what they want and make a fuss if they don't get it.

Consequently there are three problems the informed learner is required to address:

- A lack of the confidence to demand what is needed. If the learner is talking to a private training provider they would have no difficulty specifying their training needs but universities have an aura that intimidates.
- University academic staff have relatively little experience of the non-academic workplace. As indicated above, the workplace is a complex and fast-changing social environment and the needs of individuals relate to their situation in this environment. Unless the university lecturer is working very closely with an organisation in a well-established relationship, he/she has little hope of understanding this context.
- Education and organisational learning theoretical underpinnings are disconnected and lacking a common language for relating the two processes. Hence, the full-time employee participating in a university course has often to be two different people.

The suggestion here is that the way forward is for those in employment to become informed learners who 'buy' the university services they need. Employers have a role in facilitating this process by supporting their employees with information and resources. Universities have to unbundle their services and stop promoting the 'one size fits all' model. Governments need to recognise that their funding regimes are discouraging this liberalisation and change accordingly.

So how does the informed learner stand up for his/her rights?

A learner needs to understand his/her requirements and the first step is to separate knowledge from understanding. Gaining deeper understanding implies reflective learning whereas gaining knowledge suggests exposure to discreet information. Academic progression can be characterised as deepening understanding and that is what universities do best. Contrary to expectations, universities are often not up to date on specialist knowledge (unless it is the particular specialisation of the faculty).

Documenting what is known and understood is critical for the informed learner. The APEL process does help in this area, though much needs to be done to make these processes more user-friendly. The key here is to document experiential learning and the expression of deep understanding that was derived from the experience. Qualifications may be only partial evidence of what someone has learnt. This is an area where a learner will need professional help, either from an employer or an academic institution.

The third step is to agree the learning journey, that is personal development planning (the PDP process) is which is essentially a gap analysis. It is important to articulate the goal(s) in terms of competence and capability; describe the areas of shortcoming; and then define the learning outcomes you need to achieve. As our case study learners discovered, university courses tend to be badly aligned to the needs of experienced employees.

The fourth step is to decide what personal support systems are needed and how to establish them. The key elements will be a trusted mentor and a learning community of likeminded individuals who you can learn from. There may be other areas such as family and friends too. These support systems could come from the employer or the academic institution. Understanding what is on offer from various sources and checking how well it works is important.

The final step concerns itself with the question of brand. Universities and their qualifications are perceived to have varying reputations in the eyes of the public. The universities with the strongest reputations tend also to be the least flexible in terms of accredited work-based learning. However, it may be that a brief exposure to some of the world's leading researchers at a top university counts for much more than a degree from another university.

These are, however, very different learning experiences and the key for the informed learner is to know which to buy and for the university is to know which to supply.

References

Alleman E., Cochran J., Doverspike J. & Newman I. (1984) 'Enriching Mentoring Relationships' *The Personnel and Guidance Journal*, 63, pp. 329–332.

Argyris, C. (1992) *On Organisational Change*, Oxford: Blackwell.

Argyris, C. & Schon, D. A. (1978) *Organisational Learning: A Theory of Action Perspective*, California: Addison-Wesely.

Australian National Training Authority (2003) *High Level Review of Training Packages*: Phase 1 Report. Available at: www.dest.gov.au.

Billett, S. (2000) 'Guided Learning at Work' *Journal of Workplace Learning*, 12(7), pp. 272–285.

Billett, S. (2003) 'Workplace Mentors: Demands and Benefits' *Journal of Workplace Learning*, 15(3), pp. 105–113.

Bligh, J. (1999) 'Mentoring: An Invisible Support Network' *Academic Medicine* 77, pp. 377–384.

Blunkett, D. (2000) *Modernising Higher Education*. Speech at the University of Greenwich, DFEE, London: HMSO.

Boud, D., Cressy, P. & Docherty, P. (Eds) (2006) *Productive Reflection at Work*, Abingdon: Routledge.

Boud, D. & Solomon, N. (Eds) (2001) *Work Based Learning: A New Higher Education*, Buckingham: SRHE and OUP.

Boud, D. & Symes, C. (2000) 'Learning for Real: Work-based Education in Universities' in Symes, C. & McIntyre, J. (Eds) *Working Knowledge: The New Vocationalism and Higher Education*, Buckingham: Buckingham University Press.

Brennan, L. (2005) *Integrating Work Based Learning into Higher Education.* Report, Bolton: University Vocational Awards Council (UVAC).

Brennan, J., Lyon, E. S., McGeevor, P. A. & Murray, K. (1993) Students, Courses and Jobs: The Relationship between Higher Education and the Labour Market, London: Jessica Kingsley.

Brown, P., Hesketh, A. & Williams, S. (2003) 'Employability in a Knowledge Driven Economy' *Journal of Education and Work*, 16(2), pp. 107–126.

Bryan, C. & Clegg, K. (Eds) (2006) *Innovative Assessment in Higher Education*, London: Routledge.

Cabinet Office (1993) White Paper: *Realising Our Potential: a Strategy for Science, Engineering and Technology.* (Cm. 2250) London: HMSO.

Cabinet Office (2001) In Demand: Adult Skills for the 21st Century, London: HMSO.

Charles, D. R. (2003) 'Universities and Territorial Development: Reshaping the Regional Role of English Universities' *Local Economy*, 18(1), pp. 7–20.

Claes, T. (2002) *It was not a bad idea… Defining the University: From Ivory Tower to Convenience Store.* Paper presented at The Idea of Education Mansfield College, Oxford, 3rd–4th July, 2002.

Confederation of British Industry (CBI), Universities UK and HEFCE (2008) Stepping Higher: Workforce Development through Employer-Higher Education Partnership: A Joint Report, London: CBI, p. 20.

Confederation of British Industry (CBI) (2009) *Future Fit: Preparing Graduates for the World of Work*, London: CBI.

Clutterbuck, D. (2004) *Everyone Needs a Mentor* (4th Edition), Chartered Institute of Personnel and Development, London.

Coghlan, D. & Brannick, T. (2001) *Doing Action Research in Your Own Organization*, London: Sage.

Collot, A., Pagnani, B. & Guteskunst, E. (2003) www.transfine.net.

Connor, H. (2005) *Workforce Development and Higher Education*, Council for Industry and Higher Education: London.

Connor, H. & Hirsch, W. (2008) From Influence to Collaboration: Employer Engagement with Higher Education for Learning and Skills. Draft Report for Consultation at CIHE Seminar, London: CIHE.

Costley. C. (2001) *Different Methodologies in Work Based Learning, Making it Happen*. Conference Papers, Anglia Polytechnic University, March 2001, ISBN 1-84308-060-5.

Council of Ministers of Education (CMEC) (1998) *The Relevance of Education to the World of Work, with a Focus on Youth Employment*. Toronto: Council of Ministers of Education, Canada CMEC. Citing OECD (1998).

Cowling, M. (2003) *The Contribution of the Self-Employed to Employment in the EU*. Report to the Small Business Service. SBS: London.

De Grip, A., Van Loo, J. & Sanders, J. (1999) *Employability in Action: An Industry Employability Index*, SKOPE Research Paper No.5, London.

Department of Innovation, Universities and Skills (DIUS) (2008) 'Higher Education at Work, High Skills: High Value' Consultation Paper, In: Wiesner, R. & Millett, B. (Eds) *Human Resource*.

Department for Education and Skills (DFES) (2005) *Skills: Getting on in Business, Getting on at Work*, White Paper (Cm 6483), London: HMSO.

Drucker, P. F. (1993) *Post Capitalist Society*, Oxford: Butterworth-Heinemann.

Dunn, C., Mumford, J. & Roodhouse, S. (2008) 'Employee Attitudes to Workplace Learning: An Insight into Large Organisations'. In: Garnett, J. & Young, D., (Eds) *Work Based Futures 2 Proceedings*, UVAC, Bolton, ISBN 978-0-907311-26-3.

Durrant, A., Rhodes, G. & Young, D. (2009) *Getting Started with University Level Work Based Learning*, London: Middlesex University Press.

Evans, K., Guile, D. & Harris, J. (2009) *Putting Knowledge To Work, The Exemplars*, London: The WLE Centre, Insitute of Education,University of London.

Evans, K. & Kersh, N. (2006), *Competence Development and Workplace Learning: An Overview for the UK and Ireland*, Project Report, Institute of Education, London: University of London.

Faithorn, B. (2005) *Learner Progression into Higher Education*. Bolton: Universities Vocational Awards Council.

Friday, E. & Friday, S. S. (2002) 'Formal Mentoring: Is There a Strategic Fit?' *Management Decision*, 40(20), pp. 152–157.

Garnett, J. (1998) 'Using APEL to Develop Customised Work Based Learning Programmes at Postgraduate Level'. In: *Beyond Graduateness*, South East England Consortium for Credit Accumulation and Transfer, London: Page Bros.

Garnett, J. (2000) 'Organisational Cultures and the Role of Learning Agreements'. In: Portwood, D. & Costley, C. (Eds), *Work Based Learning and the University: New Perspectives and Practices*, SEDA Publications.

Garnett, J. (2005) 'University Work Based Learning and the Knowledge Driven Project'. In: Rounce, E. & Workman, B. (Eds), *Work Based Learning in Health Care*, Chichester: Kingsham.

Garnett, J. (2007) 'Employers and University Partnerships'. In: Roodhouse, S. & Swailes, S. *Employers, Skills and Higher Education*, Chichester: Kingsham Press.

Garnett, J., Costley, C., & Workman, B. (2009) *Work Based Learning, Journeys to the Core of Higher Education*, London: Middlesex University Press.

Garnett, J., Portwood, D. & Costley, C. (2004) Bridging Rhetoric and Reality: Accreditation of Prior Experiential Learning (APEL) in the UK, Bolton: UVAC Report.

Garrick, J. & Usher, R. (2000) 'Flexible Learning, Contemporary Work and Enterprising Selves' *Electronic Journal of Sociology*, 5(1), p. 15. Available at: www.sociology.org/content/vol005.001/garrick-usher.html.

Gay, B. (1994) 'What is Mentoring?' *Education & Training*, 36(5), pp. 4–7.

Geuna, A. & Nesta, L. (2003) *University Patenting and its Effects on Academic Research*. Brighton: SPRU-University of Sussex.

Gray, D. (2001) 'Work-based Learning, Action Learning and the Virtual Paradigm' *Journal of Further and Higher Education*, 25(3), pp. 315–324.

Gibb, S. (1999) 'The Usefulness of Theory: A Case Study in Evaluating Formal Mentoring Schemes' *Human Relations*, 52(8).

Gregory, G. (1988) *Decision Analysis*, London: Pitman.

Gumport, P. (2000) 'Academic Restructuring: Organizational Change and Institutional Imperatives' *Higher Education*, 39, pp. 67–91.

Hansford, B. C., Ehrich, L. C. & Tennent, L. (2003) 'Does Mentoring Deserve Another Look?' In: Wiesner, Retha & Millett, B. (Eds) *Human Resource Management: Challenges and Future Directions*, Milton Keynes: John Wiley & Sons, pp. 219–228.

Higher Education Funding Council for England (HEFCE) (2000) *The Foundation Degree Prospectus* 00/27.Available at: www.hefce.ac.uk/pubs/hefce/2000/00_27.htm.

Higher Education Funding Council for England HEFCE (2004) *Strategic Plan 2003-8 (Revised April 2004)*. Higher Education Funding Council for England, 04/17.

Higher Education Funding Council for England (HEFCE) (2007) *Research and Evaluation Reports*. Available at: http://www.hefce.ac.uk/pubs/rdreports/2007/rd16_07/.

Higher Education Funding Council for England (HEFCE) & Quality Assurance Agency for Higher Education (QAA) (2007) *Foundation Degrees: Key Statistics, 2001-02 to 2006-07*.

Higher Education Funding Council for England (HEFCE) & Quality Assurance Agency for Higher Education (QAA) (2008) *Quality Assurance and Employer Engagement in HE Learning*.

Godin, B. and Gingras, Y. (2000) 'The Place of Universities in the System of Knowledge Production' *Research Policy*, 29(2), pp. 273–278.

Kay, D. & Hinds, R. (2007) *A Practical Guide to Mentoring* (3rd Edition), Oxford: How to Books.

King, M. (2007) *Workforce Development*, London: CIHE.

Kerr, C. (1963) *The Uses of the University*. Cambridge, MA: Harvard University Press.

Kerr, C. (1987) 'A Critical Age in the University World: Accumulated Heritage vs. Modern Imperatives *European Journal of Education*, 22(2), pp. 183–193.

Learning Through Work (2009) *Introduction*. Available at: www.learningthroughwork.org.

Leitch, S. (2006) Leitch Review of Skills: Prosperity for all in the Global Economy – World Class Skills. Final report, December 2006.

Little, B. & Enhancing Student Employability Coordination Team (ESECT) Colleagues (2004) *Employability and Work Based Learning*, Learning and Employability Series, York: Higher Education Academy.

Lord Mandelson, Secretary of State for Business, Innovation and Skills, set out his vision for higher education in a speech to university Vice Chancellors today, Monday 27 July, at Birkbeck, University of London, Press Release 27th July 2009 from Birkbeck College.

March, J. G. (1999) *The Pursuit of Organisational Intelligence*, Oxford: Blackwell.

Marginson, S. & Considine, M. (2000) *The Enterprise University: Power, Governance and Reinvention in Australia*, Cambridge: Cambridge University Press.

Megginson, D., Clutterbuck, D., Garvey, B., Stokes, P. & Garrett-Harris, R. (2005) *Mentoring in Action: A Practical Guide for Managers*, London: Kogan Page.

Miller, E. (1993) *From Dependency to Autonomy; Studies in Organisational Theory*, London: Free Association Books.

Mould, O., Roodhouse, S. & Vorley, T. (2006) *Realising Capabilites: Academic Innovation and the Creative Industries*. Paper presented at the RGS-IBG Conference, 1st September, 2006, London.

National Skills Task Force (1999) *Second Report of the National Skills Task Force*. Department for Education and Employment, Sheffield.

New Zealand Ministry of Foreign Affairs and Trade (2006) *Glossary*. (Definition no longer available). Accessed in 2006 at www.mft.govt.nz/support/tplu/tradematters/glossary.html.

Nonaka, I. & Takeuchi, H. (1995) *The Knowledge-Creating Company: How Japanese Companies Create the Dynamics of Innovation*, Oxford: Oxford University Press.

Osborne, C., Davies, J. &Garnett, J. (1998) 'Guiding the Learner to the Centre of the Stakeholder Curriculum: Independent and Work Based Learning at Middlesex University.' In: Stephenson, J. & Yorke, M. (Eds), *Capability and Quality in Higher Education*, London: Kogan Page.

Parsloe, E. (1999) *The Manager as Coach and Mentor* (2nd Edition), London: Institute of Personnel and Development.

Quality Assurance Agency for Higher Education (QAA), (2002) *Handbook for the Review of Foundation Degrees in England 2002-03*. Gloucester: The Quality Assurance Agency for Higher Education.

Quality Assurance Agency for Higher Education (QAA) (2003) *Overview Report on Foundation Degree Reviews*. Gloucester: The Quality Assurance Agency for Higher Education.

Quality Assurance Agency for Higher Education (QAA) (2004) *Handbook for the Review of Foundation Degrees in England 2004-05*. Gloucester: The Quality Assurance Agency for Higher Education.

Quality Assurance Agency for Higher Education (QAA) (2005a) *Report of a Survey to Follow up Foundation Degree Reviews Carried out in 2002-03*, Gloucester: The Quality Assurance Agency for Higher Education.

Quality Assurance Agency for Higher Education (QAA) (2005b) *Report of a Survey of existing HNDs converted to Foundation degrees since 2001*, Gloucester: The Quality Assurance Agency for Higher Education.

Quality Assurance Agency for Higher Education (QAA) (2005c) *Learning from Reviews of Foundation Degrees in England Carried out in 2004-05: Sharing Good Practice*, Gloucester: The Quality Assurance Agency for Higher Education.

Quality Assurance Agency for Higher Education (QAA) (2006) *Section 7 of the Code of Practice for the assurance of academic quality and standards (the Code)* (Revised edition). Gloucester: The Quality Assurance Agency for Higher Education.

Quality Assurance Agency for Higher Education (QAA) (2007) Code of practice for the assurance of academic quality and standards in higher education – Section 7: Work based and placement learning. Gloucester: The Quality Assurance Agency for Higher Education.

Quality Assurance Agency for Higher Education (QAA) (2008) Section 9 of the Code of Practice for the assurance of academic quality and standards (the Code): Work-based and Placement Learning. Gloucester: The Quality Assurance Agency for Higher Education.

Quality Assurance Agency for Higher Education (QAA) (2009) *Thematic enquiries into concerns about academic quality and standards in higher education in England,* Final report, Gloucester: The Quality Assurance Agency for Higher Education. Available at: http://www.qaa.ac.uk/standardsandquality/thematicenquiries/FinalReportApril09.pdf.

Ramani, S., Gruppen, L. & Kachur, E. K. (2006) 'Twelve Tips for Developing Effective Mentors' *Medical Teacher*, 28(5), pp. 404–408.

Roodhouse, S. & Swailes, S.(2007) *Employers Skills and Higher Education*, Chichester: Kingsham Press.

Ross, D. J. (2007) Mentoring. Available at: http://login.learningthroughwork.org/ufiresources/mentoring/intro/p1.html

Schon, D. A. (1983) *The Reflective Practitioner*, London: Arena.

Shapiro, N. & Levine, J. (1999) *Creating Learning Communities: A Practical Guide to Winning Support, Organizing for Change, and Implementing Programs,* Paris: Lavoisier.

Slaughter, S. & Leslie, L. (1997) *Academic Capitalism: Politics, Policies and the Entrepreneurial University.* Baltimore: John Hughes University Press.

Standard and Poor's (2008), Revenue Diversification and Sustainablility: A Comparison of Trends in Public Higher Education in the UK and US, London, CIHE Publications.

Stewart, T. (1997) *Intellectual Capital*, London: Nicholas Brealey.

Taherian, K. & Shekarchian, M. (2008) 'Mentoring for Doctors. Do its Benefits Outweigh its Disadvantages?' *Medical Teacher* 30, pp. 95–99.

University Vocational Awards Council (UVAC) (2002) *The New Vocational Initiatives*. Proceedings of the UVAC Annual Conference, Bolton: Universities Vocational Awards Council.

University Vocational Awards Council (UVAC) (2003a) *Review and Development of Graduate Apprenticeship*: A National Higher Education and Employment Bridging Programme, Bolton: University Vocational Awards Council.

University Vocational Awards Council (UVAC) (2003b) *Widening Participation in the Workplace: A New Agenda for Further and Higher Education*, Bolton: University Vocational Awards Council, Annual Conference Proceedings.

University Vocational Awards Council (UVAC) (2005) *Integrating Work Based Learning into Education: A Guide to Good Practice,* Bolton: University Vocational Awards Council.

Unwin, L. & Fuller, A. (2003) *Expanding Learning in the Workplace: Making More of Individual and Organisational Potential*. A NIACE policy discussion paper, London: NIACE.

Von Krogh, G., Ichijo, K. & Nonaka, I. (2000) *Enabling Knowledge Creation: How to Unlock the Mystery of Tacit Knowledge and Release the Power of Innovation*, Oxford: Oxford University Press.

Wailey, T. (2002), *How to do AP(E)L*, London: Southern England Consortium for Credit Accumulation and Transfer (SEEC).

Wall, T. (2009) Imagining a Beautiful Mosaic – Flexible Learning Practices for Access, Diversity and Participation, *International Council for Adult and Experiential Learning Conference*, November, Chicago.

Waterhouse, R. (2002) 'Widening Participation and the Distributed University'. In: Roodhouse, S. & Hemsworth, D. (Eds) *Widening Participation in the Workplace, a New Agenda for Further and Higher Education*, Bolton: Proceedings of the University Vocational Awards Council.

West, M. A. (2000). 'State of the Art: Creativity and Innovation at Work' *The Psychologist*, 3(9), pp. 460–464.

Wilson, R. (2006) Vocational Qualifications: Current Issues, Government Responsibilities, and Employer Opportunities, London: Institute of Directors.

Workman, B (2009) 'The Core Components: Teaching, Learning and Assessing'. In: Garnett, J., Costley, C. & Workman, B. (Eds) *Work Based Learning: Journeys to the Core of Higher Education*, London: MUP.

York St John (2009) Independent and Professional Studies Validation Documentation, York: York St John University.

Index